Flanders in Australia

Flanders in Australia

Australia

A Personal History of Wool and War

JACQUELINE DWYER

Kangaroo Press

FLANDERS IN AUSTRALIA

First published in Australia in 1998 by Kangaroo Press
an imprint of Simon & Schuster Australia
20 Barcoo Street, East Roseville NSW 2069

A Viacom Company
Sydney New York London Toronto Tokyo Singapore

National Library of Australia
Cataloguing-in-Publication data

Dwyer, Jacqueline.
Flanders in Australia: a personal history of wool and war.
Bibliography
Includes index.
ISBN 0 86417 969 3.
1. Wool industry - Australia - History. 2. Wool industry - Flanders - History. 3.
World War, 1914-1918 I. Title

636.3145

Set in: Bembo 11/13.2, Bodini Book, Plantin
Printed by Griffin Press, Adelaide

10 9 8 7 6 5 4 3 2 1

Foreword

As a nation matures and moves towards a sense of true identity, its history comes increasingly into focus. And so it has been for Australia as its many ethnic strands have mingled with its early Anglo-Saxon heritage. In this context can be placed the significant ties with Flanders and especially with France — cultural and economic, and spanning many generations. While some features of this francophone connection are well known in Australia (witness, for example the exploits of French explorers whose names now grace our coastlines), others are less well remembered. It is the latter which provide the theme for Jacqueline Dwyer's well researched book — an historical record inspired by a personal family quest across the decades which saw our nationhood take shape.

I still remember the magic of the wool trade when I was a boy. It was an era when the sheep was said to carry the country on its back, when stories and myths of station life fuelled childhood memories, when the grazier was aristocracy and the stockman a legend. Not least among the forces which made wool a symbol of Australia and for years its largest export item were the buyers from Flanders — men who came from afar, often with families, over a period of 50 years from around the turn of the century. Some settled permanently in Australia, bringing with them a francophone culture which must be among the richest influences that have gone to make up modern Australia.

The author's father, Jacques Playoust, around whose lifespan this book is written, stands out among that select group of Franco-Australian pioneers — loyally Australian yet unmistakably French, almost entirely educated here and serving with distinction on the Western Front during the World War I. I might add that there can be no more moving experience for an Australian than to visit those memorials and graves in Flanders where so many young compatriots gave their today for our tomorrow.

It is not difficult to feel a special regard for those Franco-Australian immigrants and the link they created between Australia's Anglo-Saxon origins and the francophone world beyond. No doubt they were sometimes filled with a sense of isolation in their new world and a nostalgia for that part of themselves with roots across the seas. Yet in reality they were always within and contributors to a community of shared values —

values that were and remain today of more lasting significance for the nation than the commercial fruits of their profession. That depth of association and contribution deserve the recognition and respect which this book offers.

As far as I am aware, Jacqueline Dwyer is the first author to describe and record that part of Australia's history which belongs to the wool buyers from Flanders and their families. She thus adds a dimension to, and fills a void in our knowledge and understanding of the ongoing evolution of Australia's cultural heritage. And in a broader sense her book bears striking witness to a major relationship between two countries which have so much in common that they unhesitatingly stood side by side in the two great conflicts of this century.

Peter J. Curtis
Former Ambassador of Australia to France and Belgium

Contents

Acknowledgments

When my sister Annette Mezo was staying in Paris in 1983, she was given a bundle of letters by our cousin, Marie Delos-Leplat. These had been written by our father from the trenches in World War I. Combined with other letters to his family in Australia, and a diary written at Verdun, this seemed a body of papers worth preserving. Laboriously I typed them up. It then seemed necessary to widen the picture by describing the wool buyers' world to which he belonged.

Many people have responded with courteous and generous co-operation during the years of curious questioning that lie behind this work. My own children, Nicholas, Julia, Dominic, Sophie, James and Vincent, slightly surprised, were behind me from the beginning. They bullied me into buying a computer and helped me work its magic; kind neighbours gave me further tutoring. René Vandervaere supplied me with a list of names, and David Knight opened the Melbourne window.

Endless telephone calls to family and friends too numerous to name, to active and retired wool buyers, produced precious information which in time created a picture of their extraordinary fraternity, and I thank them all.

I am specially indebted to descendants of the pioneer buyers named in the text, who were more than generous with their time: Roger Pelletier, Jeanne Renault and Paul de Pierres supplied me with first hand recollections of the Indochina campaign; Jean-Paul de la Motte, Maurice Blackman and several hospitable people in Forbes gave me the background to Paul Wenz. Two French consuls-general, M. Thierry Viteau and M. Jean-Claude Poimboeuf, in turn showed their interest by contributing to the pile of information. George Franki researched the St. Aloysius College magazine, and the school archivists at Xavier, Riverview and Genezzano provided valuable clues in piecing together the chronological puzzle. Staff at the Australian War Memorial were helpful in finding the Diary of the 13th Field Artillery Brigade. Most recently, the skilled and patient editing of Helen Young tidied and groomed the text.

Most of all I thank my husband and best friend, Brian Dwyer, who unselfishly has underpinned the whole enterprise from beginning to end, and to him I dedicate this book.

Introduction

The first centenary of British settlement in Australia was celebrated in 1888 in an epoch of substantial prosperity. Australia had the golden fleece to sell, and the world was keen to buy it. Her prime market had been Britain until this time, but what was loosely called 'The Continent' was becoming increasingly interested.

A little-known movement of people to Australia had its origins in the wool trade. They came from Europe to buy wool from this new source but were not recorded in immigration figures of the period, for they were not immigrants but self-supporting business expatriates. However, their commerce in wool left behind a sizeable number of people who gradually became Australians, almost by osmosis.

Those expatriate wool buyers who were born around the time of Australia's first centenary lived during a significant period in its history. They enjoyed sharing in Australia's good fortune; they also shared with Australians the sufferings of two world wars and the hardships of the intervening depression. In particular, the years 1914–18 created an enduring bond.

The following story is a personal history of this period, seen through a small window during the lifetime of one man. His name was Jacques Playoust, who was born in Tourcoing in northern France in 1883 and who died in Sydney in 1947.

PART I
The Sheep's Back

I

Wool

In the period when blue denim was worn only by French peasants and American cowboys, when synthetic fabrics were unknown, when the middle classes dressed stiffly and formally in suits and topcoats, the woollen textile industry had an importance far exceeding our present understanding. In the last years of the 19th century Australia was producing the largest wool clip in the world and was the chief provider of raw wool for the mills of northern England, northern France, Belgium, Germany and other countries exporting textiles, blankets and carpets internationally.

The export of wool had been of the greatest consequence to the economy of the colony of New South Wales since 1803, when John Macarthur accompanied to London his first shipment of unusually fine wool, the product of rams of the Spanish merino breed and his own mixed-breed ewes. Five years later he again sold high quality wool in London by private treaty at Garraways, a long-established Coffee House in Exchange Alley near 'the Cornhill'. Here merchants gathered for pleasure and to conduct their business. Subsequently a commercial shipment of fine merino wool was sent from the Rev Samuel Marsden's farm near Parramatta. In 1839 wool auctions were inaugurated at Garraways and Australian wool was sold to Yorkshire manufacturers and dealers, who praised it for its softness and suitability for worsted yarn.

The crossing of the Blue Mountains opened up good sheep country west of Sydney. Far to the south, squatters from Tasmania settled in the area of Geelong by Port Phillip Bay, then pushed further on to Portland and the western districts of what was to become the separate colony of Victoria. By 1839 Victorian wool reached England, and a shipment arrived from good sheep country in South Australia and Western Australia seven years later.

Pastoralists were now producing large quantities of wool. About 150 fleeces would be compressed into bales by hydraulic presses, stamped with the name of the station, and piled high onto bullock drays to be hauled on the long and costly annual journey to the ports. An alternative was to send the bales down the Murray on barges. In Sydney the wagon drivers left their wool bales in the Haymarket, or drove further on to have them loaded onto ships at the 'Semi-circular Quay'. They camped there a while by the wharves before taking on general supplies for the return journey to the distant sheep stations.

By the mid century the quantity of Australian bales at the London sales surpassed those sent from Germany, and Australia rapidly became the primary source of wool for the textile mills in the north of England. Quality was dramatically improved by skilled selective breeding of sheep by Australian graziers, so that in that half-century the weight of the average fleece was almost doubled. Australian wool bales were favoured as they were reputed to be fairly graded and packed, unlike those of certain other countries which sometimes were of erratic quality. By this time buyers from the Continent were attending the London sales, with France as the major client, followed by Belgium, Germany and to a lesser extent the United States.

As the consumption of wool in Europe was increasing rapidly, Australian resentment grew at the virtual monopoly held by the London wool auction houses. It was felt that colonial sales held nearer to the areas of wool production would avoid double transport costs and also by-pass London financial interests. Pressure from Australian sellers and European buyers encouraged the formation of Australian auction houses. The first Australian sales of consequence took place in Adelaide under the direction of Elder Smith and Co. In Melbourne Richard Goldsbrough, who had trained in Bradford, set up wool sale rooms. Dalgety's, which had its origins as an importing firm in Melbourne, became interested in establishing similar sales. Wool was also sold by auction in Geelong and Ballarat. In 1843 the versatile entrepreneur Thomas Sutcliffe Mort instituted general auction rooms in George Street, Sydney for all kinds of goods, as well as wool which later gathered more importance. Australian Mortgage Land and Finance (AML&F) became one of Australia's largest woolselling brokers when it was incorporated in 1863.

A pioneer of direct selling to Europe was Jules Renard, the adventurous young son of a Flemish wool merchant in Antwerp. This important port on the Scheldt was now the centre of international trade for the newly created country of Belgium. In 1852, aged 19, Renard had arrived in Portland, Victoria accompanying a shipment of Rambouillet sheep and he decided to stay on to work on a sheep station for several years. He then used his local knowledge to buy wool for his father's mill in Antwerp, thus becoming one of the first European buyers to attend local sales. Relinquishing country life, he became a wool buyer for the firm Berkx and Co. in Melbourne, and three years later, in 1865, he established his own company. Within 12 years he sent possibly the first direct cargo of wool from Australia to the Continent, addressed to his father's company in Antwerp. Jules Renard became a British subject in the 1870s. He married the daughter of a Bradford wool merchant and founded a family in Australia.

When the Suez Canal was officially opened in 1869, the distance to Europe was considerably shortened by the elimination of the long haul around the Cape of Good Hope. Three years later a cable link was established between Europe and Australia, enabling manufacturers to give telegraphic orders and set price limits immediately. These fast communications with Europe greatly facilitated colonial sales. London sales were soon to lose their monopoly as Australian brokers were approached directly by English mills to buy wool on their behalf and perhaps to accept return orders for their finished product. Australian buyers such as Henry Austin Sr who was chairman of the Sydney Wool Buyers Association, and W. H. Chard were now executing orders from Belgian and German firms. Austin is credited with encouraging a modern system of selling, holding auctions in the colony rather than in London. He related how he had once asked an English broker: 'Has it ever occurred to you that it might be to your advantage to send your son to Australia to start a selling business there?' A scornful laugh was the reply.[1]

London brokers attempted to protect themselves by sending circulars to growers protesting at the 'baneful influence of dual markets for colonial wool'[2] and claiming that growers would get better prices if they sold in London; Henry Austin and prominent buyers from Europe argued forcefully to the contrary, that the price of wool was no longer expressed in London but in Sydney and Melbourne by hourly cable communications with France, Germany and Belgium. In time manufacturers from Bradford saw the light and sent out their own buyers.

The Australian market was now coming into full maturity and reducing its dependence on London agents while Australian Chambers of Commerce and associations of stock and station agents were refining the whole process. A photograph taken in 1881 of a wool sale at Harrison, Jones and Devlin shows rows of formally dressed bearded gentlemen sitting on wooden benches preparing to bid, possibly still using the silent bidding system of winks, nods and signs that prevailed in the early days.

That year saw the establishment in Australia of a French bank. It was officially named the Comptoir National d'Escompte de Paris, but generally referred to as the Comptoir, and is now the Banque Nationale de Paris or BNP. It was said to have been underwritten by a group of French merchants, thus enabling European buyers to overcome difficulties encountered with English banks in obtaining the necessary credit to cover the time elapsing between purchase and arrival. In 1882, a French shipping line, the Messageries Maritimes, opened a mail and freight service to

Australia and New Caledonia, leasing a Sydney wharf the following year. This company had already pioneered the Red Sea route by sending the first commercial steam ship through the Suez Canal in 1869,[3] which hastened the demise of the picturesque many-sailed wool clippers which had raced their cargoes through the Roaring Forties and round the Cape of Good Hope.

The number of foreign buyers increased rapidly. Europeans came, sometimes by sailing ship, with order books for a year's purchases, attended the sales, which lasted about three months and then returned home. In time several European firms sent out permanent representatives.

Belgium acted as a clearing house for Europe, doing much of the early processing of wool and employing a number of buyers in Australia. One of the earliest, arriving in 1878, was Toussaint Dewez, who came from the vicinity of Verviers, an important wool centre in eastern Belgium.[4] Five years later another Belgian, Alfred van Rompaey, from a Flemish village near Antwerp, joined forces with Toussaint Dewez later combining with a Mr Ostermeyer to create a firm using their joint names. The company acted also as agents for the German Norddeutscher Lloyd Shipping Line since these were natural associates, as shipping lines depended on the highly profitable exports of bulky woollen bales. Frederick Hentze arrived from Antwerp in 1899 for the firm of Ostermeyer Dewez in Melbourne. In 1901 he transferred to the Melbourne office of the Basle firm of Haerle Simonius Strohl.

There are conflicting reports as to which of the French firms first opened permanent offices in Australia. Leroux opened in Sydney, sending two buyers, Emile Dervillée in 1876 and Emile Odon in 1880.[5] Masurel Fils and Henri Wattine were two of the first merchant houses from Roubaix-Tourcoing to open permanent offices in Australia. Masurel from Tourcoing sent C. Maquet as their representative[6] to open an office in Sydney; it grew to be one of the largest French buying firms and lasted more than a century. Emile Wenz visited Australia in 1884 to assess the possibility of establishing a branch of the Rheims wool merchants, Etablissements Wenz, and some years later offices were inaugurated in Melbourne and Sydney.

The great adventure of launching an enterprise on the other side of the world required momentous decisions in human terms. Edmond Delvas, a buyer for the Roubaix combing firm of Allard Rousseau, spent the early years of his career in the 1870s travelling enthusiastically for six months a year to buy at the wool sales in Australia and Argentina. But he married, and after the birth of their first child his wife protested at his lengthy absences. His employer suggested a solution to this problem by offering him a more stable and responsible position in setting up a permanent office in Australia for Allard Rousseau. His wife's family, however, strongly opposed the idea of sending their daughter to this distant land of savages and kangaroos. Edmond Delvas renounced the opportunity, and remained sedately in Roubaix as a *négociant* (merchant) for the rest of his life. Some 40 years later one of his daughters was to seize the opportunity that he had missed to live in Australia.

The companies of Richard Goldsbrough and Thomas Sutcliffe Mort amalgamated in 1888, and in the 1890–91 season Goldsbrough Mort's records show that 'Continental' interests bought 56% of the wool offered, England and Scotland 28%, USA and Canada 6% and others 10%.[7] America at this stage was protecting its own industry with heavy tariffs. Central sale rooms opened in Sydney in 1892, controlled by a unified Wool Brokers Association whose task was to look after the marketing of the clip for the growers, storing the wool in warehouses and organising the sales, for which the brokers charged handling fees and commissions. Quantity and quality were improving, and huge flocks were managed by a handful of men on horseback aided by skilfully bred kelpie and border collie sheep dogs. Sydney now took the lead from Victoria, and benefited from the wool boom which succeeded the depression of the previous few years.

By the late 1890s, wool was by far the nation's chief export; Australia was now said to be 'riding on the sheep's back'. A class of wealthy pastoralists had emerged who owned immense sheep stations employing large numbers of people, particularly at shearing time. In some cases the properties were run on an almost feudal scale, with homesteads surrounded with smaller cottages, stores, chapels, schools, post offices, even racecourses. The owners were highly esteemed and held great political power.

Queensland wool sales were inaugurated in Brisbane in 1898; wool stores and wharves were built along the north banks of the newly deepened Brisbane River so that the bales could now be shipped directly. The Boer War of 1899–1902 raised prices for a time, but only temporarily. In time the responsibility of the National Council of Wool Selling Brokers in a federated Australia was to estimate the clip and to chart a program for the sales in each state.[8] On the whole prices remained steady even as production rose, and the wool trade was both peaceful and stable until the upheavals of 1914. This was indeed its *Belle Epoque*!

Buyers were commonly being sent out by European firms in the new rapid steamships to set up permanent branch offices in Melbourne and Sydney, as the wool sales were of much longer duration. (The Western Australian growers continued to send their wool directly to the London markets till after World War I.)[9] This attracted to south-eastern Australia an international group of people who were prepared to take on the experience of settling for long periods, and in effect to make their lives with their families in this new country. In time a cosmopolitan fraternity evolved, with a unique style of living which was recalled in later years with much nostalgia.

There were also many Australian buyers, a number of whom achieved great eminence; knighthoods abounded. Others came from the north of England, mostly from the wool-combing and worsted centre of Bradford in Yorkshire. Japanese buyers from firms such as Kanematsu, Mitsui and Okura bought fine wool as well as raw wool and tops. Germans came from Saxony and Silesia, and French-speaking Belgians from Verviers, where effective techniques had been developed for washing and carbonising wool.[10] Hide merchants came from Mazamet in southern France to purchase woolly skins for their fell mongers[11] and tanneries. Most French buyers, however, were northerners, some from Rheims, but the majority from the twin towns of Roubaix and Tourcoing in French Flanders, the main French centre for woollen textiles. A number of Belgians came from Mouscron, a town just across the border in Belgian Flanders, who were often employed by French merchants from Tourcoing. These northerners were following a centuries-old Flemish tradition.

† † †

The region of Flanders is a plain edged with low dunes on its western seaboard. Over time this coastline was overlaid with sediment from the rivers, so that gradually the seaports were driven further inland. Much land consists of polders, low-lying areas (often below sea level) that have been reclaimed from the sea and protected by dykes. The plain rises imperceptibly towards the east, chequered with occasional sandy hillocks, always of strategic value in the many wars fought in the area.

Flanders was settled in the 5th century by Salic Franks, who enriched its soil over the centuries to produce a countryside suited to intense agriculture. Since early times these Low Countries had been closely associated with the spinning, weaving and dyeing of wool. Traces remain of cloths from the period of Charlemagne, dyed red with madder root, and with purple obtained from molluscs. In the 12th century Phillipe of Alsace obtained a treaty to sell in Germany cloths made in Lille, Douai and Tourcoing. There had been a well established trade in the Middle Ages between the weavers of Flanders and the sheep growers in the English Cotswolds. Here Flemish wool buyers were well known as they visited farms and Cistercian abbeys where they chose the wool which best suited the various needs of the cloth weavers, just as they do now, at the lowest possible price. It is held by some that the game of cricket was first played in England in the 14th century by settlements of Flemish cloth workers,

18

the name derived from the Flemish *met de krik ketsen*, to chase with a curved stick.[12] The arcaded late gothic Cloth Hall at Ypres bears impressive testimony to this commerce, and a number of churches in the English Cotswolds contain tombs and brasses of wealthy wool merchants.

Respecting the connection, Guy, Count of Flanders, made an alliance with Edward I of England against France in the early part of the 100 Years War, when mercantile considerations played a major part in negotiations. Flemish towns had acquired communal rights and despite wars, plagues and floods they remained prosperous and independent thanks to their influential merchant class, whose trading houses communicated with others right across the continent. However, because of the vagaries of royal inheritance and success in war, the Counts of Flanders owed allegiance successively to France, then to the Holy Roman Empire, then to the Burgundian dynasty who inherited the County in the 14th century. The domains of the Burgundian princes at one stage extended as far south as the Somme. Sheep's wool was a powerful symbol; when Phillip the Good, Duke of Burgundy instituted a new European knightly order in Bruges in 1430 he named it the Order of the Golden Fleece.

Before it silted up, Bruges was the port from which ships carried the fine cloth woven in Flanders from wool grown in England and Spain. Prosperous Flemish patrons, enriched by the flourishing wool trade, made possible a great period in art which produced such masterpieces as the van Eyck altar pieces in Ghent and the Memling paintings in Bruges. A portrait of Jean of Roubaix by van Eyck hangs in a museum in Berlin. At this time fine woollen Flemish tapestries were widely exported and can still be admired in chateaux and museums throughout Europe. In a later century the port city of Antwerp produced the baroque painters Rubens and van Dyck.

Through the commerce of wool two little-known towns, Roubaix and Tourcoing, were centuries later to forge a link with the new nation of Australia, and their importance will become apparent as the story unfolds.

The tiny commune of Tourcoing, some thirteen kilometres from the city of Lille, was fortified by the Flemings in 1477 as protection against Louis XI of France who had quarrelled with Mary of Burgundy for the inheritance of Charles the Bold. Despite this, and in that very year, Tourcoing was pillaged by the French. Nearby, in 1469, Peter, Lord of Roubaix, who descended from the English royal house, had been sent letters patent by Charles the Temeraire, Duke of Burgundy and Count of Flanders which gave to 'the peasants and the citizens of this town the power and authority to licitly weave and make cloth of all wools'.[13] Peter built a chateau and enclosed the commune of Roubaix with moats; a century later the chateau was pillaged by Calvinists. Throughout this period spinning and weaving were largely a cottage industry, and the artisans often combined their work with farming sugar beet, flax, hops, and chicory on minuscule plots in this fertile plain. The finished cloth was sold through international traders in Lille. In the following century corporations were organised, and the incumbent Lord of Roubaix appointed official observers to inspect pieces of cloth to prevent fraud. There was great rivalry between Lille and its two smaller neighbours, and on one occasion the Holy Roman Emperor Charles V, who was a native of Ghent and was closely associated with the welfare of Flanders, negotiated the settlement of a quarrel. He ordered the Mayor and Aldermen of Lille to restore to the Magistrates of Tourcoing the goods they had seized from several inhabitants of this town, and to set free the prisoners they were holding.

Following periods of Spanish and Austrian Hapsburg rule, Louis XIV annexed the southern part of Flanders in 1667, effectively cutting the province in two. Lille, Roubaix, Tourcoing and Douai thus became part of France, although their inhabitants at that time still spoke the Flemish language. The region suffered from invading armies from Austria and the Kingdom of Saxony in the French Revolutionary Wars, but in 1794 the army of the 'Grand Old Duke of York' was beaten on the plain around Tourcoing.

Like other provinces of France, French Flanders kept its individual culture, architecture, gastronomy, beer and *patois* as well as, in that epoch of slow communications, its suspicion of Parisian dominance. The northern part of Flanders was occupied by the French after the Revolutionary Wars and throughout the reign of Napoleon. After the Emperor's defeat at Waterloo, near Brussels, the region was incorporated into the Netherlands before becoming part of the independent country of Belgium in 1830.

The fluidity of the national borders under these successive regimes resulted in a loyalty to the institutions of the village and the province rather than to the nation.

Despite the many wars the cottage industries of the Flemish towns continued to develop their spinning and weaving of linen and wool into the 19th century, growing flax locally and buying their wool from domestic sources as well as from other countries such as Spain, Argentina and Germany. The industrial revolution taking place in England soon spread across the Channel, and the mills which had depended on horses to turn the looms now began conversion to steam power. Separate mills were built for the numerous processes of washing, sorting, scouring, carding, combing, and drawing to transform the greasy clip from the shearing sheds into the soft cream-coloured rovings[14] required by the spinners.

Great refinements were made in the design of machinery for spinning and combing in Roubaix and Tourcoing, and these two towns became the most important centres in France for woollen textiles, showing particular skills in the manufacture of soft all-woollen worsted. They now posed a serious challenge to their rivals, Leeds and Bradford in Yorkshire. The number of power looms multiplied tenfold in the 1850s as demand grew, and the removal of import duties on raw wool in 1860 became a strong incentive for considerable purchases from other countries.

French Flanders, identified as the *département* of Le Nord (the North) since Napoleonic administrative reforms, now saw the beginning of a period of unprecedented development and prosperity which brought much social and political change. Immigrants from Belgium joined agricultural workers moving from the country to the rapidly growing towns to seek employment in the mills. Crossing the border became a well established custom, so that even into the 1920s large numbers of Flemish peasants could be seen, wearing their traditional baggy black velvet breeches clipped back from their bicycle wheels as they rode from Belgium into France to work in the Tourcoing woollen mills.

This drift of people entirely transformed that damp landscape; the characteristic dark-red brick terrace houses and cobblestoned streets now spread in a wave across the farmlands of the plain. The ancient city of Lille, with its Spanish baroque Bourse and Vauban fortifications, was practically merged with the two smaller towns of Roubaix and Tourcoing, even spilling towards the north over the Belgian border into the town of Mouscron. Consequently the national frontiers at this point were physically and psychologically rather blurred. Although this did not affect the traditional rivalries that had always existed between the three towns of Lille, Roubaix and Tourcoing, this agglomeration, whose population had increased almost five-fold in a century, became known as the city of a thousand chimneys.

The administrative *département* of Le Nord had important coalfields nearby, with well developed road, canal and railway communications to the easily accessible ports of Dunkirk in France and Antwerp in Belgium. It also had the advantage of proximity to the flourishing industries of England. Like its English counterpart, Yorkshire, the region became the chief centre of the French textile industry and liked to call itself the locomotive of France, responsible for much of the country's wealth. A similar industrial development was occurring further east in Rheims which also became an important centre for combing, carding, spinning and weaving of wool.

A distinct bourgeois culture evolved in these last years of the 19th century, based on hard work, thrift and strong, extended family ties. There was much inter-marrying between the great industrial families, many of them arranged, and in time the matchmaking task was facilitated when the few surnames of the region were codified into a genealogical register called 'Les Grandes Familles de Roubaix-Tourcoing'. A daughter required a dowry. If she were really plain, the dowry needed to be sizeable, otherwise employment had to be offered to the prospective son-in-law; he in turn had to prove himself to be *sérieux et travailleur*, serious and diligent. These marriages often proved successful.

Families were large and work had to be found for all the male children. New enterprises became essential, and employment had to be created elsewhere if it were not available in the region. After the end of the Franco-Prussian War in 1870 manufacturers reopened their mills, now equipped with modern machinery. As international exports grew, the volume of wool from domestic sources no longer sufficed. A number of large merchant houses now emerged in Roubaix and Tourcoing to oversee the supply of wool from other sources such as Argentina and Australia. Coincidentally, in Australia there were now highly successful clips from improved strains of Spanish merino sheep, whose long fine fibre was ideal for the manufacture of worsted cloth.

So it happened that in the last years of the 19th and the early years of the 20th centuries a sizeable group of French and Belgian families from Flanders travelled for six weeks to the unknown, remote and anglophone country of Australia to launch their careers and their lives.

2

Arrivals

Queen Victoria still reigned when, in 1889, Georges and Marie-Thérèse Playoust steamed up the river Yarra-Yarra to the splendid new city of Melbourne in the colony of Victoria. The wealth generated by the gold rush had built a capital of wide avenues, traversed by cable trams. On a site where 60 years ago there were only a handful of weatherboard, slate and turf huts, there now stood imposing stone buildings, Law Courts in the Italian style, the new Princes Bridge, a newly opened cruciform exhibition building, a stone Parliament House under construction, university buildings, and perhaps the most impressive of all, the five-storeyed Federal Coffee House in Collins Street West, turreted, domed, garlanded, and with a mansard roof worthy of Haussmann's Paris. There was already a racecourse with a handsome grandstand at Flemington. There were clubs, theatres, hospitals and beautifully laid out gardens containing a high-towered Government House fit to receive the Queen. Most of the government offices were equipped with telephones. Port facilities were modern, with several commodious piers, a number of superior ware-houses such as Goldsbrough and Co. and a large steam crane. Ship repairing yards and foundries had also been established.[1]

Georges Playoust had been sent by his employer, the Tourcoing woolbroking firm of Henri Cauillez, to establish an office in Australia. He had been preceded by at least another of the large Roubaix merchant houses, Masurel Fils, and two Belgian firms. The journey would have taken about 34 days by the new steamers, and in much more comfort than a generation earlier. Contemporary P&O suggestions for a travelling wardrobe for gentlemen included half a dozen white shirts, half a dozen regatta shirts, half a dozen soft shirts, mixed silk and wool, all with studs, NO BUTTONS, five suits of clothes and a black silk coat for dinner. Passengers were also advised to 'see you are not cheated by rascally hucksters of jewellery, curios and nick-nacks at Colombo and elsewhere. Keep your temper in all places and under all circumstances'.

The cabin steward would arrange for soiled linen to be sent ashore for washing in Colombo. Since cleaning was generally performed by bashing the clothes against the rocks in the river, damage to shirts, and especially buttons, was common. Ships carried little fresh water and only salt water was available for plunge baths. It seems that when Georges and Marie-Thérèse boarded the Messageries Maritimes mail ship SS *Sydney*, bound for Melbourne via the Suez Canal, Seychelles and Perth, they took adequate precautions against these discomforts — according to family lore, they brought on board 90 pieces of luggage and two nursemaids to help look after their family of five children.

They had been married eight years earlier in Tourcoing, their birthplace. Georges was a kindly man, shortish in stature, with bright blue eyes, and his warm, genial personality was expressed by an endearing smile. He smoked cigars constantly, and was later to grow flourishing curly whiskers. Wool was not his background — he was the son of a school master at the Collège de Tourcoing — but Marie-Thérèse had a well established family tradition in the industry. Her grandfather had founded a carpet and blanket mill in Tourcoing in 1825, using horse power, then later steam; in the 1860s the mill was refurbished by her father with modern machinery from Liverpool and Manchester. At this time she had helped him with his book work, retaining from this experience a keen business sense. Travel held no fears for her, as she had often visited her Irish mother's family in Dublin and London. She was fully bilingual in French and English, was a talented piano player, and despite her reserved manner, she was a generous person interested in taking part in the social life of this new country. However, her first task on arrival in the colony was to give birth to a daughter, Eugénie, while bushfires raged through the state of Victoria. Two more children, Marcel and René, were born in Melbourne in the next five years.

They lived for a time in Kew and enrolled their children in schools where they felt their own French culture would not be too alien. They chose Genazzano for the girls, where they were taught by an order of French nuns who had recently arrived in Melbourne. Religious orders had been excluded from teaching in France by the new anti-clerical laws promulgated by Jules Ferry in order to laicise education. The two older boys, Georges and Jacques, were sent to the Jesuit College of Xavier to begin their Australian schooling.

The office representing Henri Cauillez was installed in three rooms in Oxford Chambers in Bourke Street, surrounded by solicitors, architects and accountants. However next door were the offices of Dalgety's, and Messageries Maritimes through whom much of the wool would be shipped to France. Georges immediately involved himself in the affairs of the recently formed Victorian Wool Buyers Association. There was much to discuss at the meeting in November 1891 at the Menzies Hotel, which included difficulties with different woolselling brokers and the need for a central sale room in Melbourne. Messrs. Dalgety and Co. were also to be informed of the desirability of a central sale room in Geelong.

There were serious problems that year in the economy of the colonies, particularly Victoria, where wealth from the gold rush had initiated a tremendous surge in building on borrowed money. This boom was now being followed by the inevitable reaction: financial institutions were perceived to be over-extended and investors withdrew their money, leading to several bank closures in Melbourne and Sydney. Crowds of frustrated depositors rioted in Melbourne.

Pastoral loans could no longer be serviced when commodity prices fell, and inter-colonial pastoralists held meetings in Melbourne and Sydney to discuss a plan of action. They had worries other than reduced wool cheques. The sheep shearers, fearing a reduction of their own pay as well as competition from the introduction of mechanised shearing machines, had formed unions to oppose individual contract labour and demanded a closed shop, whereas the pastoralists insisted on their right of freedom of contract. This was a constant conflict of principles. Georges learnt that in Australia the word 'scab' not only meant a disease afflicting sheep but had become a derogatory term for non-union labour (an expression imported from the USA) and, like other buyers, he was concerned that these disputes would extend to the waterfront. Maritime unions in Brisbane were refusing to ship wool shorn by non-union labour.

Feelings mounted in Queensland throughout encampments of itinerant shearers. On the grassy plain of Barcaldine, strike committees conferred under the 'Tree of Knowledge' to plan their campaign to enforce the principle of the closed shop. When armed shearers met under the Eureka flag demanding an end to non-Australian and non-union labour, the government feared further civil unrest and sent troops to deal with the threat. After six months, when the unions ran out of funds and the strike broke, there was serious violence; wool sheds were burnt down, attempts were made to derail trains, and grass fires were lit along the Condamine. As a result several unionists were gaoled.[2] Fortunately for the pastoralists, international trade began to pick up in the following year and most banks resumed business, but they were to endure one of the worst droughts on record, which lasted till the turn of the century. The first dispute was lost by the shearers, but it accelerated the development of the Australian Labor Party.

Another of the pioneer buying offices established in Australia by Tourcoing firms was that of the top maker and spinner Anselme Dewavrin Fils et Cie. They sent Paul Lamérand to Melbourne in 1892 to assess the possibilities of opening an agency to purchase Australian wool. Lamérand had been raised in the textile industry, as his family had established in the mid 19th century a *blanchisserie* where bolts of linen cloth were washed and extended on the grass to bleach. His report to Dewavrin was positive, and in the following year he returned with his young bride to Melbourne on the coal-burner *Ville de la Ciotat* to commence business. Dewavrin was one of the most important of the French wool firms, and is one of the few still in existence. Paul Lamérand's descendants were to keep a strong association with this company and with the wool trade, and were present when, in 1992, the company celebrated its centenary in Australia. Georges Playoust and Paul Lamérand, former contemporaries at the Collège de Tourcoing, were close friends and their families later intermarried.

About this time, Georges' brother Joseph was also sent to Melbourne from Tourcoing by Henri Cauillez et Cie. He settled with his wife and family in Kew, a little further along Sackville Street from his brother.

Both families moved to Sydney when in 1895 it was decided to set up another office of Henry Cauillez in the colony of New South Wales, as the auction rooms of Goldsbrough Mort had given the lead to the wool market in Sydney, which now had a population of 107 652.[3] Dewavrin et Cie followed suit, substituting the name of Lamérand in directories and auctions because of difficulty in pronouncing their own name. Jules Renard transferred from Melbourne in 1896 to oversee the Sydney branch of his company in O'Connell Street. Wool was in that year by far the largest export of New South Wales.

The new Cauillez office was established at 17 Loftus Street, in the building vacated that same year by Wenz and Co. These offices were located alongside the new pillared Customs House at Circular Quay. Here were the spacious wool stores of New Zealand Mortgage and Loan, Winchcombe Carson, Harrison, Jones & Devlin and Hill Clark & Co. These warehouses and the proximity of the offices of shipping lines attracted a large number of wool brokers and buyers to this end of the city. Circular Quay boasted facilities suitable for the largest vessels, which included the 7000 ton ship of the Norddeutscher Lloyd Line, *Kaiser Wilhelm II*. Others were owned by the French mail line, Messageries Maritimes, the P&O Steam Navigation Co. and the Orient Line. Messageries Maritimes ships left Marseilles on the first day of every month, travelled through the Suez Canal, reaching Melbourne in 34 days and Sydney in 37 days. At this time the Orient Line held the record steaming time of Plymouth to Adelaide in just under 30 days. Transport of wool bales was a core business of these shipping lines.

Sydney had developed into a fine city. The centre now contained two gothic cathedrals, an imposing sandstone town hall, a stone university building in the gothic style, an arcaded post office, two classic balustraded gentlemen's clubs, a new sandstone treasury and a Colonial Secretary's office in Macquarie Street, while an onion-towered Lands Department was under construction nearby in Bridge Street.[4] The streets were busy with hansom cabs, horse-drawn omnibuses, hackney carriages and several steam trams. Sydney Harbour was well fortified with guns of large calibre placed on North, South and Middle Heads, as well as batteries under Admiralty House and on Bradley's Head to protect it from a hostile fleet. A military road connected the forts on the north side of the harbour. Cargo ships crowded the harbour and steam ferry boats carried passengers around its bays and to more distant Manly, where the massive St. Patrick's Seminary dominated the hill. Gastronomic standards were maintained by Monsieur O. Desneux, a chef trained in Paris, at a restaurant at 173 Phillip Street called 'Paris House', where the table d'hôte was 2 shillings and 6 pence and a private room was 4 shillings. He also opened a *charcuterie* in King Street which provided delicacies such as *andouillettes* and pâtés.

Another centre of French influence was the outpost of the Institute Pasteur which had been built on Rodd Island in Sydney Harbour in 1888. It had initially been established by Louis Pasteur's assistants, Dr Loir, who was Mme Pasteur's nephew, and Dr Germont, to experiment on a biological method to destroy the rabbit population which was threatening the livelihood of graziers. Rodd Island was considered an effective quarantine area for this experiment, even serving as a safe haven for the actress Sarah Bernhardt's dogs. It failed to achieve its promise in the eradication of rabbits, but the scientists remained for some years to continue their biological investigations using Pasteur's methods, which led to useful vaccines for the diseases of anthrax in sheep and 'black leg' in cattle. These were to be used widely in New South Wales.

Two artists' camps had been set up by the water in Mosman at Balmoral and Sirius Cove. At Sirius Cove in particular, Tom Roberts, Charles Conder and Arthur Streeton were sharing the *plein air* ideas of the French impressionist movement with local artists. A boy called Harry Ervin, later to be the chief of an important Sydney woolbroking firm, used to visit the camp from his parents' home in Mosman and not only formed friendships with the artists but established a lifelong interest in collecting their work. He bought a painting called *A Souvenir of Little Sirius Cove* directly from Streeton when he was about 14, and much later bequeathed this work to the National Gallery in Canberra. Harry Ervin's interest in art resulted in bequests of his paintings to the National Gallery a number of years later. He also left to the National Trust a donation so substantial that it enabled the establishment of both the S. H. Ervin Gallery on Observatory Hill and the Norman Lindsay Museum at Springwood.

Although an extended drought was ravaging the country, Sydney was still a verdant city whose gardens spilling down to the water's edge were much admired by European visitors sailing into the harbour. For the new arrivals the contrast could not have been more marked between this sparkling blue scene and the flat grey landscape of Flanders, punctuated by factory chimneys and slag heaps, which they had left behind. The style of living of the two countries also differed noticeably. Tourcoing's austere facades concealed interior splendour, rooms crowded with antiques, carved panelling, mirrored doors, fine paintings and books. Social life there was luxurious but inward looking, whereas Sydney offered a vital outdoor existence, particularly appealing to the young.

Between the frequent and lengthy journeys back to France required by Georges Playoust's work, his considerable family lived in a number of rambling rented houses in various parts of Sydney's eastern suburbs. They chose this area in preference to the more remote peninsula of Hunters Hill which at the time was the predominantly French quarter of Sydney. This French flavour was due to the land developments of the Joubert family and the monastery of the French Marist Fathers. The Marist Père Piquet was chaplain of the French community for many years. The French consul, Monsieur Biars d'Aunet, lived in Hunters Hill at the Villa Annunziata, and Georges Playoust attended his farewell dinner in 1896.

For Marie-Thérèse 1896 was a busy year when, in addition to settling her family into a new city, she gave birth at home to her ninth child, Maurice. This did not prevent her from attending a ball to raise funds for the Bureau de Bienfaisance, the recently established welfare organisation for indigent members of the small French community. The following year Sands Directory listed the family's principal residence as Belle Vue Hill. This was probably 'Trahlee' where there was enough ground for the boys to run wild, and to keep farm animals, although it was not favoured because the steepness of the road up the hill tended to break the horses' legs. It was a healthier lifestyle than that of the inner suburbs of the city, where the bubonic plague still existed.

Georges and Marie-Thérèse participated in the affairs of the newly founded Sydney branch of the Alliance Francaise, which was operating a French language library in a very small way. As the only help received from the French Government was the gift of a few books for the library, some of which were distributed to schools and the university as prizes to encourage the study of French, it was necessary to raise funds, as subscriptions were not sufficient to cover expenses. By 1899 they had 1800 volumes in their library and were proposing to extend their operations. Language examinations were to be instituted, diplomas awarded and a public reference library to be opened. Many social functions were organised to raise funds to benefit both the Bureau de Bienfaisance and the Alliance Francaise. Wool buyers and their families became very involved

in both these institutions and were to dominate their committees for half
a century.

Marie-Thérèse formed a friendship with the capable Augustine
Soubeiran when they were co-treasurers of fund-raising functions for the
Alliance. Mademoiselle Soubeiran was a French emigrée who had joined
in the founding of Kambala girl's school at the request of Miss Louise
Gurney in 1887, both acting as co-principals.[5] She had also been one of
the founders of the Sydney branch of the Alliance and was later to become
its President. When Mlle Soubeiran was awarded its gold medal in 1911,
Marie-Thérèse gave an 'At Home' in her honour at the Australia Hotel,
receiving herself the title of 'Officier d' Académie' from the French
Government for her contribution to the Alliance three years later.

Sydney now boasted a French language newspaper, the *Courrier
Australien*. Its editorials had long deplored the lack of a French Chamber
of Commerce, and Georges, who was always active in wool buyers' affairs,
acted as one of the committee of businessmen which met early in 1899 at
the request of the consul-general to frame the constitution of such a body.
As the federation of Australia's states was imminent, it was felt that this
move was timely, to give a new impetus to trade between the two countries.
The first meeting of the new Chamber took place in June and was attended
by 30 members, who elected Georges as President. He continued to act
as 'Président Donateur' for most of the succeeding years until 1914.

The inauguration of the Chamber was celebrated by a banquet attended
by the Premier of New South Wales the Hon. George Reid, the Colonial
Treasurer Mr Carruthers, the Minister of Education, the Mayor of Sydney
and Dr Rougier of the Institut Pasteur. There were many long speeches,
during which the important issue of tariffs was the main subject. The
consul-general spoke of cordial relations between the two countries and
hoped that once federation was completed Mr Reid, who was known to
be an ardent free-trader, would use his influence in federal affairs to effect
a reduction in tariffs on French imports. Mr Reid in turn developed the
idea that commercial relations were the strongest brake on conflicts
between countries.

The Colonial Treasurer, in proposing a toast to the success of the new
Chamber, noted that in the last year direct exports from New South Wales
to France totalled £1 699 000 (mostly wool) whereas direct imports from
France totalled only £214 000.[6] The *sympathique* Georges Playoust replied
warmly to the Minister's toast, referring to the respect his French colleagues
had for the laws and the 'institutions which are the glory of Australia', and
'the love of this privileged land which must undoubtedly be destined to
hold a large place in the world'. In the reports of the banquet nobody
mentioned the quality of the food.

The *Courrier Australien* now assumed the banner of 'The official Organ of the Chamber of Commerce and of the Committee of the Alliance Francaise of Sydney', and began to report their doings with enthusiasm. One of the first tasks of the Chamber was to organise an information service for parties interested in establishing trading links.[7] The main concerns were the potential tariffs to be instituted in the following year when Australia's states were to unite in a federated Commonwealth, as already Sydney–Melbourne differences were emerging between the free-traders of New South Wales, such as the Premier Mr Reid, and the protectionist Victorians.

The early meetings of the new Chamber also discussed the feasibility of inaugurating a cargo line linking Australia directly with the ports of northern France. With increasing trade there were now insufficient means of direct transport, as freight carried on French ships had to be trans-shipped in Marseilles in order to reach these ports. The Chamber also concerned itself with an extension of the Messageries Maritimes route between New Caledonia and Brisbane.

The following year, at the beginning of the new century, the French consul-general and Georges Playoust were delegated by the Chamber to furnish the French Board of Trade with information concerning the proposed new shipping routes, in view of the rapidly growing trade between the two countries. An international congress of merchant shipping lines was timed to coincide with the 1900 Exhibition in Paris.

Georges, who was now appointed a Councillor of French Foreign Trade, combined his business affairs with a family visit to the 'Exposition Universelle'. For a whole summer Paris celebrated the dawn of a new century with this extravagant international exhibition, where countries rivalled each other with splendid pavilions lining the banks of the Seine. There was a German schloss with its own beer garden, an English manor house, a wing of the Kremlin, a Moorish café, a ceramic pavilion where Spanish art was represented by a conventional death-bed scene painted by a young artist called Picasso. There were concerts, art exhibitions, scientific meetings, football matches, car races, and the new motion pictures. The Alexandre III bridge, the Grand Palais and the Petit Palais are permanent reminders of this surge of optimism.

The family was back in Sydney by October. They had travelled on the SS *Armand Behic* with a Colonel Marchand, who left the ship in Colombo to go on to Peking. This was the former Captain Marchand who had had the temerity to raise the French flag in Fashoda, near Khartoum. Kitchener had raised the Union Jack nearby, and tensions were high, but fortunately the incident had been settled diplomatically. Marchand had been decorated, promoted, then sent well away from Europe. He charmed Marie-Thérèse, and gave her a fulsomely inscribed photograph of himself which she later displayed in an elaborate silver frame.

From its inception the Sydney French Chamber of Commerce had involved itself with French commercial affairs in Queensland, but it extended its interest to Victoria, South Australia, and Western Australia when these former colonies became states within the new Commonwealth of Australia. A variety of business men were members of the board, and included officials of the French bank and Messageries Maritimes. Another was Mr Alfred Wunderlich, the youngest of three brothers who imported the terracotta Marseilles tiles which were now colouring Sydney's skyline in orange as they replaced the old shingles and corrugated iron. It was wool, however, which dominated their concerns. Mr Learoyd, the English principal of Wenz, was elected Vice-President. Despite years of drought, wool was by far Australia's largest export, and in 1904 and 1905 France overtook Britain as New South Wales' largest customer for this commodity, a fact often overlooked in Australian histories.[8]

As a memento of this period, Australian weeds sprouted in the fields of Flanders from the seeds rinsed out of the wool during the washing process.

The Chamber deplored the fact that terms of trade were operating very much in favour of Australia, as at this time France was exporting only a few luxury goods such as pianos, religious articles, wines, fabrics, and laces to this country, and these attracted very high preferential tariffs. This is reflected in the balance of trade figures for 1905: Australia exported to France goods to the value of £5 762 904, and its imports amounted to only £510 950.[9]

The Chamber was concerned that French industrialists showed so little enterprise in developing Australian markets and even 'oscillated between imprudence and timidity', according to *Le Figaro*, a contemporary Parisian newspaper. In 1907 the committee included representatives of several wool firms, Lamérand of Dewavrin, Learoyd of Wenz and Co., P. Prenat of Picard Goulet, Lierneux of Lorthiois Frères, G. Leroux, P. Puech of Armand Guillou (skins) and Mr C. Shard of the Comptoir (French bank).

In 1905 Georges founded his own woolbuying firm to create a future for his many sons, leaving the direction of Henri Cauillez et Cie to his brother Joseph, who had come with him to Sydney from Melbourne. Joseph remained chief of Cauillez et Cie until his retirement in the 1920s and his sons Charles, Fernand and Paul later followed him into a career in wool. Joseph Playoust, his wife Blanche and their numerous family lived in a number of houses before settling in Strathfield at 'Woodside', a Victorian italianate edifice with a tower, and which had sufficient adjacent land to keep horses and a cow.

3
Wool Buyers

Henri Cauillez et Cie was prospering and was now one of the largest French woolbuying firms in Australia. Before World War I it employed some 35 buyers on contract, including Eugène Cau, who came from Tourcoing in 1909 to work in Melbourne, and Phillipe Scamps from Roubaix to work in Sydney. In time, like many of their colleagues, these men were to make their lives in Australia. The significance of the diaspora of wool buyers from France and Belgium is made evident by the 34 firms listed in Sands Directories for Sydney under the classification of 'Woolbrokers' or 'Wool Merchants' before 1914 (see Appendix I).

Anatole Paroissien and his brother Victor arrived from Rheims in the 1890s, sent by the firm of Eugène Gosset. They settled first in Melbourne, then followed the growing Sydney sales to establish an office at 63 Pitt Street. They were to have many Australian descendants, of whom several were wool buyers. Anatole's son, Marcel, and grandson, Jean, followed him in the wool trade.

Many others arrived at the turn of the century to work on contract for French firms, fully expecting to return home at the end of their term. Not all did; quite a few stayed on in the country to be succeeded by their sons in the same enterprise, within the tradition of family employment. No one was in the least concerned about nepotism; it was expected.

For example Joseph Flipo came from Roubaix in 1911, at the request of his uncle Paul Lamérand, to work for Anselme Dewavrin et Fils; his own son was to follow in the same firm.

Victor Dekyvère came from Roubaix in 1908 as a representative of Mathon-Bertrand, and remained with that company until 1912, when Dekyvère Sonneville was founded. His brother Paul followed him to Australia, but worked independently through Masurel. Loyal to the tradition, Victor's two sons, Victor Jr and Marcel, were to succeed their father in his company and all continued to live in Sydney.

Jean Droulers arrived from the northern French town of Fourmies in 1912 to work for the Belgian firm of Kreglinger, but in later years was to take over the direction of Masurel, and was followed by his youngest son.

Paul Wattel from Lille worked for Emile Lahousse, and his younger brother Benjamin was employed by Louis Kint, where he was followed by his son Raymond.

The Roubaix firm of Henri Wattinne was first represented in Australia by the Belgian Pierre Nutte. He returned to his home in Mouscron, impressing his family with the heavy gold chain which a shipping line had given him, and recruited his wife's three nephews: Joseph Parmentier in 1908, then Gervais and Georges Parmentier who arrived in Sydney on the *Otway* in 1913 to work with him. Charles Boggio worked for the Belgian firm of Fuhrmann, and his daughter married Georges Parmentier. Their descendants now live in Australia. Both Joseph and Georges had sons who succeeded them in the wool trade in Sydney.

Armand George arrived from Belgium on a German ship in 1912 to work with Toussaint Dewez, to whom he was related, then later with Moch et Odelin. His son, young Armand, followed him into this company.

French and Belgians, sharing a language and a common culture, were sometimes described as 'cousins in a big family'. The sufferings of 1914–18 were to strengthen this bond even further.

There was a parallel movement of involuntary immigration to Australia, of English buyers from 'Worstedopolis', the Yorkshire city of Bradford, the great manufacturer and trader of 'tops' (semi-manufactured wool, combed and prepared for spinning). Their names, like Beaumont, Whitehead, Laycock, Illingworth, Bywater, Yeoward, Biggin and Hill became woven into of the fabric of the country.

A unique camaraderie developed among the buyers as a result of their unusual working hours, structured by the timing of the wool sales. The location of their work also isolated them from other businessmen, so that they were seen by some to be a clan apart. Each working day at about 7 a.m. the buyers, dressed in shirtsleeves, visited the wool stores to appraise the wool. The atmosphere was very amicable as they shared the breakfast and lunch supplied in the wool stores, and in time they came to know each other very well. The francophone French and Belgians evolved a jargon of their own such as 'bidder' (to bid) — which had indelicate implications — 'le floor', 'grosse-braide' (cross-bred) and 'topper les lots' (to top the lots).

Usually the lots, already classed, were displayed under natural light on the top floor of the stores to give better visibility. The wool was then spilling out of the bales, as a portion of each lot was broken open on the display floor. The work was an interesting challenge. Wool is a highly variable material and, not unlike wine enthusiasts, the buyers came to know the product of different districts and to understand the effects on it of weather conditions. They used their hands and their eyes to assess the suitability of the wool, as buyers had for centuries past, measuring the length of the staple, feeling and counting the crimps in the fibre, assessing the colour, watching for extraneous matter such as dust or seeds, which would not be welcomed by manufacturers half way across the world. Afterwards it was necessary to clean their hands meticulously to remove the burrs, but the lanolin in the wool kept them soft.

They were fascinated by their craft, and their skills took years to acquire. A knowledgeable buyer was invaluable to his employers as he was able to evaluate to the last percentage the yield of a bale. The type of wool was gauged to meet the specific needs of the mill owners, who were so concerned to judge the 'handle' of a fabric that it was not uncommon for them to greet their fellow manufacturers by fingering the lapel of their suits before they shook hands! These traditional methods are nowadays almost superseded by objective testing with instruments which measure the diameter and length of the staple, mechanically specifying the 'microns'. Wool buyers now call themselves 'Wool Exporters' and are more remote from the action. The wool auctions have deserted their dignified urban sites, and are now held in desolate warehouses at the outer limits of the cities. The venerable wool stores such as Dalgety's, Winchcombe Carson, AML&F and Goldsbrough Mort have been demolished, set on fire or converted into apartments.

After their long mornings in the wool stores, the Sydney buyers changed into more formal clothes to meet their colleagues at the Wool Exchange in Macquarie Place at 2 p.m. for the auctions. They took their ranks in the amphitheatre, each seat bearing the name of the buyer, the more important buyers seated towards the front. Here the good humour of the morning was put aside as they focused their attention on competing to obtain at the best possible price the wool they had appraised in the morning. 'We could have shot each other', or 'We could have poked their eyes out', some related later.

The auctioneer mounted his rostrum below as though he were conducting an orchestra, announcing the number of each lot, and then listening with intense concentration. As each lot was called, the buyers consulted their catalogues, then quickly and aggressively bid against each other, rising from their seats in the curved panelled tiers, gesticulating all the while to secure the attention of the auctioneer, and increasing the bids in fractions as small as a penny, halfpenny or farthing. At the end of the bidding the auctioneer struck the rostrum with his gavel, and in a level voice announced the value of the lot with the name of the buyer.

As some 350 lots had to be cleared in an hour, each lot would be sold in a matter of seconds. Behind the buyers sat the pencillers, not unlike bookmakers' clerks, with catalogues in hand, recording the values reached by each lot, and to whom they were sold. The various signs and cries of 'arf! arf!' were incomprehensible to anyone but the auctioneer and the pencillers, although the characteristic high-pitched squeaks of the Japanese bids became familiar to the growers crowding the public gallery high up at the back of the hall.

For these graziers, who had made the long journey to town to discover the result of their whole year's effort, these few rowdy seconds decided whether they were to return home crestfallen, or bearing generous gifts. For country children accompanying their parents the sales themselves were a little disappointing, as they could not follow the action at all, but they were at least able to enjoy the fizzy drinks supplied by the brokers.

After the excitement of the auction, the buyers returned to their offices to deal with cables, informing their principals in Europe of their purchases, and taking orders for the next day's sales. On the following morning they sent representatives to the wool stores to draw samples from the bales which had been bought but not yet displayed. If this examination verified the appraisal, arrangements were then made to ship their purchases across the world. Wool shipments formed a considerable part of the business of the shipping lines, and it is not surprising that shippers and buyers often became close friends.

The buyers also travelled interstate together by train several times a year to attend sales in Brisbane. They took with them packs of cards, hampers of delicacies and fine vintages of Bordeaux and Burgundy to relieve the tedium of the long journey, before arriving covered in soot at two o'clock the following afternoon. The routine of appraisals and auctions was repeated in Brisbane, providing some equality of service to the growers from the distant parts of the huge state of Queensland.

These men from Flanders enjoyed a comparatively cosmopolitan society, augmented by diplomats, European bankers and shipping line executives from various countries and a handful of scientists and academics. Early in the 20th century few Australians had travelled to Europe because of the expense and the distance, but many of those who did showed a great deal of interest in local French institutions such as the Alliance Francaise on their return home. The Alliance in particular was to benefit from Australian participation, as its activities generated understanding between both countries.

Not all members of woolbuying dynasties followed this strict career path. One of the most interesting breakaways was Paul Wenz, who at the age of 23 was sent from Rheims in 1892 ostensibly to visit his family's firm, Etablissements Wenz, which had Australian offices in Melbourne and Sydney. His nomadic instincts had developed early; in his childhood, his favourite place to hide and play was amongst the wool bales in his father's storerooms, and at the same time he had formed an acquaintance with a man who had made and lost a fortune in the Australian gold fields. According to a school contemporary, the writer André Gide, Paul Wenz even then seemed to think only of travel abroad. At their college, the École Alsacienne, whose dormitory was in the former house of the poet and literary critic Sainte-Beuve, there had been pupils from many countries, and this further fuelled Paul's interest. He joined the family business for a time, but felt caged in by office work. After performing the obligatory military service and a period in Algeria, he sailed to Australia, where in Ballarat he met his old friend Joseph Krug of the wine family from Rheims.

He was an extremely tall man, about 6 ft 5 in (196 cm), and handsome. Already determined not to spend his life working behind a desk in the city, he set off jackarooing along the Murrumbidgee and in the Gulf Country. Enamoured with Australian country life, he bought a station, 'Nanima' in the fertile Lachlan River flats near Forbes in New South Wales, an area pioneered by other Frenchmen.[1] He received financial help from his family, on the proviso that he should return to visit them every four years. By the end of the century he had married an Australian country woman, Harriet Dunne, built a generously proportioned bungalow on 'Nanima' roofed with Marseilles tiles, and had already embarked on a literary career.

This kindly man had a good facility in English which enabled him to meet a variety of people and befriend many in the district. He drew on them to form the characters in his short stories and novels which were published over the years in the French magazines *L'Illustration*, and *Nouvelle Revue Francaise* under the nom-de-plume of Paul Warrego, the name of a Queensland river. He was not afraid of a little mild mocking, referring to Forbes as a town that had one hotel to every 100 inhabitants, but the tone was gentle. Although he wrote in the French language, his prose was simple, without the customary literary flourish of his contemporaries. In these tales he evoked an authentic Australian atmosphere and was sure of his facts, unlike certain other transient French writers. He depicted Henry Lawson-like personalities in his shearers, rouseabouts and immigrants, and wrote about Aborigines with a sympathy ahead of his time. Parts of his work seem autobiographical, describing the caged-up feeling of the office worker who longed only to travel, and he openly admitted to his dislike of city life. His *Diary of a New Chum*, first published in Melbourne in 1908, was his only novel written in the English language, although a short story also appeared in the *Bulletin*.[2] He had many literary acquaintances in Australia, and befriended the American novelist Jack London, whose work he translated into French. He also maintained a long literary correspondence with the French novelist and old school mate, André Gide.

With such a fertile mind, Paul Wenz had many interests. He shared his brother's enthusiasm for aerial photography, which at the time meant attaching a camera to a kite. He also took very competent photographs of the countryside with an enormous wooden box camera. He still had a passing concern for the woolbroking affairs of Etablissements Wenz, through whom he shipped his own clip. He and his wife visited their agencies in various places such as Argentina, Chile and Uruguay. They also went to the Pacific Islands, South Africa, China and the East Indies, and crossed Russia on the Trans-Siberian Railway, becoming a source of wonder to their more static neighbours in Forbes.

4

The Kangaroo Cousins

Few wool buyers had planned to emigrate permanently, but over the years when their children went to school they adopted the language of their friends and felt themselves to be part Australian. After the Playoust family's move to Sydney, the girls were enrolled at the Sacré Coeur Convent at Rose Bay. Like their previous teachers the Genazzano nuns, these French nuns had also arrived in Australia in 1882 after being exiled by the new and rigid anti-clerical laws relating to French education. They brought with them precious carved choir stalls for their chapel from their former convent in Paris.[1]

The older Playoust boys, Georges (13) and Jacques (12) were enrolled as boarders at St. Ignatius College, Riverview in the first term of 1896 for the joint sum of twenty-eight pounds and seven shillings per term and they were allowed to bring wine for their evening meal. The following year Jacques received a prize, a leather-bound copy of the works of Milton, with its book-plate inscribed in Latin *In classe iii Grammaticus Ex Insigni mento*. He also shone in a school debate.

More sombrely, their medical records indicated problems which were to plague the two boys for the rest of their lives. Georges was sent home after a serious abscess complicated an injury to his arm. This in turn led to osteomyelitis, a common problem in the era before the discovery of antibiotics. His arm was so severely damaged that in later years he was rejected for military service. Jacques received a sporting injury to his hip which similarly became a chronic disability.

Georges remained at Riverview till 1898, but Jacques became a day boy at St. Aloysius College in Bourke Street, where he completed his senior year. The college then moved to Milsons Point, where a sequence of younger brothers — Stéphane, Marcel, René, Maurice and Roger — were enrolled, as well as Joseph Playoust's sons. The extended family remained close, with the children meeting their cousins frequently to play tennis. They all spoke English with each other but they habitually spoke French to their parents. Some had problems in pronouncing the letter 'R'. To their friends at school they were 'Froggies', but they were nevertheless *les cousins kangourous* to their relatives, whom they met on their frequent journeys home to France. This dichotomy was too much for Jacques' spelling, which remained erratic all his life, even though he was very well read. With the birth of Roger in 1900 the family of ten was now complete.

Every second year there were long journeys to Europe by coal-burning steamships distinguished by several funnels. Entire families of wool buyers travelled together compatibly, as both children and parents knew each other well. The children revelled in the rituals of Crossing the Line in the Indian Ocean, followed by a day ashore in Colombo with carriage rides to Mount Lavinia, always under firm direction by parents to wear solar topees as a precaution against sunstroke. At Aden the destination was usually the Queen of Sheba's Wells, then as they sailed through the Suez Canal in burning heat, the children peered out the portholes to see men riding camels along the bank, or perhaps even a mirage.

Being bilingual, the children were capable of reverting immediately to European ways once their ships emerged from the Suez Canal into the Mediterranean for the final lap to Marseilles. A reverse process took place during the return journey after the long crossing of the Indian Ocean as the first Australian voices were heard in Fremantle.

At the turn of the century a number of wool buyers living in Australia chose a defined European educational stream to form their sons to succeed them in their enterprises. For example, Alfred van Rompaey, a Belgian, had married in Sydney a French-born girl not long out of schooling at the Sacré Coeur Convent. This couple had a deliberate policy to arrange the family's journeys so that their children should be born in Australia as British subjects, but be educated in Europe. Consequently two sons were born in Bowral, NSW. These 'Australian' boys were toddlers in Geneva and were later educated in London at Dulwich College, followed by an extensive further education in the German woollen centre of Leipzig.

One son, Leslie, returned to Australia at the age of 19 in 1910 to join the family firm, commuting between Sydney and Melbourne. He was fluent in English, French with a Belgian inflection and the classic Hanoverian German in which he had matriculated in Leipzig. A 1911 Ostermeyer Van Rompaey wool-type book still exists; it sets out 355 basic wool types and is printed in English, French and German. He married the daughter of an immigrant from Wurtemburg and an English woman, and they founded a family in Australia. Meanwhile his brother was sent to Montevideo to set up his own woolbuying business.

In Australia their agency for the Norddeutscher Lloyd Shipping line was flourishing. Their company secretary, W. H. F. Adena, was also acting as honorary consul for Germany when war broke out in 1914. This benevolent gentleman had been living in Australia for 30 years, but these were xenophobic days and he was sent to internment camp.

The patriarch, Alfred Van Rompaey, after spending two periods acting as honorary Belgian consul in Sydney, in 1882–90 and again in 1897–98, seems later to have visited Australia only for the wool sales, living alternately in Geneva, Kent and Leipzig, and interesting himself in the trade of sheepskins with the Mazamet fell mongers.

His compatriot, Frederick Hentze, who had arrived in Melbourne from Antwerp in 1899, married an Australian, Edith Berry, the daughter of a former premier of Victoria. Like other wool buyers, his occupation required regular journeys to Europe, and their eldest son Phillip was born in Leipzig. However Phillip was sent first to Melbourne Grammar to be educated, then later to a school in Switzerland. He was not allowed to go on to university, but was encouraged to undergo four years of practical experience in Italian and Austrian woollen mills before joining his father's firm in Sydney. By this time he was fluent in French, German and Italian as well as English.

Jules Renard and his Australian wife had three sons. The eldest, Clement, attended Melbourne Grammar for a time, but at the age of 15 went to Belgium before joining a large firm of wool merchants in France. He was to work with his father for 17 years until 1901, when he was appointed general manager of the Melbourne branch of a large German trading company, Lohmann.[2]

The sons of Toussaint Dewez were educated at Melbourne Grammar, Belgium and later on in Germany. They attended a type of finishing school in Leipzig which expected hard work from their students; 'Tue', who was said to have a talent for languages, complained to his family that he was obliged to attend a Russian class at 8 a.m. His brother 'Gus' followed him there some years later, with two other Australians, Oscar Kraefft, afterwards a buyer with Wenz, and Harry Benson. 'Gus' later worked for a period in Belgium. As a result the brothers became adept in French and German, with some Russian and Italian, and sufficiently knowledgeable about the wool industry to fit them for work in their father's company with its international affiliations.

One might wonder how the multilingual education these young men received might have affected their acceptance by other business circles in what was then a very parochial Australia, wary of foreign tongues and customs. Recent years have brought far-reaching changes.

After Georges and Marie-Thérèse Playoust's eldest son, Georges Jr, had completed his schooling, he was sent by his father to Leipzig to gain some experience in the wool trade, but his heart was not in it, and anxious reports were sent back to Australia by his tutors. Jacques followed him in

1904 but, being better adjusted, he settled down to learn. Leipzig was the foremost centre of the woollen textile industry in Germany, which at the time was a substantial importer of Australian wool, in third place after England and France. Jacques became proficient in the German language, their music and culture. His lifelong interest in these subjects resulted in warm associations with German wool buyers in Sydney. He also gained insight into the mentality of the Germanic people, whom he appreciated without being blind to the dangers of Prussian militaristic values. Tensions were surfacing at the time in the Balkans and in the European colonies in Africa, which were reflected by the strengthening of alliances among European powers.

Jacques returned to Australia to join his father's firm in Sydney and Melbourne, regretting this a little as he would have preferred to study law. He adapted to his career in wool, however, and was photographed in a Melbourne showroom in 1907 examining the bales alongside his father, with whom he had an excellent rapport. In 1912 he was attending sales in Geelong. His brothers Georges, Stéphane and Marcel were also recruited to the wool trade. This was not an age where children were given a choice, as parents decided for them what they considered the most practical career path.

The Playoust tribe made yet another move to Milford Street, Randwick to a Victorian gothic pile which still exists as 'Nugal Hall'. Here in December 1908 the two eldest daughters were married in a double wedding ceremony — Marguerite to Alfred Decouvelaere, a French wool buyer from Tourcoing working for Alphonse Six, and Marie-Thérèse Jr to an Australian, Ernest Polin. The two couples were to have less than six years together before the outbreak of war. The brides wore the elegant high-necked dresses of this new Edwardian period, and the six bridesmaids were crowned with enormous hats laden with flowers. Hats in fact dominated the wedding photographs; Georges beamed with pleasure under his silk top hat, and Marie-Thérèse appeared very much the matriarch in her large plumed cavalier version. Jacques was a cheerful unhatted groomsman.

Because Jacques and his brothers were domiciled abroad, they were exempt from compulsory military service. Despite this they were registered in classes according to their year of birth, *avec sursis* (with delays) and were liable to be called up for service in a national crisis. Since 1898, notices had appeared in the *Courrier Australien* requesting men of 20 and over who had not fulfilled their military obligations to appear at the chancellery of the French consulate with their identity papers to regularise their military situation. Those who did not conform, whether forgetful, insubordinate or refractory, exposed themselves to the penalties provided by French law.

Conscription for military service was then unknown in Australia and England, but had been an established institution in certain countries in Europe for more than a century. At a time (1998) when France is planning to phase out compulsory military training by 2000, it is interesting to look back on the history of this system, which was introduced during the Revolutionary Wars. In 1793, the year King Louis XVI and his Austrian Queen Marie Antoinette were guillotined, the new Republican Government conscripted 300 000 men to fight the Austrians. The Directoire Government in 1798 passed the first conscription laws requiring the registration of able-bodied men. This was further developed under the Napoleonic Empire and the idea was taken up by Prussia and other European powers. Subsequent regimes in France had modified the rules, but when Prussian forces invaded France in 1870, laid siege to Paris, defeated Napoleon III, and annexed Alsace and Lorraine there was a profound change in the French mentality.

Bismarck's military regime in Germany was seen in France as a permanent menace. Remembering the invasion of 1870, measures were taken to withstand another such experience. In 1872 a five-year term of military training for all able-bodied Frenchmen was established, though the period of service was later reduced. Germany and France now had large numbers of trained soldiers in reserve, but with a comparatively small professional standing army. France was divided into 19 military regions, with Algeria and Tunisia as the 20th region. There was a military government in Paris, while each region had the necessary magazines and stores to enable it to take to the field. This dispersal was to enable France to continue the fight in the coming war, even though part of the country was quickly occupied. The levies of 1910 were for men between the ages of 20 and 45. In August 1913 the situation was tense enough in regard to the German threat that an army law was passed lengthening the period of military service to three years, thus increasing the army's strength by one third.[3]

In this way the general mobilisation declared in 1914 meant that Germany, Austria and Russia were able to mobilise large numbers of troops, while France was able to muster nearly eight million men, augmented by 500 000 colonials. In contrast, Great Britain kept a comparatively small professional army. Since the days of Cromwell's 'Ironsides' the British people had felt a deep aversion towards the idea of a large standing army. The Island Kingdom was to depend on its powerful navy to defend its shores.

Far away in the antipodes the newly federated Australia had never known an external threat. The only wars known to Australians had been fought half-way across the world, where in response to the call of Empire,

contingents of volunteers were sent to the Crimea, the Sudan and South
Africa. In the same spirit of loyalty they were to respond massively to the
call of the 'Mother Country' in 1914.

When Lord Kitchener of Khartoum visited Australia in 1909 to inspect
military installations, he recommended the formation of an army of 80 000
men, the establishment of a training school for officers, and for military
training of one to two weeks in camp for young men between the ages of
12 and 25 years. A number of schools formed cadet corps, and Maurice
Playoust was photographed in his St. Aloysius cadet uniform in 1912 before
a first general review and march through the streets of Sydney by the
combined corps.

His older brother Jacques, who is about to assume a central place in
this story, still lived at home and was pursuing a carefree bachelor life. He
had a new camera, recording events in photographs now fading in their
Art Nouveau albums. He photographed his games with the 'I Zingari'
cricket team,[4] a new open 'motor car' trip along rough dirt roads across
the McPherson Ranges to Brisbane, long-skirted skiers at the Hotel
Kosciusko, gaff-rigged yachts, and Snowy Baker, the Olympic all-rounder,
in boxing gear. He took a picture in profile of his father, 'the Boss', for
whom he had much affection, sitting at his desk wearing shirtsleeves, a
pince-nez on his nose and a pencil behind his ear. He travelled alone to
France on the *Otranto* in 1911, returning on the *Mauretania* via New York,
where he photographed the revolutionary new triangular skyscraper, the
Flat Iron Building, before taking a train journey across the Canadian
Rockies.

This was the year in which his family moved into the newly built
'Murrulla' in Martin Road, opposite one of the monumental gates of
Centennial Park, where the young trees were gaining height. The park
had served in 1901 as the venue for the ceremony proclaiming the
Commonwealth of Australia and the swearing-in of the first Governor
General, Lord Hopetoun. 'Murrulla' had the advantage of a great deal of
surrounding land, with a bush house for the younger children's games
and a tennis court, where the ladies played in long skirts and large hats.
The house still exists, though now greatly embellished. It is said to be the
setting chosen by Patrick White for his novel *The Eye of the Storm*. The
house also had stables where Jacques kept his horse 'Starlight', on which
he rode in Centennial Park. He was a keen horseman and occasionally
rode to the Blue Mountains, stopping to water the horses by the Nepean
before riding on to the fine new hotel at Medlow Bath or to stay with
friends at Mount Wilson.

In 1913 Jacques was in Europe again, travelling by the SS *Otway* to
Naples, then making his way slowly north through Italy. In Switzerland

he climbed the Jungfrau before facing his clients at the mills of Roubaix-Tourcoing and Yorkshire. On the return journey there was the ritual rickshaw ride to the Galle Face Hotel at Colombo. The good times were not quite over when a 'motor trip' to Goulburn was photographed some time in 1914, with picnics by the side of the road, and a high-shouldered bottle of Bordeaux in the foreground. As the women were wearing winter clothes, the assassination at Sarajevo (28 June) could not have been far away.

PART II
War

5

The Call to Arms

Crown Prince Franz-Ferdinand, the heir to the throne and his morganatic wife were making an official visit to Sarajevo in the province of Bosnia-Herzegovina, then part of the Austro-Hungarian Empire, when they were shot dead by a Bosnian Serb student, aged 19. Local troubles broke out immediately, and the leading French magazine of the time, *L'Illustration*, recounted that Serbs in the city were 'attacked and brutalised, their shops pillaged by gangs of Croatians'. Similar unrest developed on a global scale. Complex networks of alliances had evolved over the last decades, at this stage resolving into two blocks: on the one side the Triple Alliance with France, England and Russia, later joined by Italy and Japan, on the other the Central Powers of Germany, the Austro-Hungarian Empire and later Turkey.

Power plays, regional rivalries, wrongs to be avenged, and premeditated military strategies all created a perilous situation. A month later Austria declared war on Serbia, then the action began. Expressed in the simplest terms, events proceeded thus:

August 1   France, Germany and Belgium called up their reservists, and within 48 hours 2 million men were mobilised. Germany declared war on Russia.

August 2   German troops entered French territory.

August 3   Germany formally declared war on France.

August 4   Germany declared war on neutral Belgium and immediately crossed her frontier with one million men. Britain, as Belgium's guarantor, issued an ultimatum expiring at midnight. This was ignored and accordingly Britain declared war on Germany.

Australia, as a self-governing Dominion of Great Britain, was automatically at war and, jointly with New Zealand, offered to send an expeditionary force, to be known as ANZAC, to support Britain. Australia also put her naval force under the control of the British Admiralty.

This was far from being exclusively a European war. Australia took measures to protect her regional security, for Germany had a wide presence in the Pacific. The island of New Guinea was divided between Papua, which was administered by Australia, sharing its northern border with the German possession of Kaiser Wilhelmsland, and its western border with Dutch New Guinea. To the east was the Bismarck Archipelago whose fine harbour at Rabaul was potentially useful to the German Navy. Western Samoa and the phosphate island of Nauru were also German possessions. Within weeks, and at the request of the British Government, an Australian naval and military force landed on the eastern coast of the Gazelle Peninsula,[1] taking control of the German wireless station and administrative centre of Rabaul. Six Australians were killed[2] and were thus the first Australian casualties of the war. The German presence surrendered and gradually Australian patrols and district officers pushed further into the interior, taking over permanently the whole German-controlled territory. Had Germany won World War I, and had the British Navy been defeated, the consequences for Australia's security would have been serious.[3]

A New Zealand force occupied Western Samoa, while Australians took the island of Nauru and evacuated the German inhabitants. The equator was seen as the limit of Australian influence, as north of the equator the Japanese, now allied to Britain after declaring war on August 28, occupied the German-held Mariana, Caroline and Marshall Islands, together with Palau. The Japanese also besieged and took a German naval base on China's Shantung Peninsula near which Germany's Far East naval squadron, consisting of two 11 600 ton cruisers, the *Scharnhorst* and the *Gneisenau* and three light cruisers, including the infamous *Emden*, had been deployed. The squadron was commanded by Admiral Graf von Spee, and his flagship, the heavily armed *Scharnhorst*, was equipped with up-to-date wireless enabling the ships to play an effective game of cat and mouse with Allied navies. The light cruisers were directed west to the Indian Ocean to raid Allied shipping. The threatening presence of these ships was a source of anxiety to Australia, who was entirely dependent on merchant shipping for her international trade and, in time to come, for transporting troops. This devastating possibility later became evident when the SS *Troilus,* carrying 2000 bales of wool to England, was sunk by the *Emden* off the coast of India.

While an Australian squadron was searching for the *Scharnhorst* and the *Gneisenau* off the coast of New Guinea, these two heavy cruisers were hiding in the Mariana Islands, before heading well east to the remote French outpost in the Society Islands, which was still without wireless and unaware that there was a state of war. The two ships arrived outside the coral reef of Bora Bora with their names painted over and the headbands of the sailors' caps turned inside out. When the sole representative of France on the island, a simple gendarme, arrived to inspect the ships he was received personally by the Admiral, who requested provisioning of meat, fish, eggs and fruit which would be paid for in English gold. The Admiral even offered to take a delivery of mail, but the gendarme demurred when he observed sacks labelled AUSTRALIAN MAIL stored under a secret deck.[4]

When the crew went ashore to collect the provisions the natives, with traditional politeness, also gave them two hundred coconuts. The following day the cruisers made for Tahiti, but were refused entry by better-informed authorities. The Germans responded by shelling the town of Papeete, causing damage and some casualties. They then collected more provisions and money from neighbouring islands and sailed through the Straits of Magellan into the Atlantic. *Scharnhorst* and *Gneisenau* received their retribution in December — the British had acquired a copy of the German naval code and the German cruisers, lured to the Falkland Islands by a false radio signal, were sunk by a waiting fleet of Royal Navy vessels.[5] Graf von Spee, in heroic naval tradition, went down with his flagship.

Within days of the declaration of war, the port of Sydney was shut at night, with daytime restrictions on the movements of steamers and sailing ships. Military censorship was imposed on cables, and there was a temporary cessation of wool and mineral exports. Enemy aliens were interned, including a number of German wool buyers who were imprisoned in Berrima gaol.

Mobilisation was an unknown practice in Australia, but it soon became a reality for many young expatriate French and Belgian men called up for service in Europe, who were now to experience radical changes to their lives. Like most of the young Australian-born wool buyers in Sydney and Melbourne, the Playoust boys had not performed military service at the age of 20 as they were domiciled abroad, but they had been registered at the consulate as reservists according to their age groups 'with mobilisation suspended'.

The following announcement was made by the French consul in the *Courrier Australien* of 7 August 1914:

> Mobilisation has been decreed by the French Government and takes effect from August 2. All those Frenchmen capable of serving must consequently rejoin at their own expense their assigned military corps as quickly as possible. Those who have not the means to do so should deposit a written declaration to this effect. They will then receive a requisition for a French ship. The next departure for Marseilles will take place unless otherwise advised on 29th of this month.

Never one to delay, Jacques Playoust, who had just turned 31, had already booked his own passage on the first available ship sailing to Marseilles.

P&O had advertised the departure of the 10 000 ton ship, SS *Malwa*, sailing on 22 August for Marseilles, Plymouth and London. It had electric ventilators and reading lights installed in all the cabins, and the ship was equipped with wireless. The price of the passage to London ranged from £41.16s to £82.10s.

The household in Centennial Park was in understandable disarray. Father and Mother (Georges and Marie-Thérèse) were in America on their way home from France, accompanied by their third son Stéphane, who was 26 years old and also a wool buyer. Stéphane turned back to France immediately, as directed, to join his assigned military corps, while his parents continued on their journey across the Pacific, at some risk from the roving German naval squadron whose whereabouts were unknown.

Those now living at 'Murrulla' were Eugénie (Ninie) 24, René (19), Maurice (17) and Roger (14). Their older sisters Marie-Thérèse (Marie) Polin and Marguerite Decouvelaere came to join the group with their small children when their husbands were posted overseas — Alfred Decouvelaere with the French army, with whom he had already performed two years of military service, and Ernest Polin with the Australian army. Georges (32), was married and lived elsewhere in Sydney. He had been rejected for military service because of his arm disability, and instead was to serve his country in a civilian capacity by buying wool for the French government. Marcel's (23) whereabouts were not mentioned. He was also a wool buyer. 'Uncle Joseph's' eldest son, Jean, was an employee of the shipping line Gibbs, Bright and Co. and was liable to be called up in September, as was his cousin René.

The *Malwa* sailed as planned, carrying what was probably the first French contingent to leave Sydney for Marseilles. It was a group of 21 reservists, many of them wool buyers, and several of their wives. Among them was Jacques' friend Joseph Flipo, who had already completed his military service and attended an officers' training school before arriving in Australia in 1912. Marcel Paroissien was another; he was a near contemporary of Jacques and worked at Wattine-Bossut. His wife and two children were to follow him to France in January on the *Mooltan*. Other colleagues among the passengers were L. Dutriez, Aristide Desrousseaux, who worked for Masurel, and Georges Wauquiez, an employee of Motte Meillassoux, all merchant houses from Roubaix and Tourcoing. Armand George, a buyer with Toussaint Dewez, was returning to fight in the Belgian Army.

The *Courrier Australien* reported the departure of the Messageries Maritimes steamship *Sydney* a week later, carrying a large number of reservists, and the crowd farewelled them at Millers Point by singing the

'Marseillaise'. Jacques' brother-in-law, Alfred Decouvelaere, embarked on this ship, as did more of Jacques' woolbuying colleagues. Phillipe Scamps was listed as a passenger, disembarking in Marseilles with his wife, two children, and a maid. Mr Lefebvre sailed with his wife and three children. Paul Wattel, who worked for Lahousse and had been vice-president of the Wool Buyers Association, was part of the group. These ships also called in to Melbourne and Perth to pick up other reservists. They were to have an adventurous journey to Marseilles in their fully blacked-out ship dodging the German light cruiser *Emden* in the Red Sea. The *Emden* continued to prey on shipping lanes and to cause considerable damage until, in early November, HMAS *Sydney* destroyed it near the Cocos Islands.

Victor Dekyvère was on his way home to Australia when war was declared. He had already performed his military service in France 14 years ago, and was still in the army reserve. He immediately returned to France on the SS *Maloja* to report to his unit, leaving his expectant wife with her sister and friends in Adelaide. Gervais Parmentier went back to join the Belgian army, while Eugène Cau returned with his wife and their children. When war broke out, Jean Droulers had been on his way back to Sydney accompanied by his bride, but unfortunately they had chosen to travel on a German ship. They were put ashore in Java, their wedding presents were confiscated, and they were left to find their own way back to France, where Jean reported for military service.

Paul Wenz had only a passing interest in the family woolbuying company, as he was fully engaged in his property in Forbes, his writing, and his travelling. He was actually in France with his wife when war was declared. Now 45 and too old to fight, he volunteered to work with the Red Cross and was assigned to the Franco-British military hospital service, where his knowledge of both languages would be invaluable. He worked for a time at a military hospital in Versailles, where he met a number of wounded Australian soldiers who served as characters for later stories.

From his cabin on the *Malwa* on the night of his departure, Jacques anxiously wrote to the family at home, mostly in English. His spelling mistakes are retained:

22 Aout (August) 1914

My very dear Brothers and Sisters,

A line to wish you again goodbye & as elder brother permit me to give you a little advice. In a critical moment like this everybody has got to do his little best and I'm sure that everything is going to run smoothly at 'Murrulla'. If anything goes wrong ring up Uncle Joseph. He is a friend indeed and I'm sure he will do everything for you. But I do hope that

Father and Mother will not be delayed too long. If you get any news of his whereabouts wire me at Fremantle. As regards funds for the present at least you need not worry but the greatest economy 'est à l'ordre du jour' [is the order of the day].

As for René I don't know what to say. I cannot help but admire him for volunteering but I must say his underhand way of doing it is not by any means praiseworthy. If I am right he will be called under the colours this year and in wartime there is no 'sursis' [delay of call-up] & in France he would be considered a deserter. Anyhow Uncle and Alfred [Decouvelaere, husband of Marguerite] will talk the matter over and in Father's absence he must abide by their decision. Its no use objecting because they can absolutely block him as he is not 21 years old.

Wire me at Adelaide what has been decided.

With very best love to you all
I remain your devoted brother
Jacques

René, who was only 19, had still to wait several weeks before he was liable for French military duty, which at that stage was 20 years, but later reduced to 18. Impulsively, he had volunteered for the Australian Army without considering the implications of being classified as a deserter by the French authorities. In September he submitted to the official course and accepted being sent to France as a reservist.

Father and Mother arrived safely home to their disrupted household, and set to work immediately to help in the war effort. In October Marie-Thérèse was elected president of a committee to raise money for the Red Cross by giving a concert at the Sydney Town Hall which would include a series of *tableaux vivants*, a characteristic form of entertainment at the time. At this concert, Georges made a 'patriotic and vibrant appeal to the audience to participate in the auction during the interval'.[6] He would have had many dramatic events to refer to, as Paris had recently been saved from the German advance by the Battle of the Marne, and the first Australian contingent was to leave for Egypt shortly afterwards on November 1. The concert raised £1600 for the Red Cross.

In Sydney an issue of the *Courrier Australien* of the 20th November 1914 publicised an appeal for donations of money and materials with which to make warm clothing, to be sent to Madame Georges Playoust of Centennial Park. Two shipments of clothes had already been sent by the *Medina* and *Mooltan*, and two donated ambulances were to follow. Support was rallied and social fund-raising events were planned. This appeal marked the beginning of what was to become a significant charitable institution.

The French-Australian League of Help was formed at the request of the War Chest Fund with the aim of providing comforts for the troops in France. At a well attended public meeting held at the Hotel Australia on 22 December the first speaker was the noted economist Mr H. Y. (later Sir Henry) Braddon, chairman of Dalgety's. He asked: 'How is the burden of the war being borne? On the sea Britain is doing her duty grandly. But on the land, for every Briton in the trenches there are three if not more French.' Mr Holman, the Labor Premier of New South Wales, then asked for support, stating 'It is not sufficiently recognised that were it not for the two and a half million men France put into the field, the military avalanche which Germany was prepared to let loose upon Europe would have been unchecked. I believe the people of Australia will do all they could to forward the present worthy movement.'

Mr Holman and Mme Georges Playoust were elected co-Presidents of the new and very large committee, under the patronage of the French consul; among its nine vice-presidents were Mr Braddon and Mme Joseph Playoust. They were fortunate to have the participation of the two very capable women co-founders of 'Kambala', Mademoiselle Augustine Soubeiran who was elected one of the two hon. secretaries, and Miss Louise Gurney who became co-treasurer with Mr Braddon.[7] And so the two friends, Marie-Thérèse Playoust and Augustine Soubeiran who had worked together in the Alliance Francaise, were once more united in a cause.

Money was raised throughout the country. A workshop was made available for ladies to sew warm clothing for the troops and for their families in need, while depots were set up throughout the state for the collection of new clothing to be packed into bales. Shipments were sent fortnightly via the Director of the French Red Cross in London, Madame Brazier de Thuy, whose husband had been the representative of the Messageries Maritimes in Australia. One may wonder whether the writer Paul Wenz might later have been involved with the work of the League when he was posted to London in 1916 to work with the French Committee of the Red Cross. He wrote to André Gide from London that his wife Hettie was busy making up parcels for soldiers out of articles sent from Australia, all of the best quality and accompanied by notes saying 'From your friends in Australia'.[8]

During the war years the Alliance Francaise went through a difficult period, as there was a shortage of money available for their work. The possibility of closing was even discussed at a committee meeting. The Sydney branch was able to continue with the help of a few donations, and was staffed entirely by female volunteers, who took over the entire responsibility of the library for the duration of the war. They had familiar names that were closely associated with wool: Mlle Boggio, later Mme Parmentier, Mlle Lamérand later Mme Flipo, Mme Henri, and Mlles Eugénie and Antoinette Playoust. Paul Lamérand was President in 1917.[9]

Unlike the Sydney branch, the Western Australian branch of the Alliance, which had been founded in 1911, was not dominated by the wool trade, as the western pastoralists shipped their wool directly to the London markets. In Perth many of the Alliance members were associated with the teaching profession, both secondary and tertiary. When war broke out the committee organised very popular French classes which were attended by a number of soldiers preparing to leave for the Front.[10]

6

1914: Invasion

By now the situation in France and Belgium had seen sensational changes, as the German invasion had been extremely swift. Belgium could offer little resistance and was pillaged and burnt; Brussels fell on 20 August 1914. The first patrols of *Uhlans* (German soldiers) were reported near Tourcoing three days later and as the fighting raged between there and Ypres, convoys of automobiles were sent from Tourcoing and Roubaix to rescue the French and British wounded to bring them to newly established Red Cross hospitals. But the way to Paris was now open, as required by the German plan recommended by Schlieffen, a former German Chief of Staff, which had stressed the importance of the rapid seizure of the capital. In fact, by the end of August German troops had reached the Marne and were advancing towards their goal.

The 6 September issue of the French journal *L'Illustration* describes the provisioning of Paris, for the Germans were now only 35 kilometres away. Bridges across the Marne were dismantled. The racecourses of Longchamp and Auteuil were requisitioned for grazing cattle and storing hay; the Bois de Boulogne became a pasture for sheep. General Galliéni, the military governor of Paris, announced that the government had been obliged to leave the capital for Bordeaux, and declared himself ready to defend Paris to the end. He commandeered the taxis of Paris — 700 small two-cylinder convertible Renaults — to transport thousands of men in record time to attack the right flank of the invading army, a decisive move which stemmed the advance.

In the following week's report the situation was completely transformed, with French and British troops taking the offensive all along the line in what was quickly called the Battle of the Marne. The cover of *L'Illustration* showed a drawing of an infantry soldier with bandaged head and bayonet drawn, and the caption *Et maintenant, en avant!* (And now, forward!). The Germans were driven back to a high point behind the river Aisne, the natural citadel called the Chemin des Dames. This 'Way of the Ladies' had been built along the ridge for the daughters of Louis XV, to ease their journeys from the royal chateau of Compiègne to visit friends in the east. These chains of hills, which dominated several river valleys and the city of Rheims, were to be fought over frequently in succeeding years, as had happened since the days of Charlemagne.

It was in the Battle of the Marne that a new phenomenon was observed which was called the 'War of the Moles'. With reluctant admiration *L'Illustration* describes the perfectly organised trenches and tunnels that the Germans had burrowed into the white chalk hills of the Champagne region, just as the wine makers had carved out their deep layered cellars in past centuries:

> With their artillery to protect them, their pioneers arrive to the chosen positions furnished with light tools with short handles, followed by wagons with long-handled tools. The work is carried out with rigorous method according to precise principles like an equation. Each fusilier has a mathematically designed space, with no room to fall over if he is shot dead. Behind the trenches, troglodyte dormitories, kitchens, depots connected by passages. Sometimes the ground is cemented. One would imagine that these people have sworn to stay the winter. The machine guns have their place. Behind is installed the artillery. Let's hope our bayonets will win out!

This was the beginning of the trench warfare that was so characteristic of the 1914–18 conflict. The Germans had more than a year to fortify their positions with remarkable skill during the stalemate of the Front, using modern building methods to line their trenches with materials such as concrete reinforced with steel wire. The following week's issue of the journal contains photographs of Rheims Cathedral aflame, and recounts German attacks on Albert and Peronne further west in the Somme, and in the Aisne.

Such was the troubled situation when the first reservists from Australia arrived in Marseilles on the *Malwa* and the *Sydney*, hoping to find the appropriate authority to whom to report for duty. As most of the reservists had their origins in Flanders they had orders to report to their regional military depot at Cambrai near Lille, but it had been evacuated further south after Lille had fallen to the enemy on 20 October. The sea journey from Australia normally took a little over a month to reach Marseilles, but with the disruption of communications and train services Jacques might well have faced the difficulties on arrival described by Phillipe Scamps, who took nine weeks to find his regiment. Such delays in reporting for duty were simply not understood, and Jacques Playoust related a less than friendly welcome when he finally reached his military depot, now based in Aubusson, some 400 km south west of Paris. His reception was particularly hostile as he had not waited for the official shipping arranged by the consulate in Sydney; he was all but imprisoned as a deserter.

Jacques was now a *poilu*, a rough equivalent of the terms 'Tommy' or

'Digger' for the common soldier, and indicated a shaggy or bearded person. He was identified on the back of two postcards by a photograph of himself wearing his newly issued ill-fitting uniform, new rifle and bayonet, and looking serious but not yet quite military. The French infantry uniform in the early part of the war was a navy blue double-breasted overcoat worn over red trousers, which proved too easy a target for the enemy. However, General Galliéni was pictured in November in his new more functional grey-blue 'Bleu Horizon' outfit and gradually the men were issued with similar dress. It was not till July 1915 that they were provided with steel helmets to protect their heads in battle, although many had already improvised metal linings for their caps out of lids from their drinking mugs. The beautifully designed new leather-lined steel helmets bore the regiment's insignia in front, but the crest at the top covered small ventilation holes. A leather strap held them in place. These came to be worn as a second skin all the time the men were in the trenches, and greatly reduced the number of head wounds from shrapnel and stray bullets.

The first undated and anxious postcard was sent by Jacques to Tante Mathilde Leplat, his mother's widowed sister-in-law, who lived in Paris with her 16-year-old daughter, Marie. These two women became very generous and firm friends to Jacques, and he visited them every time he went on leave to Paris; Marie preserved all his letters. This card is translated into English:

Compagnie [Depot]
162eme de Ligne, Aubusson, Creuse

A little French 'piou piou' [footslogger] who greets you. It is a fortnight since I arrived. I have written frequently to the North without being able to obtain a reply. Can you give me any news? Is Stéphane in France? He was in America with Father and Mother when mobilisation was declared, and I did not see them again before leaving. I am getting quite used to my new trade. There are about 110 in the company, reservists and convalescents.

A new convoy is being prepared which is expected to leave soon. If I am to leave with them, even though I am far from knowing my job thoroughly I will try to manage, and perform my duty as a good Frenchman. With my very affectionate good wishes,

Jacques
Compliments to Marie

A similar postcard with Jacques' photograph was sent to a wool buyer in Australia who had worked for a German firm. The Sydney postmark seems to be 7 December 1914 so it would have been posted about six weeks earlier.

Dear Schuster

Still all well though it's pretty cold here at Aubusson some 1500 feet above sea level. Our depot was originally at Cambrai but it was transferred here when the Germans took it. We are being kept very busy and am beginning to feel quite hard. I don't think we will delay long here as they want every man.

Greetings, yours sincerely
Jacques Playoust

The training required to form a recruit into an efficient soldier had been estimated to take two years, but the period was now reduced to just a few weeks. There was no smart drill nor ceremony, only rough and practical instructions. Fresh from his training camp, and formally issued with his dull grey metal identity medal engraved with his name, his 'class' according to birthdate of 1903, his region of origin, Lille, and his recruitment register number, 5110, Jacques was posted to the area of Ypres, in Belgian Flanders.

Ypres was a quiet moated, ramparted market town with a precious collection of gothic buildings, whose finest jewel was the huge arcaded Drapers Hall, which had served as a centre for the cloth trade in the 13th century. It measured 133 metres in length, with two storeys of elegantly pointed ogival windows, and was capped by a massive belfry, the most beautiful in Flanders. Unfortunately for its architecture, Ypres was also strategically positioned to protect the port of Dunkirk, which was now a German objective. The port was all the more important to the Allies as Antwerp had already fallen to the Germans. No family letters survive from this time, nor any details of Jacques' experiences here, but a later newspaper interview indicates that Jacques was 'in front of the famous Hill 60 in December 1914'.

The battle had raged through October and November with French, Belgian and British troops resisting the German attack. The result was a stalemate, so when winter set in there were hundreds of thousands of casualties, a ruined city of Ypres, and the loss of many hectares of reclaimed land where the Belgian army had opened the locks, using the floods to halt the German advance. The original British Expeditionary Force (mostly regular army) was so decimated that for the future it had to rely on volunteers.

This indecisive battle initiated the phenomenon of the great trench deadlock, fixed in place for years across northern France, while the war raged on in other parts of the world. It was made possible by the characteristic Cretaceous rock formation of this area of Western Europe, stretching from the South Downs in England and the white cliffs of Dover, across the Channel to the low hills north and south of the Somme river, and eastwards to Champagne. As the Germans had done in Champagne, the Allied forces burrowed through the soft, chalky rock to create a complex system of manned trenches, one in front, a second support trench behind, then further back a reserve, as well as communication trenches and subterranean shelters.

The pioneers and sappers with their spades and mattocks now played as important a role as the gunners by excavating the communication trenches and tunnels. Engineers built systems of road and rail to transport men, food, guns, and ammunition to the front line, and to bring back the wounded. Thick networks of barbed wire fringed the trenches. Both sides faced each other across No Man's Land, an area between them stretching from 50 to some hundred metres. Both sides burrowed deep, sloping shafts attempting to mine enemy trenches or to establish listening posts, but for years neither side was able to pierce the opposite line to any significant extent, and then only at great human cost.

From aerial photographs the double line could be observed stretching to the horizon like the Great Wall of China, with an arid desert landscape at its core, but bordered in summer by leafy trees and ripening crops. The cord-like line scarred the landscape for some 700 kilometres across the map, starting from the north in the flat, boggy sugar-beet fields of Belgian and French Flanders, some of it below sea level, where an occasional hill was a strategic object, then extending south through the high plains of Picardy and the winding, peaty Somme river valley. The Front then took an easterly direction towards the Aisne river flowing parallel to the long ridge of the Chemin des Dames which, at its eastern limit, overlooked the city of Rheims in the chalk country of Champagne. Still further east came bleaker, colder country in the wooded hills of the Argonne, then on each side of the Meuse river rose the heights whose forts protected the city of Verdun. The line became attenuated near the forested Vosges Mountains and the border of neutral Switzerland, which marked the end of what came to be known to the Allies as 'The Front', and to the Central Powers as 'The Western Front'.

For three years this snaky cord curved to and fro, each slight change in the line leading to the loss of thousands of lives. Each sector of the Front had its own story. Regiments were moved from one sector to another, with rest periods in between which allowed the battalions to be 'reformed', a euphemism for replacing the casualties. The Belgian army, led by Albert their admired 'Soldier King', defended the tiny triangle of low land remaining free in western Belgium. To the east, some sectors such as the Verdun were manned by French troops, or their colonial regiments, largely African; other sectors, especially to the west in the Somme area, were assigned mainly to British regiments because of their proximity to Britain.

In time came regiments from the Empire: Canada, India, Australia, New Zealand and South Africa. North of the Front were the occupied territories, who had to endure the German yoke until 1918.

A newish invention, the telephone, was the crucial link between the trenches and their command posts, also between the front line troops and the artillery which supported them. The telephonist, which Jacques Playoust was to become, had the risky task of repairing the vital telephone wires, often under fire in No Man's Land, in order to maintain the chain of command.

The rapid invasion of Flanders had alarmed and horrified northern French and Belgian families living in Australia. After several days' bombardment, German troops had entered Lille in October 1914, and Roubaix and Tourcoing were occupied at the same time. This meant a loss of a crucial rail junction and canal communication centre as well as an important sector of France's industry.

By January 1915 pitiful accounts of the German occupation were appearing in Sydney papers. Immediately after the arrival of German troops, hostages from amongst ecclesiastical and industrial notables of Lille, Roubaix, and Tourcoing had been taken to German Headquarters, the Kommandatur, but later they obtained permission to take it in turns to remain in their town halls under surveillance. Soldiers with bayonets guarded the gates of the textile mills as huge requisitions in kind, including millions of francs worth of good Australian wool, were carried away in large horse-drawn wagons to the railway stations to be sent to Germany. All petrol, coffee and coal was requisitioned, causing great hardship as the first cold blasts of winter were being felt. The Germans later relented and sold sacks of coal in the street at an inflated price. Coffee was now non-existent. Animals, harnesses, carts and trucks were plundered from the farms while large quantities of groceries were requisitioned from shops. Fortunately a type of bread was still available. White bread had not been long in disappearing altogether, and the ersatz (substitute) was a sticky grey loaf made from flour of dubious origin, rationed to 1 kilogram a day for seven people.

The Germans then exacted a sum of 5 million francs from the municipality of Roubaix, to be found in 24 hours. This was levied from private citizens, who were later reimbursed in an almost worthless new currency. At least sanitation remained good and there was no typhoid fever. At first electricity and gas were still available, and breweries were very busy. Roubaix and Tourcoing had become a thoroughfare for German soldiers and trucks travelling to and from the battlefields.

English soldiers wounded in the first battle of Ypres were rescued, sometimes by the women volunteers of the Red Cross, who took them to their hospitals in Roubaix and Tourcoing. They were very often young women whose sheltered lives had limited their skills to embroidery and domestic tasks, but who in time became vital and resourceful nursing aides. One of these was Evelyne Delvas, who was later to marry Jacques Playoust. She nursed many English 'Tommies' at the Ambulance Saint-Louis for several months until they were removed to captivity in camps in German territory. All her later life she kept an album with their autographs, tenderly dedicated drawings and reminiscences of their battle experiences. She also kept her identity card issued by the Kommandatur demanding personal details like 'Grösse, Haare, Augen, Nase' (Size, Hair, Eyes, Nose). Fortunately her status as a Red Cross nurse in those years protected her from being commandeered for forced labour in Germany, although she and her family were subjected to danger and privations for the whole period of occupation.

German soldiers and their horses were billetted in private houses and gardens and the proprietors were obliged to leave their front doors unlocked to allow immediate access to the occupying forces. Newspapers were shut down and there was an 8 p.m. curfew. It seemed from later reminiscences that quite a few people of occupied zones had made prudent preparations; the folk memory of earlier invasions was still vivid. Knowing German appetites, the finer wines were walled up in secret cellars, and the silver and gold buried in the garden.

7
1915: Let's Not Think! It's Better!

From Ypres Jacques' regiment was moved to the Argonne, where he contracted typhoid fever, a potentially fatal disease of the small bowel which was caused by infections directly related to unsanitary conditions. If the bowel perforated it caused peritonitis, from which patients usually died, as antibiotics did not yet exist. Jacques was later to describe regaining consciousness in the hospital and becoming aware that, in the 'triage' of patients, he had been assigned to the third group of men who were expected to die, and for whom little treatment was given. He also suffered from a recurrence of his schoolboy hip problems which in later years were to cause severe arthritis with a pronounced limp.

Fortunately his mother, Marie-Thérèse, was now in Paris and could look after him during his convalescence. She and her husband had left their other children in the care of their older daughters, and were now settled in an apartment in a hotel in Paris, where they could see more of their sons during their leave. They were also active as members of a committee distributing donations sent by the French–Australian League in Australia.[1] Georges was at that time making a return journey to Australia to keep in touch with his Australian family and to wind up his business affairs; he was to return to Paris by the *Persia* in August.

There remains no correspondence from Jacques during early 1915 till a letter written in English to his sister in Centennial Park:

Hotel Métropole
Champs-Elysées, Paris
1st April (1915)

Dear Ninie

As you will see by above address I am now in Paris. How pleased I am you can't imagine. Liberty once more & finished with those horrid hospitals. Mother pets and spoils me like she never did. Under this regime I am progressing satisfactorily. I'm putting on weight every day, too quickly for my poor legs which still give me trouble. A few days ago after a very disagreeable night I called in the doctor. He was very comforting. He could not do anything. I had only to grin & bear it, have patience & not take too much exercise. He told me that my thigh muscles were more or less atrophied. I had a little épanchement de synovie [discharge of synovial fluid] He called a lump I have on my ribs periostite etc. For the form he gave me some medicine that tastes like wine. Its the most palatable I've had since the beginning.

It's simply wonderful with what rapidity my congé [leave] is going. Only 19 days more. I very much fear I shall make a sorry soldier if I have to go back to the front at once. They have been asking for more interpreters of late. Only last week I sat for a written exam. I must have got through for I'm to go tomorrow & pass the oral. I think I'm pretty sure of a job. First my English is very fair, then I've been to the front & already am fairly old. (I feel a 100 some days now). I got a tremendous lot of letters lately that had accumulated at my depot during my sickness. I'm a very busy man answering them all. I don't think I should have managed only the Doctor says I'm to be quiet. I got a long letter from Father from Gibraltar & was delighted to hear he had given the German submarines the slip. Its pretty risky job travelling nowadays. I shall answer it next mail.

Mother appears to be a very busy woman. She has a frightful lot of correspondence. Parcels to make for her soldiers take time too. You ought to go through her wardrobe. She has a big stock of all sorts of things buisquits, figs, caramels, butter and jam in tubes etc. A young grocers shop in fact. She gets things by the dozen, 'Its cheaper' she says. Then Aunt Mathilde comes every day for an hour or two. She is just as nice & kind as ever & thinks of nothing but giving pleasure to others. We see quite a lot of Marie too. She has not much to say yet & really wants more the company of young people. Father will have given you all the latest news by now so I'm going to conclude.

Give my love to everyone at Murrulla & Parisian. I'm quite keen to see my little godchild again. Won't she howl if she has the pleasure of seeing me again.

Things are going satisfactorily here. Premylzs has fallen & the Russians are on the move once more. I have not the slightest doubt that we shall get through the Dardanelles. The English who up to now had done very little on land are sending heavy reinforcements, 80,000 a week says Mr Moore.[2] We will win without the slightest doubt but it's going to take months yet. I doubt very much that we will get back to Australia before the new year.

Kisses galore from
Jacques

The year in which the letter was written was not indicated, but it could be deduced by his allusion to the fall of Przemysl in southern Poland (then a Russian possession) after a five-month siege by the Austrian army. This had one beneficial effect for Russia in that three of their Corps were thereby released to fight their way back to the Carpathian passes which led to the Hungarian plain.

Jacques' reference to the Dardanelles related to the Anglo-French naval contingent which at the time was trying to force a passage through the narrow Dardanelles straits, which were controlled by the Turks. Turkish mines blocked the movement of Russian ships from their Black Sea ports to the Mediterranean, and unless Russia had access to warm weather ports it would be difficult for her to be an effective partner in the war. Allied battleships shelled Turkish forts, but the naval battle which followed was abortive; three British and one French battleship were sunk, and others damaged.

Army landings were then deemed necessary in an attempt to control Constantinople and to put the Ottoman Empire out of the war. A joint force from Britain, France, Australia and New Zealand was collected on the Greek island of Lemnos, thereby giving the Turks plenty of warning of the coming invasion. (*L'Illustration* published a photograph of Australian and French tents pitched alongside each other on the beach of Mudros Bay, Lemnos — the Australians' accommodation was much more palatial than that of the French!) The dawn landing of the Australians and New Zealanders on 25 April took place at what came to be called Anzac Cove. After the landings, heroic battles were fought on forbidding terrain, and in their first engagement in the war the Anzacs demonstrated to the world their superlative fighting qualities.

On the same morning British troops landed near Cape Helles. Across the straits, on the Asian side at Kum Kale, 3000 French were landed as a diversionary measure; after three days' fighting the force was re-embarked after heavy losses. They were then reassigned to the right of the British in the Cape Helles area, where British, Indian and French reinforcements were sent in May.

The ill-planned and uncoordinated campaign dragged on fruitlessly for the rest of the year, while changes of priorities became necessary as the Central Powers overwhelmed the Serbs. It was decided by the Allies to abandon the Dardanelles campaign and the final successful evacuation from Cape Helles took place the following January. The campaign had been a splendid failure, but for Australians and New Zealanders it served as the fulcrum for their national identities.

Accurate casualty lists are difficult to obtain, as so many historians differ, and the Turkish records in particular were said to be uncertain. The following figures of lives lost are displayed in the Australian War Memorial in Canberra, and are ranked here numerically:

Turkish	86 692	Australian	8 709
British	21 255	Indian	7 594
French	9 874	New Zealand	2 701

These figures may surprise those who know only of the Anzac involvement in the Gallipoli legend and the tragic landing at Anzac Cove. They certainly reveal how dearly the British troops paid for their leaders' misjudgments and, indeed, the very heavy losses of the French. Few Australians seem to be aware that hey were at Gallipoli at all.

Maurice and Marcel, two more of Jacques' brothers now appeared in France. Maurice, who was 18, paid his own passage to France to enlist, as attested in official consular papers. His school magazine, the *St. Aloysius College Journal* described his departure thus:

> Before Maurice Playoust left for France and war he visited the College to bid farewell to his old chums and to the various masters. He brought Ludo Lamerand with him who is also off to fight. Maurice was presented with a beautiful gold mounted cigarette holder in a case by the boys, whilst the College gave Ludo a handsome pocket book. In spite of the difficulties of speech-making, everybody felt happy about the whole affair, especially as school was dismissed at 1.15 p.m. for the rest of the day. We have since received two most manly letters from Ludo and Maurice in appreciation of their gifts. On the Saturday the cadets marched to see them off and sang 'The Marseillaise' as the boat drew out from the wharf; and much was the patriotism thereof'.

On arrival he was assigned to the 3e Régiment du Génie (Engineers) based in Rouen.

How Marcel came to France is not known, nor how he happened to be in the photograph of a very motley group on the front of a postcard sent to his mother. The photographs was taken in Marseilles, probably the regiment's place of disembarkation before it proceeded for training at La Valbonne, a military establishment near Lyons.[3] The laconic message was written in English.

> Dear Mother, arrived Lyon yesterday. Nothing settled yet but we will probably go to Laval Bonne about 30 kilometres from here. We belong to the 6e Colonial. For the present its no use writing as we may be moving any time. I am in this photo taken in Marseille. I have put a cross against myself. Love & a kiss, Marcel.

The following letter to Marguerite Decouvelaere was written by Jacques while he was still convalescing in a hotel in Bourganeuf, a small town close to his army depot in Aubusson. The *poilu* was paid only 5 sous a day, but he seems to have supplemented this by a few comforts:

21 Aout (August)

Dear Marguerite,

Your letter of the 12th July came along with a letter from Marie & Ninie. Things are pretty good with me just now. I'm beginning to mingle a little in the Bourganeuf higher circles. It all came about in this way. By chance my lieutenant asked me to come and have a game of tennis with him. In spight of my side that still gives me a little trouble & my utter lack of form I beat him fairly badly & became thereby champion of Bourganeuf. Now I give lessons to the Captain's wife and daughters, the Doctor's wife, the lieutenant & several other members of the Bourganeuf grand monde. Its sometimes pretty trying but it all helps to pass away the time. Moreover it has got me quite a lot of little favours from the officers. 'Noblesse oblige' so I have had to get rid of my shabby old uniform & get one made at my own expense. For here at the depot we get old clothes only & it is only when we go to the front that we get a new rig out.

I have just got a note from poor Paroissien. He has earned the Croix de Guerre but paid very dearly for it. In an attack he got not less than 14 wounds, his face disfigured, most of his teeth knocked out, his arms, hand and legs badly endomagés [damaged] After six weeks in bed he is again on the mend & has a morale excellent. I don't know whether I told you poor G. Wauquiez had died from Typhoid at Bar le Duc & Aristide Derousseaux is dead.

Mother I suppose has written to you all details about her travels. She promised me to return to see me in Bourganeuf but is now hesitating owing to an attack of neuralgia.

Love to all at Murrulla & Woodside. Kiss the kiddies for me. I suppose by now they have forgotten all about uncle Jacques. They tell me my little fieulle [Marcelle Decouvelaere, his 'filleule', god-daughter] is very spoilt. Beware Marguerite for you will have to pay dearly for it later on.

Best wishes from brother Jacques

Marcel Paroissien was convalescing from his wounds in a hospital at St. Germain en Laye, near Paris. He, Aristide Derousseaux, and Georges Wauquiez were all part of the group of wool buyers who had sailed to France with Jacques on the *Malwa*.

In an attempt to break the deadlock a great offensive with 800 000 British and French troops was launched on 25 September around Arras and in Champagne. There were tremendous casualties but only a slight gain in ground. Jacques took part in the Champagne offensive and remained in this sector for the rest of the year. He wrote to one of his sisters in an English which was becoming a little rusty:

13th November 1915

Dear Ninie

I'm afraid it will be some time before the North is rid from the Germans. We who are in front of this splendid combination and trenches and fortins [small forts] have no longer any illusions specially after our last attack, we advanced t'is true & took prisonners but not without enormous losses. We are going to win, I have not the slightest doubt but its going to take sometime yet. It will not be a brilliant victory but by usure [attrition].

Winter has started. It is cold and it snowed all the morning.

Love,
Jacques Playoust

It was in Champagne that the first member of Jacques' family, his younger sister Marguerite's husband Alfred Decouvelaere, lost his life, earning the Croix de Guerre and the Médaille Militaire. Marguerite was left in Sydney with the responsibility of three young children to raise alone. Jacques had been in line in this same area, and responded to her letter with a card sent from St. Hilaire au Temple, a small village north of Chalons en Champagne. He wrote to her in English:

21st January (1916)

Dear Marguerite,

What a brave little woman you are! May your sacrifice be of avail. We have still very heavy work in front of us & may the 'casse' [damage] be not too dreadful. We must screw our courage to the sticking point and hope for the best. What a great consolation religion must be to you! As for me I've thought on matters seriously, in front of death too, & I'm quite satisfied, so please dont worry about me. It does not make me love you the less. Courage.

Jacques

He wrote in French to his cousin Marie about this time (translation):

7th January 1916

Dear Marie,

Thank you for your letter of 3rd January. Here too we have seen the sun from time to time but its appearance was very ephemeral. Fortunately we are at rest for some time at about 10 kilometres from the front. We are lodged in barns and in stables. My billet is in one of the latter, well aired, there are holes on all sides. Still the 'Totos' [lice] are less terrible. These good little beasts don't care much for manure. Anyway we are resting and are organising ourselves for a new offensive. It is not much fun but since one must have courage, we will try to have some. The mail I have received from Australia is not too cheerful. That poor Marguerite has just received the sad news, and how many poor young women are finding themselves in the same case. Let's not think! It's better!

I embrace you very affectionately,
Jacques Playoust

The French-Australian League in Sydney was by now becoming well established and provided a valuable supply of comforts for the troops and for civilian refugees. By September 1915, 33 000 articles of clothing had been dispatched, such as shirts, knitted socks, pyjamas and dressing gowns for wounded soldiers, each garment bearing the greeting 'Made in Australia by your friends'. Cash donations arrived from individuals and a wide variety of groups throughout the country, such as the cheque which was sent regularly by the ladies of the Queen Adelaide Club. Generous support was given to the League by country people who raised the money in original ways, from a huge sheep sale in Wagga Wagga, for example, which resulted in a vast profit of £1000.[4]

Cash subsidies were sent to a variety of charities looking after war orphans and widows, or to equip ambulances. An orphanage called 'Waratah' had been established on the coast in Normandy with funds from the League, but its activities soon became overstretched. Later on the sum of £5000 was raised by an appeal in the city of Newcastle to purchase a neighbouring house to increase the capacity of the orphanage, which would be called 'Australie'. Long lists of donations of money appeared weekly in the *Courrier Australien*, and a decision was taken to devote half the subscriptions for the purchase of automobile ambulances for the Allies. The state of New South Wales contributed the sum of £5000, and there were donations from a significant cross-section of city and country people.

Since the beginning of the year Madame Joseph Playoust (Blanche) of Strathfield had assumed the co-presidency with Mr Holman after her sister-in-law Marie-Thérèse had left for Paris with her husband Georges. Now appointed a *Présidente d'honneur* or patron, Marie-Thérèse acted in close collaboration with French military and civilian charities, putting them in touch with Mademoiselle Soubeiran in Sydney so that they could benefit from grants from the League. The Paris headquarters at 372 Rue St. Honoré grew to a committee of seven people, including the London Director of the Red Cross, Mme Brazier de Thuy, Mme la Générale Michel, wife of the military governor of Paris, and Georges Playoust acted as Treasurer.

A letter of thanks was received by the League in Sydney from the Mayor of Vauxbain, via Soissons (Aisne), dated 20th April 1915, which recounts a personal connection with Australia; it was a curious link, as the mayor's name was R. Hawke. In this long letter he acknowledges receipt of the sum of 4000 francs and a quantity of clothing sent to alleviate poverty in the commune. 'The generosity of my co-citizens has by far surpassed my most optimistic expectations. It has been very agreeable for me to prove that I was not mistaken in thinking that the people of this country my parents loved to tell me about, and of which they had such excellent memories would respond to the distant voice of one of their own because of his place of birth'. He would have liked to entertain Australian troops but the British Army was too far to the north of them. With the Germans now as their 'near neighbours', their village could be annihilated one of these days, but when he could convene the Council again, he felt sure that they would pass a special resolution to make known to Australians and to the League the gratitude of those who have been helped.

Mr W. A. Holman, the Premier, made an official visit to their workshops and depots to observe the collection of goods to be shipped. He remained co-President of the League and a faithful supporter of its work for years to come. A handsome man, a master of oratory and a fluent French speaker, he had won the admiration of Sydney's French business community despite his less than conservative political ideas. He also showed himself to be an ardent Francophile when in an address to the Sydney University Union early in 1916 he spoke of the originality of thought amongst French intellectuals in opposing German domination of philosophic reasoning, and acknowledged 'our cultural debt to France'. The French government conferred the Légion d'Honneur on Mr Holman in June 1916.

8
1916: Verdun

The rain and fogs of autumn put an end to most military activity in France, apart from desultory artillery fire. By the end of 1915, 'l'année stérile', it was clear that, because of poor teamwork, the Allied efforts had been ineffective and that an overall strategy was needed to break the stalemate. With this in mind the British Prime Minister, Mr Asquith, accompanied by Mr Balfour, First Lord of the Admiralty, and Lord Kitchener, the Minister for War, crossed the channel for a meeting in Calais with the French Prime Minister, M. Briand, and General Joffre on 4 December.

Two days later, in Joffre's Headquarters in Chantilly, just north of Paris, Joffre, Field Marshal Sir John French and their colleagues from Russia, Serbia, Belgium and Italy met to found a War Council destined, according to the official note, to create a permanent link between the Allies. The meeting lasted several days, and it was planned that a simultaneous offensive would be launched on the French, Russian and Italian fronts. If they attacked together, it was reasoned that the enemy could not transport reserves from one front to the other.

The main offensive in France was to be a massive Anglo-French assault in Picardy, north and south of the Somme. This was to be deferred till summer, due to the inexperience of newly conscripted troops. Until now, British troops had consisted entirely of volunteers, but military ranks were now so depleted that on 5 January 1916 Mr Asquith introduced a Conscription Bill initiating compulsory military service.

Three days later the failed Dardanelles venture ended with the evacuation of the last troops from Cape Helles. These included Anzacs from the Gallipoli landing, who were now sent to Egypt to rest, reform and train for the Western Front.

However, the Germans were to take the initiative. In his famous Christmas memorandum to the Kaiser in 1915, the German Chief of Staff, General von Falkenhayn promoted the idea of an attack concentrated in such a way 'that the French General Staff would be compelled to throw in every man that they have. If they do so, the forces of France will bleed to death'. The aim was that in bleeding France white, the England so detested by the Kaiser could be persuaded to end the struggle.

Falkenhayn recommended a massive attack on the fortress of Verdun, the strongest in France, which protected the most direct route to Paris. It was also of symbolic value, fought over since the days of Charlemagne, fortified by Vauban in the reign of Louis XIV, and further defended and modernised after the defeat of France in 1870 by Prussian forces.

The city of Verdun was protected by a series of wooded ridges, with escarpments rising to 400 metres, each topped by forts, on both sides of the sinuous Meuse River. The most powerful of these forts, Vaux and Douaumont, were thickly lined with concrete, deeply tunnelled, and had already withstood several attempts at penetration.

The Kaiser endorsed Falkenhayn's choice of Verdun, before which his eldest son, the Kronprinz, was already established with his Fifth Army. For this extraordinary operation, code-named *Gericht* (meaning tribunal, judgement or execution place) the generals planned a *trommelfueur*, a deluge of fire unknown in history, on a 24-kilometre front. The ingredients of this infernal recipe consisted of 13 of Krupp's 'Big Berthas', 2 long-range naval guns, 17 305 mortars and a lavish distribution of field guns. To add spice, there were also the new flame throwers.

New railway lines were built to bring in the munitions, in addition to road-building equipment and barbed wire, sandbags and general supplies for the pioneers. Assembled for the attack were 140 000 men, hidden away in the long *stollen* (galleries) constructed with habitual German skill.

The bombardment from this assembly of huge guns, the most intense of the war, began at 7.15 on the morning of 21 February and was concentrated onto a pocket handkerchief of hillside, churning the earth into a moonscape. Nearly 2 million shells fell into 20 square kilometres, resulting in enormous French casualties. Late that afternoon, accompanied by suffocating and tear-inducing gases, 80 000 German men advanced in successive waves, expecting Verdun to fall rapidly.

Joffre's second-in-command, General de Castelnau, was rushed to the area to assess the rapidly deteriorating situation, and General Phillipe Pétain was ordered to follow with his Second Army, which was in reserve after the hard autumn battle in Champagne, to defend the left or west bank of the Meuse. In the most inhumane battle ahead, Pétain, a dour northerner from the Pas de Calais region of Flanders, proved to be an efficient organiser whose humanitarian qualities were exemplified by his attention to the wellbeing of the common soldier.

After receiving his orders from General Joffre at his General Head-quarters in Chantilly on 25 February, Pétain set off by car eastwards towards Verdun. Jacques Playoust was to trudge along this same road just two days later, when returning from furlough in Paris to rejoin his regiment. Alistair Horne vividly describes Pétain's journey, and how he found his progress impeded by ice and snow.[1] Beyond Bar-le-Duc the human effects of the horrendous battle now raging further north became visible. The General was seen to be moved to tears at the sight of the wounded *poilus* held up in their makeshift ambulances by streams of civilian refugees, marching troops, and horse-drawn carriages skidding on this narrow minor road.

Pétain reached Military Headquarters at Dugny, a village on the Meuse a little south of Verdun, where he was informed of the fall of the fort of Douaumont. The command post was in complete disarray. He retreated further west to Souilly, a small village strung along the main Verdun–Bar-le-Duc road, where a bleak stone house containing the town hall and school became his headquarters for the campaign. Here he met his superior, General de Castelnau, who extended Pétain's command to the whole area on both sides of the Meuse. Castelnau gave him orders to defend Verdun *coûte que coûte* (at all costs) on the east bank, the area beyond Fort Douaumont which had resisted attacks earlier in the war.

Pétain retired late and spent the night in an armchair in an unheated room in his billet. The next morning he woke up stricken by pneumonia, and for the first day of his command, without the knowledge of his subordinates, operations were directed from his sick-bed. Morale had been greatly lifted by news of Pétain's arrival, as he had a good rapport with the *poilus,* who recognised his genuine interest in their welfare. For the first time since the inception of the battle, German reports on 27 February claimed no success.

The retreat was halted. Cool and methodical, Pétain informed himself about the resources available, food, water supply, telephone networks, transport, airfields. German prisoners were interrogated to assess the strength of the opposing army. One of his first acts was to delegate a capable engineer to build a railway, and to re-organise the road from Bar-le-Duc to Verdun to ensure communications and supplies. From all over France 3000 civilian trucks were requisitioned to form a continuous chain to bring men to the battlefield, along with their supplies and munitions, and to return with the wounded. Trains were to run in rotation every five minutes. From a vantage point in his tall stone headquarters at Souilly, Pétain could observe this constant movement. By the end of the year two-thirds of the French army, metropolitan and colonial, passed along this way to fulfil their tour of duty. Verdun remained an entirely French sector.

† † †

The story is now taken up by Jacques Playoust's diary, written between February and August 1916 in a small notebook with a cardboard cover. He wrote, mostly with a blunt pencil, on squared paper and, again, his punctuation and uncertain spelling have been left in their original form.

At the front of the notebook he wrote the Morse code alphabet and codes for signals. The Author's notes and translations are shown within square brackets.

Jacques was now a hardened *poilu*, and his responsibility was to transmit signals, which often required him to go 'over the top' to repair telephone wires. The diary was written in English, possibly for reasons of privacy, and begins with his journey to the Front on 25 February. On that day, after heavy fighting on the periphery, the great fort of Douaumont was taken by an ingenious group of Brandenburgers who formed a human pyramid, climbed in through a gun turret, and opened the doors. This news took some time to filter through to Jacques, who was now marching eastwards from Champagne.

25th [February 1916] Leaft Paris after delightful but too short furlough snowed all night quite 6 inches of snow everywhere. It appears Paris has not seen so much for years. In the country more still. Misery & cold starts again. For how long?

26th Arrive at Chalons at 7 last night about 3 hours late owing to enormous movement of troops. Get instructions to go to Seirry to rejoin our regiment. We arrive there only to find it gone. Obtain hospitality in a grange, bitterly cold, no rug. At 7 a.m. fortunately find cart to take us back to Chalons. Towards evening sent to Vitry la Ville, again find regiment gone. Fortunately find a bed, warm room and hearty welcome at post office. During my stay see about 300 prisonners taken in neighbourhood of Tahure. The poor beggars look a sorry lot, thin, worn out boots etc. etc.

27th Off to Pagny sur Somme [not the Picardy Somme, but another small river with the same name near Chalons] about 10. Trains anyhow. There get instructions to go to Bussy le Repos some 26 kilometres further on. Do about 20 that afternoon & rest about 6 miles from destination in a grange with some troops of the 94. under circumstances fairly comfortable.

28th Start about 7.30 & arrive early at Pagny where I find regiment. All sorts of nasty rumors about Verdun. Everybody on the 'qui vive'.

1st March 1916 Normal life. Exercise de Spécialités as usual. Examination in afternoon by Captain of Génie [captain of sappers, who were responsible for the building of fortifications and trenches] Just my luck after no practice for 10 days.

2nd Nothing special.

3rd Leave Bussy le Repos at 7 a.m. Arrive at Muville en Bois only 15 kilometres but all the same fairly tired. En route for the trenches. Off again tomorrow. [He was now in the Argonne forest, heading north on minor roads towards St. Menehould. The direct road from Rheims to Verdun was now too close to the Front.]

4th Reveil 4 o'clock, on the road at 6.30. Arrive Verriere, muddy road dog tired. Much to our disgust get orders to return 4 kilometres to a village further back that we had passed. Enough to break anybody's heart. Start St. Menould at 3 arrive 4 heures & après avoir grelotté à l'entrée pendant une heure et demie on nous envoit dans les Casernes des Cuirassiers pour cantonner. Palais luxueux après les granges qui nous abritent depuis 2 mois. [After shivering at the entrance for one and a half hours we were sent to the barracks of the Heavy Cavalry for billetting. Luxurious palace after the barns which have been sheltering us for two months.]

5th Repos that is well earned. Clean up. Inspection by Gl. Develle. [Possibly Nivelle, in command of the 3rd corps, and in Verdun from March.]

6th Off at 7 a.m. To Pretzs about 7 kilometres from Thiaucourt. Cross country where heavy fighting took part at the beginning of the war. Hundreds of tombs. French generally have a crown, the Boches just a simple cross just 2 or 1 Allemands [Germans]. Little hamlet where we are most uncomfortably billeted. Was practically destroyed. We have walked 32 kilometres during the day. Distance fair enough but with some 30 lbs. on your back killing. Weather wretched & cold & country God forsaken.

7th Visited ruins empty cartridges & shells laying about specially in destroyed church. Won't the tourists find interesting souvenirs. Rest which is sorely need by everyone.

8th Start 7 Ville sur Cousance. Cold Frosty still God Forsaken country. Arrive about 2 p.m. watch stopped. Many évacués civils [civilian evacuees] on road. We are billeted in a stable full of sick horses. Our mansion labelled horses à évacuer [horses for evacuation] & we sleep alongside the poor mangy animals.

9th Reveil 6 ready to march at 7. Only off at 4 o'clock. Told off as Cyclyste to make cantonnement [billets]. Snow & cold. Pretty exciting time on road, shells all round. Company arrives midnight all dog tired. Bombardment incessant all night, no lights of any description allowed.

10th A couple of nice spells. I have billeted Jeanne d'Arc. During the day several of the Regiment go & empty the cellars. Result many, many drunk & they tell us we must hold coute que coute [at all costs]. Let us hope the Boches give them time to recover. Affected as homme de liaison adjoint to commandant [liaison officer assisting the commander] as liaison will be difficult. No communication trenches. Off at 8.15 arrive at 12 p.m. company in order about 3 p.m. We must stop the Boches from coming up the ravin Louvemont which the 156 were occupying.

A map in *L'Illustration* indicates that Louvemont was on the right bank of the Meuse about 3 km north-west of the fort of Douaumont, which was now in German hands. The *French Army Bulletin* wrote (translation):

> The battering ram of the enemy on the right bank did not use the central breach through which he expected to reach Verdun. The German fighting units ... had to be brought back to the rear to be reconstituted with important reinforcements ... and the order of the day from the Kronprinz read on the 4th March to his troops at rest prescribed taking advantage of this pause to prepare for a supreme effort allowing the taking of Verdun 'the heart of France' ... 8-10th March: the battle is renewed between Douaument and Vaux — the enemy is making a considerable effort.

Jacques' diary again takes up the story:

11th Uncomfortable night, rotten gourbi [dug out, slang of Arab origin] no shelter at all in case of bombardment which is even now commencing. We are here for a fortnight. We have 'vivres de reserves' [reserve victuals] for three days. At night change our headquarters. Our position too dangerous. Sent at 10 to get a corvée [fatigue party] 2 or three miles from here near Bras [a village downhill on the banks of the Meuse]. Boches rain shells on all roads & villages have several narrow sqeak Back about 12.30. Helmet dented by shrapnells.

12th Up at 4.30 Pretty tired & specially thirsty all liquid at a premium little or no rest cannot even stretch limbs to rest & bitterly cold.

13th Situation no worse our secteur gradually getting organised. Heavy bombardment as usual, many aeroplanes Boches about. Casualties increasing. Several Boches aeroplanes were allowed to fly about our lines for a couple of hours & we are paying the penalty.

14th Heavy bombardment early morning we were on the alert for a while. The 151 who went to the ravitaillement [went for supplies] had 8 killed and several wounded. The Boches still continue & pour shells on all roads of approaches. Just at present no safety for a radius of 10 kilometres.

15th Heavy bombardment during the night. Have to be pretty sly getting about as a mitrailleuse [machine gun] on the Côtes du Poivre sent bullets in our directions, one of our chaps was wounded in the arm. The abris de mitrailleuse [machine gun shelter] was located and the 75 destroyed it. Yesterday one of our saucisse [observation balloon] broke its cord and flew away over the German lines. Fortunately the observateur came down by parachute in time. This was more than compensated when one of our little Nieuports brought a big German Armatik down in our lines.

16th Heavy cannonading during the night. Usual casualty list amongst the corvée We are certainly happier here than those on 3rd line. Same monotonous weary day.

17th Things seem to be getting quieter. Is it the calm before the storm. received a letter from new marraine [godmother, in this case a pen-friend] Quite a charming little note. Relieving myself in a wood close handy that afternoon a bouquet of 77 burst all round. I pulled up trousers in hurry & made a dash for trenches in double quick time much to amusement of camarades. I could not help laughing myself when in safety.

18th Busy most of the night only a few hours sleep. Getting quite accustomed to it again. Since the 10th have not averaged more than 4 very uncomfortable in 24. During the morning heavy combat of d'artillerie. They leave us fairly quiet in first line. They shan't loose anything by waiting. Aeroplanes galore ahead. A French & German met this morning, exchanged their ribbon of shots & each went his way none the worse. Afternoon & evening quiet.

19th Awaken early about 4.30 by terrific bombardment by our batteries of German lines. Boches answer more weakly but enough to make us feel uneasy in our little gourbi. As usual at daylight German aeroplanes over out lines. They were keen to see what we were about. At about 8.30 the 1er on the Côte du Poivre take [illegible] artillerie and hell is let loose but the Germans answer and we have quite an exciting time. Only 5 wounded, mirabile dictu [strange to say].

20th Awaken 5 o'clock by a new bombardment. 1st day of Spring. Indeed the weather has been fine of late (last 3 or 5 days) At 11 by order from the general our men get instructions to fire for 5 minutes. Result, the Boches sent us a 77. The Boches must have had the laugh. Several German aviators about as usual & easily keep French aviators coming too close. Some of them are not too game.

It looks more and more as if the general attack on Verdun is dwindling down anyhow this side. The Germans have been withdrawing troops and cannon north so say our aviators. It has been noted that they are bombarding less the roads on neighbourhood & lines of communications.

Unknown to Jacques, 20 March also saw the first of several Anzac Corps contingents land in Toulon, and later in Marseilles, the arrival port he had known so well before the war. The Anzacs had spent a period of tough drilling in the heat of Egypt before making the crossing through the submarine-infested Mediterranean. A group of Anzacs arriving several weeks later were in time to participate in a grand parade of Imperial troops through the streets of Marseilles, together with Indian Lancers and South Africans. General Birdwood addressed them in his crisp manner, firstly expressing great pride in his Army Corps and also encouraging a show of discipline, particularly in regard to the female sex and to 'drink'. They were given 24 hours leave to savour the tree-lined boulevards, the open-air cafés, shops and theatres of the city. Before their departure they marched for 2° miles through the streets through showers of flowers.

As they travelled towards the north they marvelled at the new spring foliage of southern France after the arid landscapes of North Africa and, for some, the Dardanelles. At train stops they were offered wine and flowers by the inhabitants, and there were many more such happy encounters to come. The smiling Australians were attractive to many people during their years in the country as they were so adaptable, and a particularly good rapport developed between Diggers from rural areas and the farmers behind the Front, whose livestock they even tended from time to time. This was the first Australian presence in France and was part of the build-up for the coming summer offensive in the Somme.

Jacques' diary continues:

21st Not much sleep. Days beautiful but nights bitterly cold. Our secteur comparatively quiet during night. Within half an hour 2 French aeroplanes came down in flames. Seems to shake aviators up a bit for in the afternoon the Boches are allowed to come within 100 metres of our lines. Mitrailleuse [machine gun] fire on them, result they are seen & unpleasant bombardment in afternoon. Shall we ever get out of this hole alive? Only 5 wounded. Boyaux full of déchêts d'obus [trenches full of waste from shells].

22nd About 2 p.m. heavy bombardment with big calibre for an hour. Little damage done, 1 killed and few wounded but how a séance like that tells on one's nerves. Rain afternoon, pitch dark at night. Corvée de ravitaillement [fatigue party for revictualling] get lost.

23rd Up most night, rain, as usual artillery comparatively quiet. Some compensation for the mud & wet.

24th Rain damp & muddy same monotonous bombardment getting pretty tired of it all.

25th More uncomfortable night than usual, new guests and just barely sitting room. Congratulations from Joffre the way we are holding on, everything seems to show that troops that were to relieve us are required elsewhere. We are informed that a new effort is required of us.

26th Nothing startling, usual bombardment, rain in morning, snow at night.

27th Comparative quiet night cold received 3 parcells Totos [lice] appear again, getting filthy. Three weeks now since last wash, no sign of relève [relief troops] yet.

28th Very disagreeable bombardment this morning. They are employing a new kind. They don't explode till they get well in the ground. They play hell with the trenches and dug outs & are most weird things. Our adjudant [adjutant] wounded. Afternoon bombardment again, They have shown more life today than they have for some time. Orders come through for a probable relève tomorrow night.

29th Awaken at daylight to bring officers of the C2 to their different secteurs. So we are going to be relieved! Cold morning, snow sets fine afternoon. Usual intermittent bombardment mostly small calibre. Gugust [possibly a diminutive of Auguste] rather annoying. At seven go to meet C2 who relieve us over the Bois des Allemands. They arrive at 10, as usual an hour late. Crossing Bois des Allemands a rafale [burst of shots] of 77, little bit of stampeed but nobody hurt. Relève finished about 2 p.m. En route for Verdun at 3. Arrive exhausted at 6 p.m., couple of hours sleep, eat, then en route again. Boches notice our movements & bombarded on way, fortunately only a couple wounded. Arrive Belenville rest a couple of hours then take cars for Moulinville en route for Bar le Duc. Get into quarters about 10 p.m.

30th Awake at 9 a.m. much refreshed, enjoy first wash for three weeks.

More use was now being made of the recent innovation of motorised transport. The road from Bar-le-Duc to Verdun was to be reserved exclusively for motor transport and carried a continuous stream of trucks bearing men and supplies to and from the Front. Day and night the convoys rolled on, with orders that any truck breaking down should be pushed over into the ditch. The traffic was so heavy that road menders were on permanent shifts. This road came to be referred to as 'The Sacred Way'.

The rapid conquest of Verdun on which the German High Command had counted was now reduced to a reciprocal war of attrition. In 'bleeding white' the French, the same loss of life was imposed on their own men.

On 12 March the Allied military chiefs, including the Serbian, Italian, Russian and Belgian generals, met again at Joffre's headquarters at Chantilly. A week later in Paris the second Inter-allied Conference was held, which included the British and French Prime Ministers, and the Russian, Japanese and Portuguese ambassadors. A permanent committee was established with the aim of ensuring unity of military, economic and diplomatic action.

The date for the great summer offensive in the Somme was set for 1 July. For the French High Command the problem was to find fresh troops for tours of duty in the continuing Verdun battle, yet still meet its commitments for the planned offensive in the Somme.

9

1916: The Mort Homme

Jacques Playoust's diary continues:

1st April 1916 Rest clean up still very stiff. Beautiful Spring weather. How delightful to enjoy the sun again without fear of the éclats [burst of shots] It appears we go back to the trenches on the 4th. Mort-Homme so they say.

2nd, 3rd, 4th Ditto.

5th En route again but only move on 5 kilometres to Fleury en Ayr. Fairly well billetted.

6th En route at 12 to embark in cars at 2 arrive near Dombasle which is burning, eat soup then en route for somewhere near the Mort Homme about 21 kilometres. Bombarded in the Bois of Bourrus rather exciting 10 minutes, horses block the road, usual excitement noise etc. Arrive dead tired just as I'm beginning to despair.

This time Jacques had been sent to the west bank of the Meuse. The Kronprinz, blocked on the right bank, had broadened the battle front. German troops had now crossed the flooded river and were attacking French positions on the tactically important Mort-Homme *(Dead Man)* Hill and Hill 304 alongside without much result, as they were being countered by artillery fire from numerous French batteries. The German Command therefore planned to make a full scale assault on 9 April with intense bombardment and fresh troops.

L'Illustration described the Mort Homme thus:

At the junction of the road from Bethincourt to Chattancourt and a track curving from Cumières to Esnes there was once a cross. It marked the place where the body of an unknown man was found, cause of death unknown. Hence the name of this area, which will be remembered in history. Formerly grassy fields, this hill became brown, bare and torn up by trenches and shell holes, with not a tree left.[1]

That week's *Bulletin of the French Army* stated: 'To the German Command it seemed necessary that in order to reach Verdun they must seize positions on the Mort Homme.'

7th Sleep in bottom of trench terrific artillery duel but they leave us quiet enough just as well. No homme de liaison required. Have to rejoin my section.

8th Ravitaillement [rations] blocked on the way. No feed, no wine, no nob [?tobacco]. We have to live on dry biscuits, singe ['Monkey' — slang for 'bully beef', tinned boiled stringy and greasy beef] & water which we find in a little stream some 400 yards away. Spend the day making some kind of shelter but hard work with little portable tools. Outside [apart from] a little wood which we brought from the ruins of Betingcourt nothing. Feeling rather slack on regime. Last night 3 men with others from other companies went over in 1st line to retake part of a boyau [literally gut, communication trench] which the last regiment left. The 75 was to destroy it then the men were to advance with bombs 40 metres & establish another barrage. The 75 fired too short & left barrage intact. The men had a go at it all the same but found job too stiff for them.

Boulogne, a most decent chap, was killed, Leroy, en prevention de conseil de guerre [committed for trial by court martial], wounded slightly. Why is it always the good chaps that go? Spent afternoon making a little niche where I am at least sheltered from the 'cracknells' as some of the men call them. They are pretty abundant in this part of the world.

8th Kitchens arrive today but the cooks to save trouble reheated the tucker which they were not able to recover. Result food not eatable, but bread, pinard [army slang for wine] duly appreciated. Letters and parcels did not arrive. Night again go to Chattancourt in ruins to get some wood to boise our saps [timber our communication trenches] which are beginning to take shape.

9th Up at 5 p.m. to continue sap. At 9 p.m. Terrific bombardment starts. Alerted, bags got ready, men at parrapets await orders to go 1st line, any moment. At 8 p.m. counter order we are to remain there. Midnight new orders & before get order to start at any moment.

10th About 3 p.m. after hurrying to get in 1st line get in trenches (practically finished) just before renewed bombardment which did not cease till 7. No shelter at all we all lay down in bottom of trenches with bags on our head. Splinters & stones fly all round semi burried several times. Impossible eat or smoke besides no desire. Worst day I have ever spent. Immediately bombardment finishes get work build up again our destroyed trench & make little abris [shelter] Everybody à bout [at the end of their tether] We learn what happened the day before. The 2nd Bn [battalion] who was occupying a salient was surrounded & destroyed or taken prisoner. Ditto for Bn of 51 result: perte du Mort-Homme [Loss of Dead Man Hill] But everywhere elsewhere the Boches attacked 6 times consecutively they were repulsed with heavy losses. At midnight we have to abandon work again. The Boches attack with inflammable liquid the 16e Chasseurs [light infantry soldiers] & bomb & win the two trenches. We are now in a critical condition. Fortunately we are able to hold them there. Bethincourt in flames.

The last entry should have been dated 9th April, rather than 10th. The day's events were described by Jacques in a later letter as having taken place on a Sunday, and Easter Sunday was to fall two weeks later on 23 April. A fine point, but the significance of the date becomes obvious in the following account from a distant observer with binoculars:

One remembers it was a sunny Sunday, a real Spring Sunday. The artillery duel was long and formidable. The Mort Homme smoked like a volcano with many craters. In front and in the rear our curtain fire and the Germans' lit up like theatre footlights. Bethincourt was almost burnt out. In the sky floated hideous green flakes made by the 105s and 130s as they fused. Under the continuous cannonade one felt the earth tremble ... The enemy was attacking on all our left bank front with five divisions ... The battle lasted until sunset, the outcome not known.[2]

French losses were considerable but, despite expending huge resources, the Germans gained only a knoll, Hill 295, of the Mort Homme. The newly appointed commander, General Philippe Pétain, issued an optimistic order of the day.[3] 'The 9th April is a glorious day for our arms. The furious assaults of the Kronprinz were everywhere broken, foot soldiers, aviators, rivalled in heroism. Honour to all. The Germans will no doubt attack again; let each man work and watch to obtain the same success as yesterday. Courage — on les aura!' *(We'll have them!)* This last line was to become a popular slogan.

11th At 2 I am sent to the colonel to bring the 154 in our position. As usual the relève arrives late, and dawn when they arrive. Our company just get away before bombardment is renewed, too late for me to get away. I am very down & don't think I will ever get away. I doubt if the Boches renew their attack these will be able to hold. 'Zigouillé' [slang for 'killed'] or prisonner appears to be the only issue. Fortunately they too seem to have had enough & remain fairly quiet. Nerves broken up but manage to get an hour's sleep. The first for three days, no food but dry bread found in trenches, liquid none. No courage [energy] however to think of that. At dusk get away, my bag [illegible] I have has been stolen. Get to emplacement where our company, they have gone to work on 1st line. Go to the emplacement of the cuisines roulantes [mobile kitchens] & wait for the Corvée de ravitaillement for information. Meanwhile have a square meal. Return with them & find the quarters of my company about 12 p.m. Find digs under the table with the officers share rugs with one of the orderlies.

Sleep like a log till 10 p.m. We are waiting anxiously for news of our relève. Our division has been badly tried & its time we got to the rear to reform. But under the circumstances they may need the few men that remain to hold on till fresh troops arrive. Never will I be more pleased to leave a secteur.

13th So far nothing new bombardment normal if anything not so intense owing to horrible weather Delightful wandering about the trenches. Still no talk of relève.

14th The attack in afternoon over but [illegible] of results. Relève evening. We are to eat at the Bois des Bourrus.

15th Kitchens not there. Twenty four hours since men have eaten & they complain. They are tired and the ground is very heavy. Only consolation we are leaving the Boches. Arrive Mercourt 7.30 where we find the kitchen. Needless to add the meal is duly honoured. Cars do not arrive till 2. They bring fresh troops from the repos [rest area] Meanwhile we have had another meal and a good drenching. Arrive Hermonville pretty habitable village south of Bar-le-Duc. Dog tired. Clean up, & sleep.

16th Ditto.

17th Ditto. Sleep & shower. Mail arrives. 1st for 3 days.

18th Revue d'arme etc. [arms inspection].

A letter to Australia:

18 April

Dear Brothers & Sisters

This mail from Australia so far has only brought me Roger's letter of the 21st February. It has found me still safe & sound & at rest but after the most terrible week I have ever speant. Even now I can't realise how I'm still alive to tell the tale. This time we went into line at the now famous dead man hill. You will have read in the paper of the terrific fighting that has been going on there of late. Well I was in the thick of it all. Sunday the 10th I will never forget. Hardly had we got into position than a terrific bombardment started. For 12 solid hours it lasted, the schweins used nothing smaller than 105 & we remained crouched in our battered trench with our bags on our heads. We did not eat & even the heaviest smoker did not think of lighting his pipe. Towards 8 things quietened down & we immediately set to work feverishly to build up again our trench. Scarcely had we started than the Boches attacked on our left with inflamable liquid & bombs. Our men had to give ground a little & for a couple of hours we did not know whether we would be cut off or no. Fortunately reinforcement came up in time. During the night we were relieved. As guide I had to go & get the fresh troops a couple of miles away. They only arrived at dawn & I had to hurry to get them in position before the Boches could see them. Personally I could not get away in time & had to remain another day in hell. I got away at sunset that night & it was only at 3 the next morning that I found my company. I had been 3 solid days with one meal, & 1 hours nervous sleep. Our company was then in reserve about a kilometre from the front. It rained & shelled continuously for the next 3 days & we were on the alirt all the time as the Boches attacked time after time. We were indeed, what remained of us, in a sorry plight when 3 days ago we returned to rest covered with mud & haggard. I've cleaned up now & although allready 3 days at rest I'm still, especially morally, upset. Many have gone mad at less. I wonder is it possible to get through this war unscathed?

Still good news from everyone at home. The Brothers with the exception of Stéphane is at the front. Mother & Father write anxiously from Paris for they know things are not well with us. J. Flipo's regiment has followed ours of late & must have had a rough time too. Rumours are that we go back on Good Friday but somehow I think they will have to leave us here a little longer to reform. Best wishes to all & my bon souvenir at Woodside.

From your brother,
Jacques

Joseph Flipo was his wool buyer friend who had sailed with him from Sydney on the *Malwa* and now held the rank of Captain. He was wounded in the head and the right hand during the Mort Homme battle, and was awarded the Croix de Guerre avec Palme and the Légion d'Honneur.

19th April Old French custom. Kiddies come round Holy Thursday with crecelle [rattle] to announce midday Angelus instead of bells.

20th–21st Good Friday. In spight of all our advanced ideas, men are not given any meat even in war time.

22nd Rain still. During my stay here have found an old woman of 88 who does my cooking. Every day I go to the butcher and choose my meat. Getting meat again & morale improves in consequence. News of the arrival of Russian troops in France has splendid effect.

A few days earlier the first ship bearing Russian troops under General Lohvitsky had drawn up at a wharf at Marseilles after a 75-day sea journey from Siberia via the Indian Ocean, thus underlining the lack of access from the Black Sea caused by the Turkish blockage of the Dardanelles.[4] The contingent was greeted by saluting officers with the people cheering and a band playing the Russian national anthem. The ceremony was viewed with astonishment by German prisoners of war on a neighbouring pontoon. The contingent marched through the crowded streets of Marseilles led by two soldiers bearing large bunches of flowers in the national colours of the Allies.

The following September the Russian soldiers were photographed as they were visited in their trenches in Champagne by General Lohvitsky, who joined them at an Orthodox Mass, during which the sound of the canon echoed the bass voices of the choir. The General greeted them as 'my brothers' and they responded by 'We wish our General good health.' After battles, it was reported, they used to sing ancient songs accompanied by the balalaika.

23rd Easter. Weather clears up a little for the occasion. No work of any kind. Afternoon concert fair show. Music specially good. Meanwhile football match not far off between our Bn. & 151. [Jacques' battalion was 162.]

It appears it was a cake walk for us 12 to nil. Evening have arranged a little dinner for myself & 2 less fortunate friends from pays envahis [invaded territories in the north of France and Belgium.] Rabbit, ham, salad, cheese, an Easter egg, sent by a little marraine [penfriend] of 12 years of age, menu. Everything is duly honoured, & old grand-mère our cook duly toasted.

24th Hear that 900 reinforcements are coming to the Regiment. Every company is brought up to effective of at least 200. We have to clear out to make room. At 2 off to Rupt 3 kilometres off.

25th Planton [orderly] at Haironville. Carry orders from our Cmdt. To our Captn. Beautiful weather, country magnificent. If there was not the thought that war is not finished it would be a real pleasure to live. Our footballers again distinguish themselves. They beat a team of Automobilistes comprising of 2 internationals by 2 to 1. They are beginning to think themselves. ['Ils commencent à se croire' means 'they are becoming conceited'.]

26th Up early to go back to Haironville where I am on duty till 11.

27th–31st Same old routine, delightful weather, country looking magnificent in this new spring clothes, but when one thinks of the dreadful tragedy that is going on yonder & still what remains in store for us, really 'le printemps magnifique a perdu son odeur' a French poet once wrote. [The magnificent Spring has lost its scent.]

1–2 May Still au repos [at rest], but rumours are increasing. We are bound to be off soon & it looks towards that Godforsaken Mort Homme. Our division evidently has not suffered sufficiently.

3rd During the night get orders for departure for the 4th. Kitchens go at 8 a.m. We are to be off tomorrow by cars for the same Godforsaken hole. I'm off as signaleur this time. A large pharre [light] etc to carry this time instead of gun & cartridges.

4th En route at 5.20. Can find no place to leave bag & gun so have to take them with me. Take cars from where we embarked last time. Go up with regiment in Sivry la Perche to rest. Beastly hot & feel load. Homme de liaison to guide looses his way & after wandering for 2 or three hours in vain we recognise road. Dead dead tired.

5th Up at 5 takes turns watching for signals, 1 hrs. duty every four, rather dangerous under intense bombardment we are experiencing, still hot & feeling thirst.[5]

6th Morning got wink that there is attack. Sent with other signallers to get fusées [rockets] Then a little rest but not for long. We are sent up in 1st with cases of grenades. Boches begin to see that something untoward is happening. Shell galore. Trenches practically destroyed. Clairon [bugler] who helped me with my case abandons me.

Anyhow get through my mission all right. Return to get ready our signalling post in case of emergency. At 6.30 the attack is let loose after a couple of hours bombardment which the Boches return. We use their methods, inflammable liquids but our artillery has not been killing enough & we fail bitterly, few killed but many wounded not only during their dreadful tir de barrage [curtain fire] which plays hell with our telephone, then I have to take duty, anything but pleasant, but again get through. What a day! All the same lucky not to have been in 1st line.

7th Up at 3 to arrange new munition depot afterwards bring up grenades in 1st line, & return tired & hot. That day starts off badly. Boches attack, take bit of trench which we retake at once. More killed & wounded, 75 in 1st Company 30 in 3rd quite 100 in whole bon. [battalion] for nothing not counting ammunition wasted, afterwards day somewhat quieter. Rabier, a real brave & generous chap, our corporal, gets his legs blown off. Heavy bombardment on our left, côte 304 in afternoon followed by attack. We see them coming out of our trenches but our mitrailleuses play havoc with them. Afterwards I learn that they had time to drink wine & [? illegible] of our men & light a fuse to the case of grenades at barrage. A sergent of ours sacrificing himself for his camarades gets blown up.

8th On duty 12 to 2. Germans must think that there is a relève for they send myriades of little 77 shrapnells. Only excitement company in front of us send fusée rouge [red rocket] Advise colonel re need for artillery. Observer has seen it too & song begins but not for long for it is a mistake. It went up instead of fusée éclairante [flare] On duty again 8 to 12.

9th Germans attack & we counter attack côte 304 [Hill 304] on our right. Install 1st thing in the morning post optique from summit of Mort Homme to communicate with the brigade. Send my first official message. Get ready for attack next day. Pal comes up to help me.[6]

10th Everything ready, artillery signallers with us. Arrange so as to signal from our gourbis with rattaches [cords] Artillery starts to give seriously about 8 p.m. We have several messages to transmit to artillery. Le service optique [visual surveillance] renders signal service for the réglage des pièces [the setting of cannons] Towards 11 activity increases crescendo, heavy pieces too when everything suddenly ceases. The men jump off the parrapet & rush the enemy's trench. In five minutes the attack was finished. half dozen wounded, booty 250 yards by 100 yards of depth which formed a disagreeable salient in our front, 80 prisonners 1 machine gun. During riposte [reply] in the afternoon, 150 falls at the entrance of my gourbi and imprison me for 3 hours, my instrument untouched & we are still able to operate from inside. Strange coincidence our 1st message to transmit 'Allongez le tir de 100 metres' [Lengthen the fire by 100 metres] It was for the French batteries, but we hoped the Boches would take the hint. On duty till 12. Both sides are nervous & fear attack. Result, mutual tir de barrages many wounded in corvées.

11th Our Bn is relieved today. They require unfortunately telephonist & are to remain another 7 days in hell.

12th Awaken at 4 o'clock after 1st few hours sleep I've had for several days to repair the line. Coming back 150 falls a few yards from me. The 1st time I distinctly see the shell coming. Cannot get communications on return. What has happened?

<u>Later</u>. Scarcely had we reached our post when a shell fell right at the entrance of post. Killed 3 telephone men, 2 signallers & 3 others, & wounded 3 more, upset all our sap. Everything disorganised but what a fearful thing this war is. Men in the prime of life are butchered what for? All peace loving men they were. Such situations drive one mad little by little & as for nerves!!! The wind is in the Germans favour & the stench of the dead come over our lines. How many corpses still between the [word omitted] how many still burried in the saps.

Afternoon very quiet & night too. During the night the Boches on our left try & take barrage but are repulsed with grenades.

13th Get our ravitaillement [rations] at last, 1st since arrival in trenches. Much rested but bad attack of dysentry. Morning very quiet only small attack of grenades in front of 5th otherwise very quiet. Quiet evening & night.

14th Lay out new line in the morning. Rain and dull. Artillery in consequence very quiet. Our work not by any means serious under circumstances. Hear that division Marrocaine attacked Côte 304 but cant get any information yet. Great discretion always observed on phone lest the Germans should hear. Towards 6 o'clock Boches attack our front with pétards. Tir de Barrage, [curtain fire] Boches answer & things hum for an hour. During the night something more serious on Côte 304. Boche bombardment, tir de barrage & mitrailleuse. It shall not be said that we were quiet for one night.

15th Rain & miserable morning, quiet. Good for us who have a fairly comfortable gourbi but for the poor chaps in the trenches pretty miserable.

16th Morning quiet, rumours of relève for Telephonist during the night. Afternoon sky clears up. Up saucisses [observation balloons] & aero & bombardment starts. They send us something tall, nothing smaller than 150. Mirabile dictu, our wires only cut once. Usual peripéties [vicissitudes] attaque à la grenade, small infantary attack which fails.

During the night another attack Côte 304. At 12 we are told that we are not relevé till tomorrow.

17th Sleep most morning. Day comparatively quiet with exception of a couple of hours between 5 & 7 in afternoon usual heavy bombardment goes on. Waiting for the relève. Do hope they will come early. The breeze comes from the Boches and the stench of dead men is awful. Evening quiet, get away nicely about 12.

18th Arrive Fromeréville [according to the map, a good 10 km behind the Mort-Homme] very tired about 3 in the morning. A few hours sleep then a substantial meal and thorough wash & shave, feel a good deal refreshed.

19th Still tired but much better all the same after solid night's rest. Did not even waken when the usual shells arrived on village. Heavy artillery duel this morning. Hear a Lt. Lietard has been killed.

Jacques found time that day to send a postcard to Marie when he was behind the lines (translation):

19 May 1916

Dear Marie

I received your brief little note of the 13th this morning, on arriving a few kilometres behind the lines where we are in reserve. Once more I have come back. Always the same good luck. I was buried for 4 hours in my dugout by a shell which fell at the entrance. Fortunately I had a battery and was able to make a little hole for air. I had just been relieved from my observation post five minutes earlier when a shell fell right into it and killed the man who was replacing me, and 7 men who were nearby. Love to yourself and mother,

Jacques.

20th Heavy bombardment during the night & day. Boches attack at 2 & succeed & take first line & even further. Our Bn. exterminated. [Jacques with his usual good luck appears to have been separated from his battalion, possibly because he had been obliged to remain in line on May 11 when the rest of the battalion was relieved] 2nd Bn. in reserve alerted to go up. Things are bad [for] us.

21st 2nd Bon goes up after soup. News are leaking out. It appears the Boches attacked 5 times in vain. It was only the 6th that they turned the position of the Mort Homme. They advanced as far as the Abris Nedterre & there the men seemed to loose their head & got lost & immediate counter attack take part of lost ground. It appears even their cavalary gone. It must have been something very serious. The few who have come back are unanimous to say the enemy lost a lot of people. We are waiting anxiously for orders. Will we be allowed to stop here? About 20 German prisonners came down this morning. A pretty haggard looking lot. So far 1 of my Cy. has returned. Cdt. & all our officers are killed or missing. It appears we have passed 1st. regiment of France. One consolation, our men defended themselves bravely. When is our relève going to take place now? A few stragglers of 1st Bon turn up. Some have had hair raising experiences.

A street map of the city of Verdun in a Michelin Tourist Guide indicates that one of the main avenues leading in to town from the east is now named 'Avenue de la 42me Division', the division to which Jacques belonged.

22nd Few more turn up, heavy fighting continues round the summit, slightly in our favour. At night we at last learn our division is releived by the 40th. We come down to Blercourt during the night. Terrific bombardment is going on. We are preparing for c-attack in the morning. A few more thousands will have been [word missing] before 24 hours are over. We are billetted in new wooden barracks along the Dombale Blercourt road. These did not exist when we went up. Now it is a little town. On arrival rumours run of victory at Douaumont [on the right bank of the Meuse]. 1900 prisoners. Compensation for our defeat at Mort Homme.

23rd Remain the day here. Things appear quieter during the day but by Gad what a night. Post available as Cycliste at the Brigade. Could obtainn if I was not now Telephonist. Having a go for it all the same. Shall know tonight.

24th No news yet. Second Bn. arrive 1st thing very tired. They were in position round Esnes, working making trenches. All have been destroyed. Bombardment continues and they loose another 1/5th of their remaining effective. We are to embark today for the rear. Start at midday for Haironville [well behind the lines, south west of Bar-le-Duc] Our billeting very fair.

25th Clean up, as usual. Town seems dead without old friends, frightfully homesick. A few are off on furlough. I wonder will my turn come around before we return. News form the front not good. It appears Douaumont belongs to the Boches again.

26th–29th Same monotonous Repos life.

30th Off at 5 to ?Longville. About 20 kilometres off I don't know where. 2 days vivres [victuals] We start at 2 p.m. To disembark at Barisé la Cote in the Meurthe & Moselle at 11 p.m. Put up in a large clean grange. If we stop here for our repos.

31st. Village about 200 inh. Little or nothing to be got bar eggs, milk, butter cheese. Inhabitants fairly agreable.

Jacques did not return to the Verdun sector. By the end of May the Germans had taken the entire Mort Homme, advancing further through July and August. But in September the initiative passed to the French, who recaptured it. Across the Meuse, on 28 October they won back Douaumont village and fort taking 6000 prisoners, and on 3 November the fort and village of Vaux. In November the French President travelled to Verdun where, with great ceremony, he distributed medals to generals responsible for the victory, to soldiers from all regions of France, and to soldiers from Morocco and Senegal, all of whom shared in the honour, and he even saluted and pinned medals onto their flags.

The cost in French and German casualties was estimated as 700 000 men along a front of just 15 miles.[7]

† † †

For many years nothing grew in Douaumont, then in the 1930s the area was planted with trees, so that today a vast new forest blankets the battlefields. The terrain is respected as a national shrine. The Paris to Strasbourg autoroute skirts this forest, but the minor road from Bar-le-Duc to Verdun, the N35, which once carried so many soldiers to and from the Front, is indicated on the road map by the name of Voie Sacrée *(Sacred Way)* whose every kilometre post bears a wreathed helmet. The stone building which had housed Pétain's headquarters at Souilly still stands, dominating the road.

Tourist buses now bring groups of French and even more Germans to visit the ruined fort of Douaumont and the chapel erected alongside the immense cemetery. Across the Meuse a small road from the rebuilt village of Chattancourt leads up to the white monument on the crest of the Mort-Homme — a sculpture of a skeletal figure emerging from a shroud and raising a furled banner. It is less visited than Douaumont but more evocative, as the young trees now surrounding it allow a glimpse of battered earth, silted up trenches and gun positions. The ruined village of Cumières on the east slope of the Mort Homme was never rebuilt, but its site is marked by a shrine. Trees surround another monument on the summit of Hill 304, but its slopes are now planted with crops.

On each anniversary of the Armistice, groups of German and French schoolchildren are brought by their teachers to the Verdun battlefields to question together how such a collective madness could ever have arisen.

10

1916: 'Thousands of Little Crosses'

After the horrors of the Verdun sector, Jacques was sent to a forest post near Lunéville, where he spent a comparatively quiet summer and continued his correspondence and diary:

1st–5th June 1916. Complete rest, go wandering about to neighbouring villages. Boutigny Caussure where there are no troops. There can arrange to have a decent meal cook. Getting fat this lazy life. Meet by mere chance the sons of the Louis Thibergien. [acquaintances from Tourcoing] They are attached to an atelier d'aviation [aviation workshop] on rails. Have several meals with them. On the whole make the most of my spare time.

6th Orders for departure. Our long rest is over, again they have told us lies. It's good that I am beginning to know what a promise in the army is worth. They treat the men like that. We only start on 8th by car, but T. R. goes tomorrow. The forest of Parow [Parroy] north of Lunéville is our secteur. Get all this news first hand as am on duty at the Colonel's today.

7th Have a last good dinner at Saussures with friends from the Telephone & the Thiberghiens. Jolly evening return only at midnight. Met nobody on the road & if we did they cant do anything worse that send us to the trenches.

8th Very tired the next morning when I have to get up and take up the line between Barisey au Plain & La Cote. Breakfast at a little pub on return just before entering village. Coffee, bread, butter, eggs, beer & rhum. Embarkment fairly punctual. We go through delightful country but towards the end go through German Villers, scene of early atrocities. The Germans burnt & sacked the village on their arrival, killed & tortured old men, women & children.

Outside see traces of heavy fighting & thousands of little crosses peep over the rising crops, protesting to heaven against the terrible butchery that has been going on for the last 2 years. Our destination is Fuimbois where we are billeted most atrociously. Those responsible ought to be shot. The laisser aller (slackness) in some branches of the French army is disgraceful. We have given up everything for our native land & we are treated no better than animals.

9th Wait for Train Régimentaire.

10th Get instructions to start for trenches at 12 after soup. Route via St. Clement (Division) Frimbois (Brigade). Our headquarters Veo. [Veho] Am told off P.C. of 2nd Bon. [He had been appointed to the battalion communications post.] Things look remarkable quiet. Within a few kilometres of the front, fields cultivated, & villages inhabited by civilians, things appear wonderfully quiet. Not an odd cannon shot on way. A slight difference with Mort Homme.

11th Arrive at 4 p.m. at P. C. gourbi, [communications shelter] the best I've seen for a long time, just an odd rifle shot. About half a dozen cannon shots exchanged towards 6 p.m. The secteur is splendidly organised, they cannot have been much interrupted in their work.

12th Same old thing only our lines are not cut by shells. Cheered up by Russian victory. [General Brusilov's troops had been victorious in Galicia against Austrian forces, taking 40 000 prisoners.]

Jacques now had more leisure to write to Australia:

14 June (1916)

Dear Brothers & Sisters

Your mail of the middle of May has brought a little sunshine in my little hole here in 1st. line. The only link that remains of our good life of long long ago. I did not appreciate how happy I was. Still I ought not to complain. We are now in the quietest of secteurs, just near the frontier in front of the famous Bois des Zeppelins near Lunéville which the Boches occupy. Just a few rifle shots & the exchange of a marmite [large shell] intermittently to make us remember that we are still at war. The secteur is wonderfully organised. Fine deep trenches everywhere, barbed wire entanglements in front of them to keep out noxious animals, & a sufficient amount of dugouts proof against anything under a 210. Telephones are everywhere & even here though only at the Bon P. C. [Battalion Communications Post]. I have 8 lines to look after. Our gourbi is fairly confortable, a little table, a bench, & untold luxury, beds of a kind. There is a spring close handy & we are able to get good water at nightfall & enjoy a daily wash. Mais la medaille a son revers [But each medal has its reverse side] & fleas, Totos & hughe big rats insist on keeping us company. What a difference all the same with the Mort Homme! Furloughs are continuing though more slowly & I hope to get away middle of July.

Strange coincidence. The other day a soldier in my Cy. got a letter from a North Sydney High school girl who wished to correspond with a French Poilu. I added a word to his letter. She will be astonished to find a Sydneyite in the same Cy. as her filleul [penfriend] Another funny one. Au repos [at rest] I met an English embusqué [soldier not at the Front] & I chatted up with him & told him I had lived for a long time in Australia. A fortnight later I got a letter from A. du Boisé, an old Riverview boy who is driving a car in the same oeuvre [Work, possibly charitable work such as the Red Cross.] He had come home to join the colours but was captured by the Emden & was only released on parole 6 weeks after but not before seeing 6 other ships sunk by the pirate. That is his reason for being embusqué.

Incidentally I got news from Mrs Hughes who is now in London with her 2 boys who are convalescent. A Melbourne friend who is with the Australians in France has also written to me. He was glad to get to France & leave Egypt but then he had not seen any fighting on this side.

The Boches are still hammering at Verdun. The Fort of Vaux is now in their hands. I'm afraid if they keep up their effort for another month they will have the town but by Gad they will have paid the price. Quite 600,000 men have fallen in the attack & defence of these ruins so far. Italy seems to have recovered herself some. Russia is doing wonders. If only the English can react sufficiently when Verdun is finished we might get a victory not a paix boiteuse [limping peace].

Love to all & bon souvenir to the cousins at Strathfield,
Jacques

Mona du Boisé, the widow of Arthur du Boisé, who celebrated her 102nd birthday in 1998 has confirmed this story. Her husband was an Australian of French descent and a grandson of Jules Joubert, who had built the grand stone houses of Hunters Hill in Sydney. At the outbreak of war he wanted to join the newly formed Flying Corps, but could only do so by travelling to England to enlist. On the way his ship, which carried a number of military personnel in mufti, was sunk, not by the *Emden* but by the raider *Moeve*.

The German Captain seems to have behaved in a gentlemanly way. As his ship was overcrowded by prisoners from several ships, he gave them the choice either of being sent to Germany as POWs or being freed, provided they signed a promise not to fight against Germany.

Arthur du Boisé chose the latter course, and was disembarked in international waters off Teneriffe. He made his way to London and told his story to the War Office, who would not allow him to break his word by enlisting but suggested that he perform some useful non-combative activity behind the lines. Being very enthusiastic about motor cars, then a relatively new invention, he decided to drive an ambulance.

15th June A little excitement. Coming back with the soup of our Post, a shell falls about 40 yards from me. It would be damn hard to be zigouillé [killed] here after escaping the M.H. [Mort Homme] Our line cut 1st time since our arrival. I mend it on the way but have to go back a couple of hours. The pionniers [pioneers] who repaired the boyaux [communication trenches] cut the line again.

16th Boches want to be nasty & send a 12 77 [? 12 rounds of 77s] round our gourbis.

A letter to Australia:

16 June (1916)

Dear Brothers & Sisters

Your mail of middle of April has reached me only a couple of days after the last & it was only a couple of days ago that I answered it.

What the dickens am I going to tell you. Life here in the trenches is monotony personified specially in a quiet secteur. I never leave my hole except to repair the lines (& they scarcely ever break) in my turn, once every two days go to the kitchen about one and a half miles from here to get our modest rations which consists of beef & beans, or beef & potatoes, or rice or macaroni, half a loaf of bread, a quart de jus [juice] a quart & a half of pinard [wine] Mother sends me heaps of parcels & I assure with that regime they come very à propos. Another very important operation that I forgot is my daily hunt for totos. They give one no rest & I catch a dozen or so every morning. Inconveniences of every kind are gone through now scarcely without a murmur.

First emotion in the secteur for me yesterday. In my turn I was returning quietly with the tucker. When one of the rare marmite [large shells] that is exchanged during the day fell right in the boyau about 40 yards in front of me. A couple of minutes saved me & as it was I only had to duck down & let the splinters fly over me. Of course our telephone lines were cut & I repaired them on the way. But I had to return a few hours later for the pionniers who came to repair the trench cut it again.

Mother as you must know is going to Vittell [a spa town in the Vosges, therefore not very far away] on the 20th where with a little luck I will go & spend my furlough with them. I'm sorry it can't be Paris but I don't want to mention it to them as it may make them delay their cure & its bound to do them good. What do you think of the lucky brothers who were all able to meet in Paris?

I am enclosing a card for little Marie [his niece Marie Polin, later McFadden] For a kid her size she writes very well. Keep her at it for its bound to come in useful later on.

Love to all,
Jacques

'Mother' at this stage was the central exchange for family meetings and communications. When she was not occupied with the French-Australian League distributions, she was constantly knitting for her soldiers with wool of beautiful quality she imported from Australia.

> **18–23** Outside the daily hunt for vermine, nothing but an attempted raid on our trenches by the Boches. We catch them as they try to cut our wires. Wound several & kill the officer. Débacle [disaster] then, & they leave everything behind them, grenades & explosives. On our right the Chasseurs [Light Infantry] whilst on patrol capture 2 machine guns & 2 men. They took up position at nightfall to harrass our corvées.

> **24th** Go down to Thebeaumenil for a few days spell, not that we need it, but a wash is very necessary. Meet cars on the way & get a lift.

> **25th** Sunday. Shower & change linnen, decent meal, feel refreshed.

While Jacques was in this quiet area in Lorraine, 1 July saw the launching of the long-planned Anglo-French offensive on each side of the Somme opposite Amiens. After months of meticulous preparation, the attack was heralded by several days of intense bombardment in which two Australian siege batteries took part.

On the north bank of the Somme were 15 divisions of *Britannique* troops led by General Haig. These included Dominion troops from Canada, India, South Africa and ANZAC. The 1st Anzac Corps, mostly Gallipoli veterans, had taken part in several victorious raids before the great offensive and, according to *L'Illustration,* had been lauded for their brilliant conduct in an official British Army bulletin telegraphed to the journal.

Facing them on a higher ridge were heavily fortified enemy positions held since the first year of the war. During this time considerable German building skills were used to delve into the chalk to build tunnels and complex trench networks up to 12 metres in depth, to equip deep shelters lined with reinforced concrete. They built railway lines to ensure supplies of building requirements as well as food and munitions, and constructed look-out posts which enabled them to overlook Allied preparations further below. They lined their approaches with bands of barbed wire. A week's bombardment by the Allies failed to destroy these positions, but instead signalled the overture. It was estimated that one million men and 200 000 horses, German, British and French, were involved in preparations for the coming battle.

On the first day of the attack, 11 British Divisions advanced in dense formation up the slope across no-man's-land, attempting to reach the high ground of Thiepval. They were largely the idealistic volunteers who had responded to Kitchener's call 'Your country needs YOU'. Far too heavily laden and still inexperienced, they followed strict instructions and advanced in formation at a walking pace into a holocaust. There was no element of surprise; German machine gunners were ready, and mowed them down in their orderly rows so that by night nearly 20 000 were dead[1] for only slight gains in ground. Thiepval was not to fall till the end of September.

Despite the ongoing process of 'bleeding white' at Verdun, the French army were still able to provide six divisions to fight south of the Somme. The more experienced French troops moved two hours later against surprised Germans in a diversionary attack, advancing with great élan and quickly reaching their day's objective. Two of Jacques' brothers were in this sector. The 1st Colonial Corps, to which Marcel Playoust was attached, were responsible for the capture of the German front line between Fay and Dompierre, bringing them closer to their goal of Peronne. René was also in the Somme and possibly their cousin from Strathfield, Jean Playoust, as they were in the same unit. The battle continued for some 4° months on a 48-kilometre front and again became one of attrition. As intended, it had the effect of relieving the pressure on Verdun, allowing the French to make several counter-attacks.

Jacques continued writing quietly into his diary. It appeared to take about a week before news of the slaughter reached his secluded position.

25th–2nd July Things seem to be brightening up a little on all the fronts. Spend a quiet & fairly enjoyable ... Boches send a few shells round the village but respect the town itself. This morning they try in vain to bring down a Saucisse [observation balloon] Raining hard today. We thought of going back to the trenches today, but get counter-orders at the last moment.

3rd A little finer. We return to the trenches in the evening. Rain keeps off & we find cars to take us back most of the way.

4th–6th The secteur is losing its charm, artillery active on both sides. It appears we are starting to annoy them.

7th–9th Secteur not improving. We can't complain when we think of what is going on North. Ideas very divided. Am fairly optimist & have supported my opinion by 2 bottles of Champagne that the Germans would be out of Peronne by 22nd inst. & by 12 bottles of Champagne that the Boches will be out of Lille before January 8th. [He lost this bet.]

10th Bombardment heavier than usual. Our 1st line liberally watered with minen. Our lines suffer badly. At 10 just as I get into bed, our gourbi shakes from side to side followed by hail-storm of shells of all kinds. Our lines cut. No communications. All sorts of rumours. Expect to see the

Buyers making a preliminary inspection Australian Land and Mercantile Company Melbourne, 1907. From left: Georges Playoust, his son Jacques, and on far right Paul Lamérand.

From back of Bourke bales of wool were sent to market by various means. Photo from the album of 'Old Vic' Dekyvère.

A double wedding in 1908. Front row: Marie Playoust (daughter of Joseph), unknown, Ninie Playoust, bride née Margeurite Playoust, Mrs Polin, Marie–Thérèse Playoust, bride née Marie–Thérèse Playoust Jr, Katie Wilkinson, Eileen Polin, unknown.
Back row: Jacques Playoust (2nd from left), Alfred Decouvelaere (bridegroom, 5th from left), Joseph Playoust, Georges Playoust, Peter Polin, Ernest Polin (bridegroom).

S.S.*Malwa*, First Contingent of Reservists 22.8.14. Jacques Playoust seated on a bollard; Armand George and Joseph Flipo 5th and 7th from right, respectively, in back row.

German propaganda postcard 'British prisoners were marched through Lille.'

French-Australian League shipment of bales of clothing to the Red Cross.

Jacques Playoust — Croix de Guerre. 'Father was more proud of my Croix than I.'

Boches arrive at any moment but they [are] content to take a few prisonners & go back to their lines. Spend night & morning repairing lines.

11th Very tired. Exact result of yesterday's coup de main [unexpected attack] known. They exploded 4 huge mines & our first lines have disappeared for 300 metres. One of the craters has actually 80 odd metres in diameter & depth 25 metres. Only 15 wounded but close on 300 men burried alive. Awful. It's expected they will try & occupy same tonight. Are on the qui vive. It's usual the people behind s'en foutent absolument [absolutely don't care, vulgar] Heard on the phone that artillery, munition scarce & grenades that we send. Evening go & repair line to Ravand Ouest in open. Things very warm on chasseurs [light infantry] on our right, but our side looks pretty quiet. It looks now as if they will not annoy us.

12th Things quieter. They still send minen fairly regularly, & to say we have no artillery to destroy these beastly things! Our killed & wounded are increasing. They say they are bringing up big guns.

13th Fair bombardment during the day but the Boches want to celebrate the eve of the 14th [Bastille Day] by a general bombardment at 10 p.m. We answer with interest & fireworks are fine for a couple. Can't appreciate view for splinters are pretty thick.

14th Things comparatively quiet. Special rations. Three extra quarts of pinard, 150 grams ham, a bottle of Champagne for 4, a ciggar. Vive la France!

A card to Marie Leplat (translation):

14 Juillet (July) 1916

Long live France. She is paying us today with 3 quarts of supplementary wine, a bottle of champagne for 4, 100g of ham, 1 cigar, biscuits, tinned peas. On the other hand, the Boches yesterday sent us a hail of shells of all calibres for the retreat. We improved the fireworks with our guns, and from 10 o'clock till midnight the fireworks were very pretty. Our good old sector no longer exists. For the last 4 days we have been fighting every night. The Boches exploded 4 mines three days ago. One of them left a crater 80 metres in diameter by 25 metres in depth, and buried 80 of our soldiers alive. What a terrible death! When it blew up I thought my dugout was going to subside.

I have received line and hook, thank you to you and your mother.

Very affectionate kiss,
Jacques

He also wrote to Australia:

16 July (1916)

Dear Brothers & Sisters,

Your letters of the 25th June or thereabouts has just come to hand. I feal pretty tired & in no form for writing. For the last 5 days we have had quite an exciting time. The Boches suddenly woke up on the 12th by blowing 4 mines in front of our lines. These completely destroyed some 300 yards of our lines and burried the occupants, more than a 100 poilus. I was at the time at the telephone in my gourbis about 800 yds. away. The earth shook so that I thought everything was going to come down on top of me.

I went to the craters the next evening. One of them has a diameter of nearly 100 yds with a deapth of 25 metres. Immediately the mines were off their was the usual tir de barrages & the rush to occupy the crater. We got there first & maintained our positions. Not as lucky the chasseurs on our leaft lost 2 lines of trenches. They counter attacked the next evening & retook the whole position. All the same it meant several hours excitement, the death of not a few, & some wounded & hell with all my lines. On the 13th July at 10 p.m. as a sort of cheering for the national day. They started to bombard us heavilly. We answered with vim. The fireworks must have been splendid but I was quite content to stop at the bottom of my dugout. They may have had the intention of making a small attack but out cannons seemed to have made them more peaceful. Things quietened down towards midnight & we were able to celebrate our fete nationale.

Rations were increased, 3 quarts of pinard supplémentaire, 100 grammes de jambon, 150 grammes of tinned vegetables, 2 biscuits, 2 ciggars, a bottle of sparkling wine for 4.

The Germans were not extra annoying. Most of us had managed to buy a little extra & we had a real jollification & yesterday some had a little mal au cheveu [sore head].

Mais c'est la guerre [But there's a war on] & then you can't help having the feeling. Today we live tomorrow we die. A current saying amongst the Poilus is 'Encore une que les Boches n'auront pas' [Another one the Boches won't get] when they empty a bottle.

Furloughs still exist in this part of the world & my turn ought to come round soon. Love to all,

Jacques

Thank Roger for Georges' photo & his baby [probably his nephew Alfred, Rev Alfred Playoust, S.J., now living in California].

The diary resumes:

15–18th July Things would be fairly quiet if we could only shut up their minen who do a lot of damage. But we have no heavy artillery at all, or if we have we can't get its help. Most demorolasing. Rain & muggy heat still continue. Mud galore. Several disagreements with phone.

19th–21st Weather improving & secteur getting quieter. On the last day we were relieved by the 16th Chasseurs & are taking up positions in the Forrêt Parroy. Quite a jog taking all our machines & passing consignes [orders] to the newcomers. Leave the Villa des Sources at nine laden like oxen to our cart who takes our machine guns away. En route at 2 p.m. & at the patelin [village, slang] before Tiebeau Menil take cars for destination.

22nd Arrive about 8 a.m. & after a walk through a lovely dense forest, stop at baraquements [barracks] hidden amongst the trees where the Colonel has his P.C. [communications post] & where a most welcome hot soup awaits us. We are sorted out & with the exception of 6 of us, all go straight up into line. We follow tomorrow. Pretty tired.

23rd Go to my P.C. about 4 miles away. Pretty little wooden barrack in middle of room. [?wood]. What a change from Les Sources. Would sign on here till the end of the War. A few lost shells fall round our quarters.

24–27th Weather beautiful. Make most of it to recognise all our lines. Delightful wandering about in the forest these times. Comparatively happy & never been so comfortable since the beginning of the War. Here where the secteur is quiet we get the visits of Berthelot & Develle [probably Generals Berthelot and Nivelle].

2nd August Nothing changed. One man killed last night, the first since our arrival whilst on patrouille [patrol]. Secteur too quiet. Very strong & well founded rumours that we are leaving for more active regions during the month. Will my turn of furlough arrive in time?

Jacques' diary ends at this point, as he changed sectors.

27th July (1916)

Dear Brothers and Sisters

Received a couple of days ago your mail of 6 & 17th & thereabouts. I thank you all specially Marie [Polin] who was the only one to remember my birthday. Since last writing to you we have again been on 'The moove' & occupy a secteur near CENSORED. [It was in the Forest of Parroy, east of Nancy, very near the border of what had been German Lorraine since 1870] We did not waist must time. We started from the trenches at 2 at night [sic], took the cars at 2 the next morning, arrived at destination about 9 & took up our positions at once. Our secteur comprises of a hughe forest about 9 miles square. It is an ideal spot for warfare on the defensive. Only in first line have we trenches & dug outs. Further back we live in a little huts only in case of bombardment have we shelters. They cant see us & only fire blindly. And all the munitions they have to spare they can use more effectively in other secteurs. I am now telephone boy at the P.C. of a commandant de Sous Secteur. My quarters are very confortable. The weather is delightful & the eternal shade is far from been out of place. Under the trees we have a little rustic table & benches were we take out meals & rest & read. We have a nice clean little barrack to sleep in, a bed of kinds, of course no sheets, & our blanket is that we always carry with us. That takes up half, the rest is our exchange [telephone exchange].

Our lines very seldom get out of order & we are about as happy as anybody could be under the circumstances & do you know what we appreciate the most is to be out of those dreadful holes & trenches. You can't imagine how oppressive they get in the long run. Forest life gets fatiguing in the long run & I should immagine in wet weather very desagreable.

I have got no news from René for some time. He is in the Somme & not far if not in the thick of things. [René was wounded several times during the war, but it is not known in which campaign.] In this like all other offensives letters are held back but it is an anxious time for anyone. From all reports the fighting is on a tremendous scale & that means a lot. How many thousands must fall daily.

I still hope to see the end of the war this year. I doubt that the Germans will be able to bear the strain of this general offensive. The Russians are exceeding expectations. The French have not said their last word. The English are putting up a grand fight at last before a very tough opposition. And the Italians are mooving too. I think that if I'm still alive & kicking in 6 months I shall have still years to come & annoy you with my hair raising war experiences. These hardships have not made too 'néfaste' [disastrous] an impression on me as you will be able to judge by the photographs I enclose. Roger has asked me for one so please give it to him.

Best love to all,
Jacques

From his quiet place in the forest, Jacques seemed well informed about the overall conduct of the War. Russian forces under General Brusilov were advancing in Eastern Galicia against Turkish and Austrian armies. Other Russian units were advancing in the Carpathian mountains, as well as in Asia Minor, near Trebizond. Italian forces were advancing against the invading Austrians in the Alto Adige near Lake Garda, and also along the

Brenta. In the Somme, British troops were bearing towards Thiepval. Le Bois Delville, aptly renamed 'Devil's Wood' was taken and retaken several times. According to Jacques' letter, his brother René was in the Somme. The French troops at this stage were advancing a little in the direction of Combles, their artillery supporting the British in 'Devil's Wood'. South of the Somme they captured several trenches.

The 5th Australian Division had recently arrived from Egypt after several months of artillery training. (It was to this division that Jacques was to be attached as interpreter in 1918). It was about to take part in the first major attack by an Australian Division on the Western Front. A diversionary attack on Fromelles, in Flanders, near the German-occupied city of Lille, was planned by General Haig in order to prevent the Germans from reinforcing their lines further south on the Somme. Together with the 61st British Division, the Australians attacked a German redoubt called the Sugar Loaf. The Germans had observed their preparations and subjected them to intense machine gun fire, eventually driving them back.

In hindsight the so-called diversionary attack seems a costly blunder, as in 48 hours there were 1708 Australian dead and almost 4000 wounded. Four hundred Australians were taken prisoner and were marched through Lille to impress the conquered population, but the people of Lille rushed forward to give them cigarettes and chocolate. The 5th Division was then out of action for several months.

Three days later, on Sunday 23 July, the Australians — this time the 1st, followed by the 2nd and 4th divisions — were in action once again further south in the Somme area. The battle for Pozières, within view of Thiepval, was renewed after a previous assault by British infantry. L'Illustration described the action thus:

> Pozières village lay on a gentle slope with a windmill. What was tactically called Hill 160 was the highest point in the region with immense views towards the boundary of Picardy. The Germans had transformed the village into a redoubtable fortress where intense bombardment failed to dispose of its German garrison. Only after midnight were the British and Australians successful in taking the outer defences and then to penetrate the village, but then it had to be taken house by house. By Monday the Germans still held several houses. 150 prisoners were taken by the Anzacs, but the Germans were not routed until Wednesday.[2]

This rather bland description gives no account of the furious bombardment then directed at the ruined village by the Germans, who were planning a counter-attack both for that time and in the weeks to come. Because of the great number of casualties suffered in these two engagements it was obvious that the greatly depleted Australian forces needed to be replenished.

The Australian Labor Prime Minister, Mr W. M. Hughes, strongly desired to follow the British example in introducing conscription, believing in equality of sacrifice. This caused a split in Labor ranks. Holman was of the same mind as Hughes, and formed a Nationalist government in New South Wales in 1916. However, as there was much opposition from the Labor party, a referendum was called for the following October to allow the people to decide. The campaign was bitterly fought and, sadly, the political, social and sectarian divisions that surfaced left scars which took at least a generation to heal. Conscription was defeated.

11

1916: The Somme

Jacques was now to undergo a period of rest and training before being transferred to the Somme sector, where French forces were fighting on the right of the British.

23rd August

Dear Brothers & Sisters

Your letters of the 10th July have just come to hand. I am en route again. We are leaving the forest tomorrow. Already we gave up our telephone post to the telephonists of the releive regt. We have come down further back & we are bivouacking as best we can for the night. My bed is a wire hamac [hammock] under a large tree. I've seen worse but hope all the same it does not rain. Things look pretty threatening.

Demain une étape [tomorrow a day's march] of 20 kilometres. Quite enough when you have to carry some 20 lbs. on your back & then we get no real training.*

The day after we have a little more to do & then rest & training for a fortnight & then 'attaque attaque' for 3 months. Many of us will not see it through. Enfin espérons. [Anyway, let us hope] It would not be so bad it was the last effort that would be required of us. Gad, people cant imagine the life that we are leading. At time the morale gets pretty low. What we would give for a broken leg, arm, now. Many would sacrifice either of them to be finished once & for all. I suppose it is right that the lives of millions should be sacrificed for the general welfare. We are all insignificant units. Mais au point de vue personel c'est atroce, c'est injuste. [But from a personal point of view it is atrocious, it is unjust]

Thank you all for your kind wishes and sympathy. Love,

Jacques

Jacques was at a particular disadvantage marching, as his legs were short. One of the stories he often related in later years concerned the ordeal of long marches, and how once when he was in so much pain with his feet actually bleeding into his boots, he sat in a gutter in a small village and wept. He was greatly touched when an old lady came out of her house to comfort him.

A letter to Sydney from his brother Marcel, who was still in the Somme with his colonial regiment, was published in his school magazine about this time:

Time is very scarce. Work is plentiful, too plentiful. We have adopted khaki. I mean we are so covered with mud, that the light blue colour has disappeared. We are now 'au repos' in a village two km. from the first line of trenches. Here, too, of course [in the village] is one interminable maze of trenches. I had an idea we were going to have our 'repos' in a village, where there would be inhabitants, where you could buy little things you wanted, and principally where there would be no work to do. No such thing! The village is in ruins, all the inhabitants have left, and there are a hundred and one things to do during the night, such as making trenches, putting up barbed wire.

It was a pitch dark night, three weeks ago, when we came to relieve those whose trenches we were to occupy. The roads, or what was left of them, were muddy, and had nice little holes left full of water. You all know the pleasant surprise it is to splash into them unawares every now and then. I experienced it more than once. It was easy to see we were approaching the lines. No cigarettes, no light of any sort, no talking! We knew we were near before receiving these orders; you could hear the shells screaming, and the 'fusées' (kind of rocket you send up to give light so as to discover wanderers between the trenches) cast gleams over us. Then all of a sudden, before entering the wood, we entered the 'boyau'.

We released the others without mishap. Between 9 at night till daylight I took six hours guard in a 'poste d'écoute' [listening post] in the end of a 'boyau' which leaves your first line of trenches in the direction of the enemy, and the end of which forms a little hole more or less protected. You can see and hear better what is going on in front.

I had expected to rest next morning, but instead, I was given a pickaxe to help dig out a new 'cagna'. A 'cagna' is really a cave dug out below the ground, where you sleep and rest when off duty. While in there working, a shell came over. It was a 105, which you hear come in the form of an uncanny whistle, just as I should imagine the cry of triumph of a vampire. I saw the men crouch down in the trenches. I did the same. It burst with much fracas about 20 yards behind us; stray bits of cast iron, copper, etc., fell a little nearer. Then, soon we heard the same wail a second time. It seemed quite triumphant this time. I had time to say a little prayer before it fell with a sickening thud two yards away from us. There was no detonation the shell didn't burst. Thank God! or I would not be writing this.

B was as white as the snow which lay around us, his lips were trembling, he wasn't able to utter a word. His cigarette somehow or other still was on his bottom lip. C, another of the 'équipe', started to rouse like H; but he never did anything but grumble. When he tells you the weather is fine, it is a way of saying that it is sure to snow. He cursed the Germans and smiled contemptuously as the shells fell. M temporarily lost some of his usual rosy colour, but he is not a funk. F, our barber, was smoking his pipe. He continued to do so, and ducked just in time. He doesn't lose his head, and times the shells well, P, who was there, too, stuttered generally for a while before being able to resume his conversation. He didn't seem to expect just that. It is his first experience in the trenches.

Shells are most demoralising things, and they have the 'rotten' and most supernatural sound you can imagine, as they go through the air. We take the asphyxiating gases very seriously. We are never without our masks, even a few miles in the rear, where they seem to think they can do damage. The horses, too, have masks.

Two weeks of first and second line, and now we are in the third. The program is a little exercise during the day, and work from six o'clock in the evening till midnight. It is a bit of a rest all the same, as in first line you average five hours' sleep daily at most. Excuse my 'talking shop', and if I am uninteresting, I am so tired that my head can't be working too well.

On 27 August Romania, encouraged by Russian advances, declared war on Austria. The next day the Kaiser removed General von Falkenhayn as Chief of the General Staff, replacing him by the ageing General von Hindenburg, with General Ludendorff as his deputy. The Germans assumed military leadership of the Central Powers, who then moved against Romania and bombed Bucharest. The Romanians appealed to London and Paris so, in an attempt to take the heat off Romania, the British and French renewed their offensive in the Somme. The British took Guillemont on the first day. Cléry sur Somme, one of the good crossings, fell to the French, bringing them closer to their objective of Peronne. The official French communique[1] issued on the night of 4 September stated: 'An attack was developed on a 20 km front near Barleux, and the first line of trenches was captured in a brilliantly conducted assault.' The communique does not tell the rest of the story, which is taken up by Marcel's school magazine:

On 4th September 1916 Marcel Playoust took place in the attack on Barleux with the French Colonials. His company went forward in the first wave of assault and penetrated to the third line of enemy trenches. There it was held up and later forced to retire on account of a failure of flanking troops. Of 180 men in the company 140 never returned, among them Soldat Playoust. Nothing has been heard of him since that day.

There is a document extant, written in careful copperplate with a pen and nib, from the chief accountant for the 5th Regiment of Colonial Infantry in Lyon and addressed to the municipal authorities of the 8th arrondissement in Paris. 'I have the honour to request you to notify, with all the necessary tact under the circumstances, Mr Playoust Georges, care of Mr Leplat, 19 Rue Marbeuf, of the disappearance of Soldat Playoust Marcel, born in Melbourne (Australia)… on 4th September 1916 in the southern region of Barleux, Somme.'

The municipal authorities were very busy in those years delivering such messages, but the news had not reached Jacques when he wrote the following letter, just as his unit was preparing to leave for the Somme:

7th September

Dear Brothers & Sisters

This mail of yours dated the 24th sees me very close to my return in line. Our period de rafraichissement [refreshment] is drawing to a close, manoeuvres of all kinds every day. The weather too has had a say in the rafraichir part of it & with the exception of today it has not ceased raining. Result I have a bad cold & feal the work muchly. But its no good seeing the Major these days unless you have something serious so I battle on. The rumor that we are to entrain on Sunday is increasing. Destination of course 'inconnu' [unknown] but the odds are that it will be the Somme.

It looks as though I'm going up again as Signaleur but this time as Signaleur de Bon. [Battalion Signaller] I don't know that I don't like it better than Telephonist because when we attack we follow the '2nd wave' & of course are much longer in the open than the soldier who has only to reach the trench. When they get there nowadays, the enemy always surrenders. The only real trench fighting that goes on nowadays is in a Boyau de Communication [communication trench] when the enemy wishes to make a barrage & then only very few men are injured. The Signaleur de Rgt follows the Colonel & that is further back. Anyhow I won't do anything one way or the other & continue to trust in my lucky star. Poor Marcel is having a rough time & perhaps even more than me he does not like the game. Stéphane is more lucky & as Mother will have probably told you he is up at la Valbonne following les cours E O de R. He is still a l'abris [sheltered] for a couple of months & then he gets 8 days furlough. You can't imagine how it is appreciated by soldiers.

I'm sorry that Roger will not be able to write to us individually regularly. But les études avant tout [studies must come before everything else] & he must not forget that perhaps before the war is over he may be one of Father's only supports. It is by no means improbable but let us hope that our lucky star will not forsake us. You may only get stingy P.C. from now on for a few months. We expect a tough secteur next time after our comparative quiet.

Love to all
Jacques

Jacques' letters have not mentioned Stéphane until this point. Stéphane would have been the first of the brothers to reach France and enlist, as he had returned from America when war was declared. He belonged to the 82nd Regiment of Infantry and, according to the *Courrier Australien* of 6 August 1915, was promoted to the rank of Sergeant on the battlefields of Neuville St. Vaast. At some stage he was wounded in the arm. At the time of this letter Stéphane was attending an officer's course at La Valbonne, near Lyon. He was the only one of the brothers to become an officer.

There is a three-month gap until Jacques' next letter. If rumours had been right he would have left his training camp on Sunday 9 September to entrain for the long journey west to Picardy. Here the Allied forces were continuing their advance each side of the Somme, trench by trench. The movement was accelerated by the end of September. The British forces, moving forwards from Pozières, collaborated with the French in an encircling movement to take the now heavily fortified village and chateau of Combles. The Germans had considered Combles the centre of resistance in the Somme, and it now contained telephone networks, stores of ammunition, etc. There was a first-aid post in the vaulted cellars of the chateau.

At the same time the strategically important redoubt of Thiepval, which had been holding out for three months, finally fell to the British with the help of the new weapon, tanks. It seems from a later newspaper interview that Jacques participated in these advances, and during this period earned his Croix de Guerre, receiving the following citation (translation):

Le Colonel de MATHAREL, Commandant la
84e Brigade, cité à l'Ordre de la BRIGADE:
PLAYOUST Jacques, Mle M1541
Soldat at la C. H. R. du 162e R. I.
Signé: de MATHAREL

' ... and a composure worthy of praise in going to repair several times over, under a bombardment of extreme violence, the severed telephone wires. Had already been conspicuous for his dedication.'

In succeeding weeks there were more attacks and counter attacks. November came with rain and fog, and the British won Beaumont Hamel, with mud to their thighs. Snowfalls ended the great battle of the Somme, but the Allies were still short of Bapaume, which had been one of the objectives on the first day of battle on 1 July. In 4° months the British front line had advanced about 12 kilometres. The French did not obtain the watery fortress of Peronne until the strategic German retreat several months later.

In his book *The First World War 1914-18* the historian John Terraine has aptly named 1916 as 'the year of killing'. He listed the numbers of casualties — dead, missing and wounded — for four months of fighting in the Somme as: British 415 000, French 195 000.[2]

In addition, across the country to the east, the numbers of French dead and wounded during the battle of Verdun had been assessed as 362 000, and of course German casualties had been comparable.[3]

† † †

Visitors to the Somme battlefields are always surprised at the small size of the area, a small triangle east and north-east of Amiens where the tragic battle was fought through the latter half of 1916. In summer sunshine among the lush fields of grain, edged still with red poppies, the scene of that earlier summer would be hard to imagine if it were not for the many cemeteries almost at every turning, with hundreds of named graves of the known dead of the battle of the Somme. Clusters of memorials British, French, Canadian, New Zealand, Indian, South African, Irish were also raised on low hills which were once redoubts, to honour the unknown soldiers who lost their lives trying to seize them.

The small Newfoundland regiment which lost 700 men in thirty minutes is commemorated in a specially evocative way by eighty acres of National Park at Beaumont-Hamel. Here the trenches are left untouched, except for the grasses growing over the earth, which is gradually silting them up. On a mound at the highest point stands a bronze caribou. Delville Wood's memorial marks the particular hell of the South Africans. From the Australian memorial at Pozières can be seen the red brick British memorial at Thiepval.

† † †

The armies now holed up in their icy trenches to endure the winter, to rebuild their dug-outs, to line their floors, to remake communications and fight the rats. The Allied General Staffs were again convened by Joffre at Chantilly to plan the following year's campaign. Joffre stated that France could only maintain its strength for one more battle, and thereafter insufficient men of military age would remain to replace the losses.

10th December 1916

Dear Brothers and Sisters,

This mail brings me a letter from Marie [Polin] and Marg. of the 29th October. I am just back from furlough & have naturally the 'cafard' [home sickness] a little. Enfin I cannot complain under the circumstances I had a splendid holiday, found the old people looking fine. Father was more proud of my Croix than I. He took me round to see our business friends, the Famille Tourquennoise [the Tourcoing family] insisted that I should get my photo taken. Of course there will be one for each and everyone of you. They will be ready in about 10 days & will get mother to send them on to you. It will give you a little patience to wait for the original but one thing can be certain, he will be more than pleased to see you.

I found my regiment in line on my return but this time in a very quiet secteur. Perhaps not so quiet as Parroy but what a change with the Somme. Those before us availed themselves of this to make their quarters as confortable as possible & we are living a trench life 'avec tous les conforts moderne' [with all modern comforts]. Our dugouts are not perhaps as solid as they might be but we have berths, tables, benches, and what is still more wonderful, electric light. We use the same force to send a current through the barbded wire in front of our trenches. Hot & cold water showers & a co-operative very well fitted indeed where you can buy almost everything a soldier wants. All this in trenches not more than 800 yards from the Boches. Are they going to leave us spend the Xmas here? In spight of rumors to the contrary I hope they would certainly never moove a division for so short a time.

The morale amongst the civilians is falling. He is beginning to feal the pinch of War. In Paris, coal, sugar & potatoes are hard to get. Everything is getting frightfully dear. Like us he was greatly disappointed with Roumania [Bucharest had fallen to German forces on 6 December]. He is beginning to realise that the Somme was not the success that could have been expected. The Allies have at last noticed that they want more unity of action, more direction, They have turned over a new leaf & going to have another try. Let us hope for the best. Best wishes,

Jacques

The balance of power was changing. Romania had fallen to the Germans, giving the enemy access to its oil wells and fertile wheat fields. As the iced trenches in winter quietened the fighting there was heightened diplomatic activity. The old Austrian Emperor, Franz Josef, died while working at peace negotiations, his own power eroded by instability in his empire and by Germany's dominance in arms.

In England, a more vigorous Lloyd George replaced a war-weary Asquith as Prime Minister on 6 December. In France public opinion had turned against Joffre's strategy of attrition, and on 12 December he was replaced as supreme commander by General Nivelle, responsible for the last successful battles at Verdun, and author of the celebrated words 'Ils ne passeront pas' *(They shall not pass).*

On that same day the German Chancellor, in a speech to the Reichstag, offered to open peace negotiations with the Allies in a neutral country. Eight days later US President Woodrow Wilson asked the Allied powers to formulate their peace conditions, but it was a vain hope; the Kaiser would not give up his conquest of Belgium. General Ludendorff urged unrestricted submarine warfare on neutral ships bringing supplies to England, France and Italy, despite the resolution of President Wilson to declare war if an American ship were sunk.

In Belgium and the occupied north of France the Germans were conscripting civilians for forced labour in German territory. In Roubaix, for example, after a 3 a.m. door-knock, the occupants of houses were obliged to line up outside their front doors while a number of young able-bodied men and women were rounded up. Machine gun posts were set at each end of the street to prevent any attempt at escape. After some weeks the women were allowed to return, but the men were sent to prison camps in the Ardennes, where they were issued with uniforms with arm bands designating them as the 'Zivil Arbeiter Bataillon' *(Civilian Worker Battalion)* and forcibly recruited into labour teams. Those refusing to work were sent to reprisal camps with conditions so primitive that many died. Later, through the intervention of the Red Cross, the children, the old and the sick were repatriated via Switzerland to unoccupied France.

12

1917: The Spring Offensive

The year began with an unusually severe winter; the Seine froze over so that the barges bringing in fresh supplies to Paris were immobilised. The cold was felt all the more by civilians as there was a shortage of wood and coal. As for life in the trenches, for weeks on end photos show men huddling in the snow. No attacks could be made until Spring.

The United States President Woodrow Wilson, who had tried throughout the war to act as peacemaker between the belligerents, was handed a note from the German Secretary of State, Herr Zimmerman, announcing Germany's decision to abolish all restrictions on submarine warfare. Any US ships approaching Allied ports, including hospital ships, would be torpedoed. On 4 February the United States severed diplomatic relations with Germany, and ambassadors were recalled.

A joyous event was pictured in the next week's issue of *L'Illustration*. At a performance of *Madama Butterfly* at the Paris Opéra Comique, just as the second act was beginning, the United States ambassador, Mr William Sharp, entered his box. He was greeted with a standing ovation and cries of 'Vive Wilson'. The performance was interrupted as the orchestra broke into 'Yankee Doodle Dandy', and the cast in their kimonos applauded and bowed. Submarine warfare was intensified and American ships were sunk. Furthermore, Germany was found to be fomenting trouble for the US over the border in Mexico. Wilson could no longer hesitate, and declared war on Germany on 6 April. It was to be a long time before American manpower could be of any help at the Front, but the psychological effect on both Germans and Allies was considerable.

Less encouraging events were taking place in Russia. Strikes, riots and mutinies in Petrograd in March set the scene for revolution both in the capital and in army ranks. This later allowed Germany to withdraw her forces from the Eastern Front to send them to the West.

During March it was observed in certain parts of the Front that the Germans were no longer retaliating, but instead withdrawing to positions about 15 kilometres back. Allied troops cheerfully attacked their rearguards and advanced to take many positions such as Bapaume and Peronne, for which they had struggled so hard in the previous year. This was in fact a precisely prepared strategy designed by General Ludendorff. His plan straightened the salients, thus shortening the line to be defended and releasing manpower and munitions. It allowed a careful withdrawal to the now strongly fortified Siegfried Line, known to the Allies as the Hindenburg Line. Ludendorff hoped to keep his forces here on the defensive in their deep forts and pill-boxes edged with tangles of barbed wire, relying on full-scale submarine warfare to decide the issue at sea.

In this newly released territory the Allies went forward with difficulty as the roads had been destroyed, the fields booby-trapped and the villages looted and ruined. Even rows of fruit trees ready to come into bud had been carefully chopped down, while many of the inhabitants were marched off to forced labour in Germany.

The Allies now had confronting them a master strategist, General Erich Ludendorff. Son of a landowner, he made his career in the Prussian army and as a young officer was appointed to the German General Staff. Here he had been strongly influenced by his Chief, Count von Schlieffen, then by his successor General von Moltke. In the years preceding the war Ludendorff had energetically committed himself to increasing the strength of the German army. It was Schlieffen's essays on strategy that had led to the surprise invasion of Belgium and Ludendorff himself had been involved in the capture of the fortress of Liège in the first days of the war.

About this time Mr Holman, the Premier of NSW, was farewelled from Sydney by a large reception held at the Town Hall, well attended by the French citizens of Sydney. He travelled to Britain and the United States, and spent a good deal of time in spring and summer visiting Australian troops in France. He reviewed the men of the 4th division with General Holmes in what had been thought a safe part of the Messines area, when a stray burst of gunfire hit them both. Mr Holman was wounded, but General Holmes lost his life.

The French General Nivelle, fresh from his success in Verdun, had an ambitious plan to end the war once and for all, and it had the support of the British Prime Minister Lloyd George. The British were first to make a diversionary attack in Picardy further to the north-west before Arras, but this plan had to be modified as a result of the German strategic retreat to the Hindenburg line. It was in this operation that the Australians took Bullecourt, suffering many casualties, and the Canadians, after a masterly scaling of the heavily fortified Vimy Ridge, captured the crest.

† † †

In 1995, 78 years after the Battle of Bullecourt, the body of Sergeant John White from Gippsland in Victoria, still wearing his clearly marked identification disk, was discovered by a farmer. He was later buried with full military honours in an Australian Military Grave in the presence of his 80-year-old daughter. To remind the world, at Bullecourt there stands an AIF memorial and museum, with a stone plinth outside the church bearing a bronze slouch hat. A farming couple from Bullecourt, M. and Mme Letaille, were recently decorated as honorary members of the Order of Australia for their work in preserving Australian relics of the war. Other memorials have been built to commemorate the Australian dead at Fromelles and Bapaume. In all such places the Australian War Graves Commission has assumed the responsibility of caring for the graves of all Australian soldiers killed in battle.

† † †

The main Nivelle thrust by two French armies, with a third in reserve, was to be launched several days later from the flat land north of the Aisne river on a front of 40 kilometres. It aimed to capture the redoubtable Chemin des Dames ridge, which had been held by the enemy since the first year of the war. During this time the Germans had had the opportunity to strengthen this natural fortress by their skilled constructions, machine gun posts and heavy artillery. Interconnecting tunnels had been dug and strengthened with reinforced concrete. They contained magazines, hospitals and a network of facilities, as well as observation posts on higher ground, from which could be clearly seen the cities of Soissons and Rheims. Their guns had been bombarding these cities relentlessly, causing much damage to their medieval treasures. Another French attack was to be made simultaneously in a sector east of Rheims.

Stéphane Playoust, 'Faf', newly promoted to the rank of Sous-Lieutenant after his officer's training school, had written a postcard to his young brother Maurice shortly before Christmas. The front of the card pictured a laughing soldier leading a charge, and calling out the celebrated battle-cry of Verdun 'On les aura!' *(We'll have them!)*.

21st December 1916

Dear Maurice

You will see by my address that I am now with my new regiment. At present the division is re-organising and reforming.

It will probably be at least another fortnight in our cantonnements [billets] The village where we are is quite decent, but as you say not gay in this rotten weather. I am lodged at the curé's [parish priest] and have a fine room and comfortable bed. A happy Xmas, with love.

Faf

When Spring came, Stéphane and Jacques were both transferred to the Aisne sector, where the Nivelle offensive was being prepared, and they met by chance.

12 March (1917)

Dear Brothers & Sisters,

I rejoined my regiment 2 days ago in line after an absence of 15 days. I found a hughe Australian mail, letters from Georges, Marie, Marg, Roger. Thank you all.

I had been living at a grand centre d'aviation to do a little signalling with avions [aeroplanes] & observation balloon. The work was interesting, not too severe, and as soon as our work was finished we were as free as birds, sleep & eat where we like. Then we were all taken up for a ride in aero & able to see for ourselves our signals from below. It beats motoring out of sight. Not half as sensational as it's cracked up to be but talk about the view up above.

On my way back here I was lucky enough to meet Faf. The first time I've seen him as an officer. He introduced me to his confreres & his Commdt. immediately invited me to stop & have dinner with them. I accepted & after dinner played a few rubbers. Steph & I played together. His extraordinary luck at cards has not leaft him & the Australians scooped the pool. Bye the bye, Faf is getting very fat.

Now I have settled down to rough times again. Our new secteur is not a pleasant one. The Boches are very [word omitted]. They have seen a lot of moovement behind our lines & give us no respite. I am here in a little dugout with shells falling all round. I assure I don't feel too happy. I have only a metre of earth & bricks above me, just about enough to stop a 77. We have had quite a lot of snow lately. The thaw has set in and to make things worse we have mud & water right to the knees in places & when you have to walk through these fully laden as I had to yesterdays you can guess the exhertion. I am pretty hard now yet I was dead to the world when I arrived.

I saw my Cl. yesterday re a leave for Sydney. He is sending my demande de permission with avis favorable [request for leave with favourable consideration] In Paris they tell me I have a chance. If only I could get away before the next offensive. But it seems too good to be true.

Love to all,
Jacques

This letter was quickly followed by another undated message:

Dear Brothers & Sisters

I must be brief this mail. We are all very busy getting the spring offensive ready. Its only a matter of days now. The artillery is about to begin the ouverture and mighty heavy its going to be. We open the dance as soon as the bombardment finishes.

I'm going to try doubly to get out of this scrap as there is a good chance of getting a furlough to Australia. The joy of getting out of this frightful life & seeing you all again. John is leaving today. I should have leaft with him if it were easy for a soldier to get his rights. But a poor piou piou [foot-slogger] is less than nothing nowadays.

Love
Jacques

John (Jean Playoust, Jacques' cousin) was indeed returning to Australia on leave. One of his sisters, whose reason for being in France was not explained, was accompanying him home. When their ship was torpedoed in the Mediterranean they both escaped unharmed, and were able to return to Australia by another ship. Jean remained several months in Sydney before returning to the Front.

General Nivelle's attack began as planned on 16 April after prolonged artillery fire. There was accordingly no element of surprise, particularly as the Germans had discovered the plans of the attack on a captured French soldier, and placed their machine guns strategically to decimate the infantry as they progressed uphill. Jacques' and Stéphane's regiments took part in this operation, starting from the plain a little north-west of Rheims, and were aiming to reach the heights of Craonne, the easternmost point of the Chemin des Dames ridge. *L'Illustration* described it thus:

> Between Craonne and Berry-au-Bac not only the first position but the second were carried off south of Juvincourt. Our advance reached 3 to 4 kilometres in depth.

There were vigorous counter attacks all along the Front, but a tank attack failed, the Air Force was outnumbered, and much of this ground was later lost. The infantry was halted on the plateau of Craonne.

On the very first day of the offensive, near Juvincourt, Stéphane earned the Légion of Honour, the Croix de Guerre and lost his life. He was 28 years old. Once more, Georges and Marie-Thérèse were to hear the knock at the door and to receive the dreaded news from a municipal official. His citation read:

> Officer of ardent bravery. On the 16th April he supported his section under a violent curtain fire, encouraging it by word and by example. Some moments later leapt on to the parapet, and drawing on his men with an irresistible movement was mortally hit.

Le Général Commandant le 5e Corps d'Armée
Général de Boissoudy

The family in Sydney was cabled, and a Requiem Mass was said by the

French Marist Father and chaplain to the French community, Father Piquet. According to the school magazine:

> The Rector of St. Aloysius College three other Fathers with twenty senior boys represented the College. Drs. Burfitt, H. Moran, and R. A. Gardner (Capt. A.M.C.) of the old boys were also present. The Fathers who taught Stéphane, recall the bright hardworking lad, who passed the old Junior among the first boys of Milsons Point ... and Stéphane that year secured the Curtis Mathematical Medal ... Stéphane, as all of his brothers, was a general favourite with masters and boys; and a hero's glorious death is a worthy crown to the dear boy's life. At the end of the Mass ... Rex Ryan sounded from the choir gallery the 'Last Post'.

The battle dragged on along the Chemin des Dames, costly in human life but with little result visible to Jacques as he departed from the Front a few weeks later. He was able to visit his parents in Paris and share their grief before leaving them to embark on a P&O ship, the SS *Mongolia,* in Marseilles for his long-desired furlough in Australia.

13
1917: 'C'est la Guerre'

Letter to Marie Leplat, translated from the French:

12 June 1917

My dear Marie,

Now that I am at ease, comfortable and out of danger I do not wish to forget my good friends who were so faithful to me during my difficult moments and I must therefore come and take up a little of your time. I hope it will not be too disagreeable for you.

If all goes well we should arrive at Port Said tomorrow towards 14 hrs. I am very hopeful; we are armed with a 150 mm. gun, and accompanied by two destroyers, and furthermore for the last three years, I have had marvellous luck. However, I do not want to pretend to be clever, and like the others, I do not take off my lifejacket.

We are only about 40 passengers in First Class, and only one lady and she is a Turk. She is travelling with her husband and baby as far as Port Said; the English are exchanging her for an English family. Of course we are obliged to boycott her since she is an enemy. Perhaps more than that, as she is French. That is the danger of marrying a foreigner. The voyage is monotonous. You have no idea how much we miss the company of ladies. Even the old chaps are complaining. The hairdresser is in despair. Not only are there no heads to wash, but he cannot sell his sweets and odds and ends. The gentlemen also are less fastidious, and care for their beards and their hair a little less well.

Reply to me in Sydney, as I do not know if I will be able to find a ship to come back. To your mother and yourself my best love,

Jacques

Having reached Port Said safely, the *Mongolia* sailed through the Suez Canal and set course for India. Just off the Indian coast the ship struck a mine and sank in 20 minutes, but Jacques' marvellous luck held. He rowed ashore unharmed, sharing a lifeboat with a former acquaintance from Mount Macedon, the amateur tennis champion and Australian Davis Cup player Norman (later Sir Norman) Brookes. Jacques' wallet was full of money because he had been just about to pay his bar bill, as required half way through the voyage.

While waiting for another ship in Bombay he sent this postcard to Marie from the palatial Taj Mahal Hotel where P&O had housed him (translation):

27th July (?June) 1917
Dear Marie,

Affectionate remembrance from Bombay. This is the hotel I am stranded in after my shipwreck. There are more amusing things to do than to spend 24 hours in an open boat in the middle of the ocean. My number is not up yet, and I am still safe and sound.

I have lost everything, clothes, handkerchiefs, war souvenirs.

Remember me to your mother, love,

Jacques

The shipping company P&O advertised in the newspapers that their Royal Mail service had been temporarily interrupted, and the *Sydney Morning Herald* published the following two articles on 31 July 1917:

THE 'MONGOLIA'

SURVIVORS IN SYDNEY: EXCITING EXPERIENCES

A number of survivors from the H.M.S Mongolia, which struck a mine and sank on June 23 last, have arrived in Sydney.

According to statements made, the disaster occurred shortly after noon. The steamer was timed to reach port five hours later. There were two terrific explosions and the passengers, many of whom had left their lifebelts in their cabins, were thrown on to the deck. A very powerful mine had been struck and the vessel soon took a list. Some men were dreadfully scalded, while several suffered from other injuries. It was not possible to launch all of the boats. One capsized, but 11 were got safely into the water. The captain did not leave the ship until the water had reached his knees. He and his officers worked well, but passengers generally were in agreement that the lascars were 'absolutely useless'.

Brigadier General Sir Robert Anderson states that his boat and four others got close to shore just at dusk, but it was by no means easy to effect a landing. One of these boats contained the late Mr F. E. Winchcombe, M.L.C. It turned turtle and two or three lives were lost. There were two deaths amongst those in Sir Robert Anderson's boat. The four other boats succeeded in landing their passengers, and at daylight it was found that the party, about 200 in all, were on Velas Beach, in Janjira, about 60 miles south of Bombay.

When Mr Winchcombe was taken ashore it was found that his

condition was critical, but he showed the 'greatest pluck right up till the last'. He died in Bombay of pneumonia.

There was no food to be obtained on the beach where the survivors were landed, and the natives did not seem disposed to have anything to do with the party. A number of the passengers then set out for a town named Dijhi, 9 or 10 miles distance. There the natives did everything they could, and arrangements were made for interviewing the ruler of Janjira. He sent food, wine and stretchers to the beach, and the sick and injured passengers, including Mr Winchcombe, were taken to Dijhi. Lady Anderson and the other ladies of the party nursed Mr Winchcombe in hospital. 'He was very brave' said Sir Robert Anderson, and 'we saw him in hospital just before he died. His death occurred 2 days after the landing'.

Rain fell during the night whilst Sir Robert Anderson's party (he was appointed leader) was on the beach. Most of the passengers lost everything with the exception of the clothes they were wearing. There was no medical chest or first aid equipment in any of the lifeboats, and many of the women divested themselves of their underclothing in order to provide bandages for those who had been injured.

But as soon as news reached Bombay a vessel was sent to Dijhi. The P. and O. Company's officials have made excellent arrangements. The passengers were in need of clothing, money and fresh passports, while some had to be conveyed to hospital. The whole of this work was attended to and those who have reached Sydney say that there was no ground for complaint at the treatment meted out to them by the P. and O. authorities at Bombay. Of course, the passengers saved hardly any of their belongings, but Sir Robert Anderson, when spoken to on the point, smiled, and remarked, 'we are lucky to be alive at all'.

That observation was fairly typical of the feelings of the majority of the survivors.

Sir Robert, who is looking little the worse for his trying experience, said that the best that could be said was not too good for the captain and officers, while the worst that could be said was not too bad for the lascars. 'They rushed to the boats' but he went on, 'but luckily the sea was calm, and they did not capsize from that cause. When the lascars got into the boats they would not row, put up sail, or do anything. We often read about the wonderful discipline of the lascars, but they were nothing like that, as far as the lascars of the Mongolia were concerned. They threatened to be troublesome, and after getting into the boats their next objective was to rush the biscuits. Had the vessel struck the mine at night time not one third of the passengers would have been saved. The wireless apparatus was shattered through the explosion, and we were absolutely helpless. Although the lifeboats had everything aboard, biscuits and water that the Board of Trade demanded, if we had been unlucky enough to have been out for some days a tremendous number of persons would have died. There were 2 deaths in my party. Both were men, and one of the fatalities was caused through burns. There were about 40 in my boat, and altogether about 300 on the beach. These last boats should be equipped with a hospital chest and first aid outfit.

'I admit that there was everything that was demanded by the Board of Trade regulations but it does seem to me that there should be food other than biscuits and water, and that some provision should be made to treat the injuries caused by an explosion. Several men were severely scalded, while others suffered serious injury to their hands. It was at first impossible to do anything for these men, and the only way to secure bandages was by using ladies' underclothing. Of course everything was in order when we got to Dijhi, where the natives were very hospitable, and no one could have shown more kindness...'

The second article read:

FROM FRANCE. SYDNEY WOOLBUYER'S WAR EXPERIENCES

'After the trenches one enjoys life ... enjoys everything. I have gained a stone and a half since I left the front' said a well proved soldier of the French Army to a 'Herald' reporter yesterday.

Over two years on active service; at Hill 60 in Flanders, in the Champagne Offensive of 1915, through the crisis of Verdun, through battlefield experiences that a civilian in Australia can scarcely realise, with this experience M. Jacques Playoust, son of M. George Playoust, of Centennial Park, a well known wool buyer, returned to Sydney, fit and smiling. He had been in the wreck of the 'Mongolia' on his way out to Australia, but that was a detail compared to his experiences on the Western Front. Like the nigger boy in the story who kept on hammering his thumb because it 'felt so good when he stopped' M. Playoust is just now enjoying a well earned leave, and when that is over he will return to the task of hammering the Germans, with all the discomforts the process entails.

It is still better to hammer than to be hammered, and, as M. Playoust stated, it is the Allies now who are doing the hammering. There was a time when the enemy fired 10 shells to the Allies' one, but now the Allies have the superiority in munitions and guns, and whether in attack or defence the foe's losses are at least as heavy and often heavier than ours.

For all that no easy or early victory is expected, unless some sudden economic crisis in Germany helps the Allies. A military decision will not be achieved quickly. The troops on the Western Front have no delusions on that point, says M. Playoust. There is little of the element of surprise in modern warfare. The continued bombardment always heralds the attack, and the enemy masses his reserves and constructs his new positions accordingly.

M. Playoust left Australia soon after the outbreak of war and was in the Ypres sector in front of the famous Hill 60 in December, 1914. Then he went to the Argonne, and later an attack of typhoid fever put him out of action. He was back in the firing line in time to participate in the French Offensive in the Champagne on September 25, 1915 and was on that front until the end of the year. Then the Germans attacked at Verdun, and nearly got through. M. Playoust's regiment, one of the crack regiments belonging to the 42nd Division, which had been under General Foch on the Marne, was sent to the Verdun Front. 'Hold at all costs' was the order, and in a nightmare of shells and slaughter the gallant French troops held on till the fury of the German onslaught had spent itself and Verdun was safe. It was a terrible struggle. In 3 months one regiment of 8,000 men, reinforced again and again, numbered its losses at 10,000. In one case the battalion was reduced to 43 men at the end of a fight. 'It was a hellish time' said M. Playoust. 'Sometimes we were without water for 24 hours or more. There were times when any man would have given £100 for a wine glass full. Once the shell uncovered a spring, and the troops flocked there to quench their thirst. The Germans spotted us, and shelled the place. The dead lay thick round the spring, but the men went on risking death for a drink of water'.

After Verdun M. Playoust went to Lorraine, near Lunéville, and spent a comparatively quiet summer. Then he took part in the Somme offensive of last year. He was present at the taking of Combles and the Thiepval Plateau. Afterwards on the Aisne he did his bit in the French attack between Craonne and Berry-au-Bac on April 16 last. On that day his brother fell fighting with another regiment in the same sector. 'It was stiff fighting. We had a certain amount of success but it cost us a lot of men' said M. Playoust. It was after this that General Nivelle returned to his old command, and was succeeded by General Pétain'. M. Playoust described how the first position was taken early in this attack. Then they had to wait for the tanks to destroy the barbed wire before the second line. In the latter attacks there was one tank every 50 or 60 yards, but according to M. Playoust, few of them returned. The French tank is a later model than the first British tank, the 2 back wheels which are very vulnerable, being done away with. Still one direct hit will destroy a tank and they can only move slowly, and cannot zigzag in their course, a well directed battery can work havoc. It was the element of surprise that made the tanks such a success when first used by the British. The French tanks, M. Playoust states, are generally of a smaller type.

M. Playoust states that while there is not much optimism in France as to an early peace there is no doubt as the ultimate result. The Germans cannot win.

Furlough lasted about three months. There were family festivities, and a grand dinner was given in August at 'Paris House', Sydney's finest restaurant of the period, for Jacques and another *poilu*, Edgar Puech. He had sailed to France with Jacques in the first contingent on the *Malwa* in 1914, and had been the first of the Australian wool buyers to earn the

Croix de Guerre. He was cited for his bravery in rescuing a number of wounded soldiers from the battlefield.

As his furlough drew to an end, Jacques took a French ship back to France.

Messageries Maritimes
Paquebot 'Australien'
21 November (1917)

Dear Brothers & Sisters

The last part of my furlough has started. I am now quite installed in this old tub and after all it is not so uncomfortable as all that. The food is not what it used to be. I have found quite a lot of friends of the family. The purser dined with us at Strathfield. The maitre d'Hotel was our cabin stewart when last we travelled. I have a large cabin to myself. Fans have been installed in them and they are big.

There is a fair crowd of passengers including a big % of ladies. I have already got a little flirt. Nothing serious but it helps to pass away the evenings. Of course all this is very fine as long as we don't get submarined. If we do 'il y aura de la casse' [There will be considerable damage] for over and above the ladies & children we have more than 600 coolies on board. Fortunately we seem to have that problem well in hand. I have heard optimistic reports from people who ought to know. Anyhow there is one thing certain that there are not many leaft in the Mediterranean.

How are you all getting on? I hope the stay at the Riji [a boarding house in Leura] is enjoyable.

Souvenir affectueux to the Joseph Playoust & best love to you all.

Jacques

We arrive at Colombo this afternoon.

14th December (1917)

Dear Brothers & Sisters

The chances look now very much that we will get to Marseilles after tomorrow. We have negotiated 2/3 of the Mediterranean safely and have just leaft Bizerte accompanied by two torpedoe [destroyers?] and a sloop to pick us up in case of accident. A couple of Hydro-avions [sea-planes] went out to scour the seas for us. How much better organised everything seems now than in the month of May. Indeed our fleet had got so big when we leaft Malta that I got frightened & thought we might have secret orders to take Kiel Harbour. Just fancy 3 merchant ships, 6 torpedoe destroyers & a sloop.

The old Australien is vibrating hard and evidently smelling the stables. She has only been going so-so & even stopped twice in the middle of the trip. Fortunately their were no Boches about. Anyhow I shant travell on the Messageries again in a hurry. Everything is running short & when you grumble the eternal excuse is 'C'est la guerre' [Don't you know there's a war on] What laisser-aller [slackness] has had recourse to it.

The permission [leave] is now almost to an end. I suppose by the end of next week I shall have heard the cannon again. For I shall certainly have to go & get my orders from my regiment. I only hope I shall be able to see the old People on my way through Paris. I shall do my best.

Best love,
Jacques

Brothers and cousins had all returned to the Front. Jacques' cousin, Jean, was back in France after an adventurous furlough during which his ship was torpedoed, and was again with René in the same heavy cavalry regiment, the 12th Cuirassiers. Jean's younger brother, Fernand, only a schoolboy the previous year, was now in a French field artillery regiment. He wrote to his former teachers that he had met his cousin Maurice when he had visited his uncle Georges and aunt Marie-Thérèse in Paris. He also witnessed a 14th July parade of soldiers returning from the Front. Jean appears to have shared Jacques' difficulties with spelling when he wrote to his young brother:

14/12/17

My Dear Fernand

Thanks very much for your kind letter and the cigarettes they pleased me very much. There is some time since I have received letters from home. I wounder what has become to them.

The weather is not very cold now so it is not too hard here in the trenches.

How are you getting on now at the baracks you must be a good artillery man now.

Good-bye old man I close wishing you the best of luck.

Your loving brother

Jean

During the six months Jacques had spent away from France, trench warfare had pursued its savage course as Nivelle's Spring Offensive lapsed into another battle of attrition. The French now had a tenuous hold on the ridge of the Chemin des Dames, but could not advance further. Pétain was appointed to succeed a discredited Nivelle.

According to the French official history, there were 137 000 French casualties in this battle, possibly much more, and the Germans had 163 000.[1] The disappointing result of the offensive which was to have ended the war resulted in a lowering of morale in the French army, though strict measures were taken to keep this secret. In May there were a series of mutinies when several units went on strike and refused to fight, complaining of starvation diets and of too infrequent home leave. These rebellions were ruthlessly suppressed. A number of secret courts-martial took place and those found guilty of mutiny or desertion were shot at dawn by firing parties. These executions of their own men were, in turn, devastating for morale. Not a word of this appeared in *L'Illustration*.

The British Army was equally uncompromising with the problem of mutiny or desertion. One of a series of letters on 'Cowardice in the Trenches' in the London *Daily Telegraph*[2] refers to 307 British servicemen who were shot by their own side. There was also the harsh Field Punishment Number One whereby a soldier was strapped to the wheel of a field gun, arms and legs spreadeagled for hours at a time, day after day, a type of crucifixion without nails. According to this letter, there were 'repeated interventions by Australian troops who, moving up to the front line, would break ranks to cut the leather straps'.

The Australian authorities took a more lenient attitude. Diggers were not charged with desertion but with being 'absent without leave', resulting in a mere prison term.

The Italians had suffered a major defeat by the Austrians and Germans at Caporetto. In Flanders the British made a number of attacks, often led by Australian and New Zealand divisions, in what came to be called the Third Battle of Ypres, or Passchendaele. The objective of the attack was to clear the Germans from the Channel ports, which were known to be U-boat bases. Those who know the damp climate of the bleak Flanders plain can imagine the effect on this landscape of the destruction of drainage, deep tunnelling and heavy bombardment. These bloody battles in persistent freezing rain ended when the Canadians captured what was left of the village of Passchendaele, putting an end to warfare till the following Spring.

The blockade of English ports and the subsequent shortage of food was palliated by American naval help in escorting convoys of cargo ships which were threatened by U-boats. American soldiers had as yet a limited presence in France. On 9 December General Allenby captured Jerusalem from the Turks, a moral victory that foreshadowed the dissolution of the Ottoman Empire. In November the new Bolshevik government in Russia, under Lenin, sought an armistice, thus freeing German troops to fight on the Western Front.

14

1918: 'Other Bloody Fields'

With the New Year Jacques' military career took a new direction. Feeling that he was now entitled to a 'cushy job', he applied for a post as interpreter with the French military mission attached to the British Army. In fact his English was so good that a bemused examiner then tested his French. He was accepted and was appointed to the 13th Australian Field Artillery Brigade, 5th Australian Division on 21 January 1918. He remained with this field artillery brigade for the last year of the war, sharing in their early near-defeats, then in their last victorious thrust. His knowledge of French and German, as well as his experience in signals, was useful to the Australians with whom he had a great sense of belonging, and his viewpoint now became that of an artilleryman rather than the *piou-piou* (footslogger) which he had been for so long.

Artillery played a key role in the battles of the Western Front. Although the infantry led the advances, they were dependent on accurate artillery fire to prepare their way and protect their movements. Field artillery, as opposed to large-bore siege artillery, consisted of smaller mobile guns and howitzers, and were under the direct orders of the Corps Commander, General Birdwood, and later of Lt. General Monash. Large guns required tractors or were mounted on rails, whereas field guns were drawn by teams of horses, often across open country, so that in the brigade diaries the physical condition of the horses was given considerable attention.

Back in a familiar atmosphere, Jacques enjoyed his dealings with the Australians, whom he appreciated for their good sense of fun. In later years he loved to recount a story of his early days with them, when they tried to take a rise out of the new little Froggie interpreter, 'Turps', as they called him. On one occasion he was brought a huge thoroughbred to ride, and when he was mounted they gave it an almighty whack on the rump. Of course the horse bolted. Fortunately Jacques was an experienced horseman, and not only brought it under control but returned to hurl a string of good Aussie oaths at the startled soldiers.

The Fifth Division was at the time on winter defensive duty in the Messines sector in Belgian Flanders, but the 13th Field Artillery Brigade had been enjoying a rest period far from the Front near Etaples in the Pas de Calais. The strength of the brigade was 28 officers, 785 other ranks, 453 horses and 144 mules. According to the brigade diary it was a cheerful time with football matches and a grand concert given by the 5th Division Concert Party and attended by the Corps Commander, General Sir W. R. Birdwood together with the Divisional Commander, Sir J. T. Hobbs. 'It was a good show'.[1]

Several days later the brigade marched back to Belgium, moving into line to relieve the 1st Division artillery. This was the Messines-Warneton area south of Ypres, immediately north of the Belgian border with France, and only a short day's march from Tourcoing, Jacques' birthplace, which was still suffering the privations of the German occupation.

This boggy Flanders plain, its drainage shattered by the shelling of the previous year's battles, continued to seep mud into the trenches. In order to strengthen the defensive positions, the trench systems required arduous works of consolidation by wood and metal framework, lining the ground with duck-boards, setting up machine gun emplacements and wire entanglements. Jacques' new unit, the 13th Field Artillery brigade was occupied in constructing gas-proof doors to dug-outs. Their duty was to cover the 15th Australian Infantry Brigade. Orders had been given to prepare for the inevitable Spring attack but throughout February there were only small patrol raids and sporadic exchanges of artillery fire.

The following letter was written in pencil:

13th March 1918

Dear Brothers & Sisters,

This last mail brought letters Dec. 20th to the 6th January. Thank you very much. I also got a nice long letter from Ernie [Polin] which I shall answer as soon as I have courage [energy]. It's a funny thing, the least I have to do the less you do.

True I have been busy since last I wrote but have been home with the old Brigade for the last 3 days after a good fortnight's absence. I was attached temporally to an Aust. Infantary Bde, who was at rest so as to help settle up before they went in again & by jove they did make it a welter. All the nice boys tend to join the artillery in Australia & you can see it in their behaviour. Why they even broke into my room, picked one of the drawers, the sideboard & turned over my bed to see if I had leaft any money behind. But they got nothing but my British Warm. It's the end of winter so I won't have to buy any before some months.

What extraordinary weather we have had this year. A heavy snow in December & 1st January & after that no more winter. Why even now it's quite spring weather, & the trees are budding for all their worth. In spight of this the German offensive is not starting. I think it is bluff. It is quite different to the Russian front that they have to pierce on this side. Things look pretty gloomy just at present however. Japan coming in at once seems the only thing to even things up. The end looks still far off.

> Best love to all,
> Jacques

It was by no means 'bluff'. Barely a week later General Ludendorff launched his long-planned Spring Offensive, aimed at annihilating the Allies before a large-scale landing of men and material could be effected. Germany was now at peace in both Russia and Romania, which meant that trains carrying 44 newly freed divisions began rolling westwards, dangerously reducing the numerical advantage of the Allies.

The Ludendorff plan consisted of successive attacks on three sectors of the Western Front. The first, code-named 'Michael', was intended for the Somme, the second, code named 'St George' was designed to be launched further north in Flanders, and the third, code named 'Blücher', was to drive south in the Aisne area, thus menacing Paris.

The first offensive in the Somme had as its target the vulnerable junction of British and French forces. The important rail and road network of Amiens was to be taken, and the British were to be separated from the adjacent French and driven back to the Channel. Between St. Quentin and Cambrai 62 German divisions were to drive forward on a 75 kilometre front.

The Germans emerged from the safety of the Hindenburg Line at dawn on 21 March. The mist was thickened by smoke, the air poisoned by gas, so that for more than 12 hours the soldiers had to endure their suffocating masks. There was a creeping barrage of epic proportions that forced both British and French to cede ground, with a resulting breakdown in communications. Four days later the enemy had reached the old 1917 trenches; Peronne and Bapaume were re-taken, and Prince Rupprecht of Bavaria's columns were pushing along the Somme Valley towards Amiens.

Field artillery were covering the retreat of French and British forces, and particular effort was put into maintaining liaison between the two. Their movements were hampered by straggling refugees from the newly occupied villages and by the scattering of long-established regimental headquarters, all too accustomed to a fixed geographic position.

With Amiens in danger, and an urgent call for reinforcements was made. Among those who were sent was the Fifth Australian Division, including the 13th Field Artillery Brigade, who left their Flemish trenches and after a day's march and another day's tortuous train journey arrived at Amiens. According to the brigade diary there was considerable delay 'on account of the primitive methods of detraining horses, only 2 ramps being provided, each in 6 parts, requiring 4 men to lift each part. Ramps had to be moved to every horse truck'. The batteries marched through Amiens to Querrieu; they were shelled on the way and there were some casualties of men and horses. 'At 5 pm orders were received to move to Bonnay, and report to G.O.C. 15th Aust. Inf. Brigade. This march was carried out in the rain. Bonnay deserted. Arrived there about 9. 30 pm. All batteries billetted.'

Bonnay is by the Ancre River, which runs into the Somme on its northern side. By 5 April the whole 5th Division was in line, filling a gap north and south of the Somme between the British Fifth Army and the northern flank of the French sector, thus protecting the vital French liaison with the British.

Prince Rupprecht's troops were now facing them astride the Somme and were attempting a massive push towards Amiens, only about 10 kilometre away. The village of Hamel fell to them and remained in German hands till the Australians recaptured it in July, but overall the Allied line held, and the Germans now found themselves at some disadvantage in obtaining supplies in this deserted area. They did not win Amiens.

There was now a period of comparative quiet, and in the Australian sector there took place a certain fraternising between the Diggers and their French *poilu* neighbours. Digger humour favoured bilingual puns such as a trench named 'Roo de Kanga', just as in the battle for Pozières they had transformed the strategic position of 'Mouquet Farm' into 'Moo-cow Farm'. To Jacques' amusement, and of interest to a linguist in a contemporary edition of *Le Figaro*, a bizarre 'franglais' pidgin evolved to meet the men's immediate needs. Some such terms were:

'plonk' for *vin blanc* (white wine)
'no compree' for *pas compris* (I do not understand)
'tray beans' for *très bien* (very good)
'delloo' for *de l'eau* (water)
'finny' for *fini* (finished)
'mungy' for *manger* (a meal)
'alley man' for *allemand* (German)
'toot sweet' for *tout de suite* (straight away)

If the shopkeeper had no chocolate he may have said that there was none left, *Il n'y en a plus*, which was quickly corrupted to 'na poo'; the ruined Ypres was then 'na poo'.[2] Its meaning was extended to 'nothing doing' or any negative reply. This pidgin was also picked up by shopkeepers and farmers behind the lines, and *Le Figaro* related an incident where a farmer's wife, angered by artillery being hauled across her crop, shouted 'You no bonne, compree dat?', to which the gunner replied innocently 'No, me no compree' and, smilingly, 'Say la guerre' (that's war).

Australian soldiers helping evacuees return to Amiens. (Australian official war photograph)

At Bray-sur-Somme the Australian Prime Minister, Mr W.M.Hughes announced that the Gallipoli veterans were to be granted home leave.

'We belong to the 6e Colonial'. Marcel Playoust is seated second from right in 2nd row, hand in pocket. Marcel and almost all the men in his company were killed in an attack on German trenches during the first battle of the Somme.

Gun captured by the Australians, exhibited in Paris on the Champs de Mars. Copied from *L'Illustration*.

Wool buyers with their catalogues, 1930s. Jacques Playoust is on far left, Gervais Parmentier far right, Desiré Carney centre.

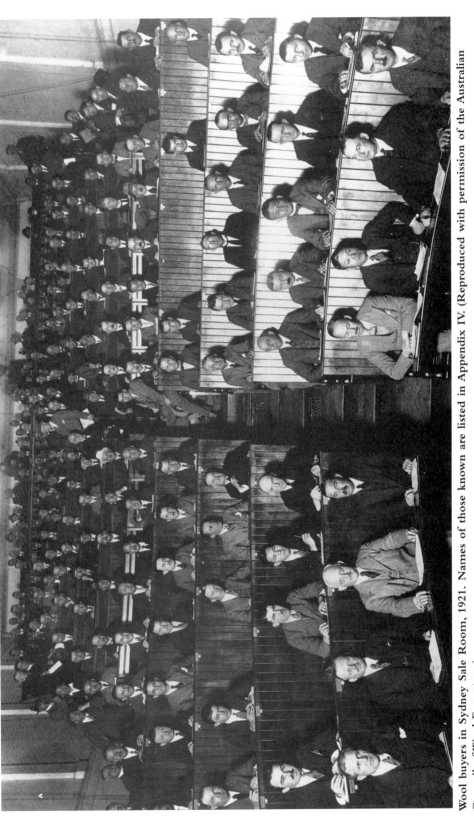

Wool buyers in Sydney Sale Room, 1921. Names of those known are listed in Appendix IV. (Reproduced with permission of the Australian Council of Wool Exporters.)

During this period the Headquarters of the Australian Corps, then under the command of the British General Birdwood, was established in the 17th century chateau of Bertangles, barely 10 kilometres north of Amiens. In this fine chateau the owners, the family of the Marquis de Clermont-Tonnerre, had collected precious furnishings and works of art, but before the fighting began these had been removed for storage in a safer place. Later Lt. General Monash planned his campaigns from this chateau.

This period of calm on the Somme was broken on 24 April by an intense bombardment followed by an infantry attack on the southern flank of the 5th Australian Division. The Division held firm, but Villers-Bretonneux was temporarily lost to the enemy in a cloud of gas, while the French further south lost Hangard. Jacques' 13th Field Artillery brigade diary records this tersely: 'Villers-Bretonneux on our left fell to the enemy but was recaptured shortly after'. Monash wrote more colourfully: 'When the sun rose on the third anniversary of Anzac Day it looked down on the Australians in full possession of the whole town, and standing on our original lines of 24 hours before with nearly 1000 German prisoners to their credit'. Hangard was recaptured and the line was re-established.

† † †

Possibly the best known Australian cemetery is that at Villers-Bretonneux, where every Anzac Day the Australian Ambassador lays a wreath in the presence of French Government officials and often a contingent of Australian soldiers as well. A bugler sounds the Last Post. This very moving ceremony is continued in the village square some small distance away, where a wreath is laid at the War Memorial, while the school children sing 'Waltzing Matilda'. Their school was, in fact, rebuilt after the war with money raised by schoolchildren in a collection throughout Victoria. Over an archway in the school there is an impressive scroll inscribed *N'oublions jamais l'Australie* (Let us never forget Australia).

The village itself was adopted by the City of Melbourne at a public meeting in 1920, with the pledge to restore the ruined buildings, in commemoration of which a street has been named the 'Rue Melbourne'. It is now *jumellé* (twinned) with Robinvale in Victoria.

† † †

Meanwhile the second part of the Ludendorff campaign, 'St. George', had been initiated in Flanders, a short distance west of the area recently vacated by the 5th Australian Division, where the 1st Australian Division had been retained to support the British. This attack was aimed at cutting off the Ypres salient, capturing the coal basin of Béthune and gaining the strategic observation point of Mount Kemmel in order to reach the channel ports. (In a subsequent letter Jacques confused the spelling of this with 'Kummel', one of his favourite liqueurs.) Nine German divisions advanced on French and British regiments, capturing Mount Kemmel in the presence of the Kaiser after bitter fighting, on the same day as the Germans lost Villers-Bretonneux in the Somme. Despite the fall of Mount Kemmel the results were indecisive, as the channel ports were not reached.

On 1 and 2 May the Inter-allied Council, including Lloyd George and Signor Orlando (the British and Italian Prime Ministers), General Foch, Field Marshal Haig and, most significantly, the American Military Commander, General Pershing held a meeting in the town of Abbeville to examine the military situation. In the previous month Foch had been appointed supreme commander of Allied forces in France, finally giving to the Allies the unified command they had lacked in previous years.

Later in May the British General Sir William Birdwood, who had been commanding the Australian forces since the Dardanelles campaign, was now appointed to command the new British Fifth Army. He had been well respected by the Australians, and when he was later raised to the peerage he took the title of Lord Birdwood of Anzac and Totnes. Lt. General John Monash was appointed to succeed him as the commander of the Australian Army Corps, which for the first time was now a separate entity and commanded by an Australian. A civil engineer by training, and well experienced in planning large projects, Monash had a clear, disciplined mind and was to weld his officers and men into a super-efficient fighting unit.

FIELD POST OFFICE 13th May 1918

Dear Brothers & Sisters

I have no more writing paper so you must excuse this short note. It is almost impossible to obtain any. I've written over to Paris for some. In spight of the month we are not having fine weather. It has some compensation. The Gothas don't come out. They are very troublesome at night & bomb us pretty regularly, so far, anyhow as far as we are concerned, without any success (touch wood). They were dropping their eggs uncomfortably close last night. I'm in doubt where Robert Dervaux [a cousin from Tourcoing] is. Mother says he is at the back of us in reserve. Father that he was [one] of those who defended themselves till the last man on Mt. Kummel.

love,
Jacques

For the third part of Ludendorff's plan of attack, code-named 'Blücher', he chose a broad front in the Aisne sector just north of Soissons and Rheims, the scene of General Nivelle's disastrous Spring Offensive in 1917 in which Jacques' brother Stéphane lost his life. Ludendorff was successful in surprising the Allies, but the area presented serious geographical difficulties, as his men needed firstly to cross the Ailette River, a small tributary of the Oise, then to climb the steep escarpment of the Chemin des Dames ridge where four French and three British divisions were deployed. Against them Ludendorff had massed 15 divisions, mostly rested and fresh, under the command of the Kronprinz.

The Blücher campaign on 27 May was preceded by several hours of intense bombardment and gassing. The Germans crossed the river and climbed the escarpment over piles of dead and wounded suffocating in their gas-masks. Once on the ridge the enemy advance was rapid, crossing the Aisne river then moving east and west, then south towards the Marne river which they reached in three days. Rheims was again threatened but not taken.

In the western section of this 'Blücher' attack the Germans quitted a base near the legendary feudal castle of Couçy, already destroyed by bombardment earlier in the war. About 5 kilometres south of the Ailette river, by a railway line, lay the small village of Epagny. It was in this vicinity that Jacques' tall cousin Jean, 'Little John', from Strathfield was stationed in a regiment of heavy cavalry. He met his death in a manner later described in the St Aloysius College magazine:

> Volunteers were asked for to form a patrol to find out the Germans' whereabouts. Jean offered his services, but soon after the patrol left the lines, it was partially surrounded. In attempting to obtain reinforcements, Jean was wounded in three places, nevertheless he managed to reach his destination and gasp out 'reinforcements' before finally succumbing to his injuries. R.I.P.

Jean was posthumously awarded the Croix de Guerre and the Médaille Militaire.

Jacques' younger brother, Maurice, wrote to his mother from another part of the front a few days later:

> Thank God that I am alive, for I have just had a very narrow escape from being either killed or made a prisoner. When in a tight corner an officer told me, 'Don't try to leave this place, for you are sure to be killed'. I thought how hard it would be for you to be without news from me for a considerable time if I allowed myself to be taken prisoner, and besides a French man prefers to die rather than to surrender. So with a prayer to our Lady on my lips I left under a heavy barrage fire. A little later I crossed a bridge with two machine guns firing at me from 20 yards away: and thanks to Heavenly intervention I came through without a scratch ...

His mother, Marie-Thérèse, was always available as a support for her sons and nephews at the Front, arranging a constant supply of gifts, and accommodation for those on leave. She was particularly protective of the youngest of her soldiers and replied quickly and appropriately with this letter, which is translated from the French:

10 June 1918

My dear little Maurice

When I think of the dangers you have been through, I still tremble, and with all my heart I thank the good God and the Virgin for having protected you and to have left us our beloved son.

Very quickly I am sending you a postal order for 20 francs which will allow you a few treats during the days you will spend behind the lines.

Fernand has just gone to the Front for a few days to lead replacement horses. Alas we are still without news of Jean! Would he have been taken prisoner? René left us on Wednesday 5th June, and through him we can hope to soon have news.

To come to Royat [a spa town] you must take the train at the station Paris Lyon Mediterranée to Clermont-Ferrand. Royat is a quarter of an hour away by tram.

I embrace you with all my heart. May God guard you.
Mother

René, Maurice's brother, was in the same heavy cavalry unit as his cousin Jean and can only have confirmed the bad news. If Maurice had spent his leave with his parents in the spa town of Royat in the Massif Central he would have learnt from them the grim news of Jean's demise, which was also communicated to Jacques in the Somme.

Jacques' unit had been recently called back into line from their rest area near Abbeville in order to join in the preparations for the coming battle to retake the Hamel salient. The following letter was written on a small piece of brown paper in pencil:

2nd July (1918)

Dear Brothers & Sisters

Excuse this brief note to answer your last mail. Nothing but bad news. Brave little John is no more. Emile is gone too. Who is going to be next. Mother tells me that René had come to his senses and will take the soft job he has a right to. Still there is always a risk, a stray shell, a bomb & even gas. We have just returned to the Front after a 2 day rest. We were to be out for a fortnight but we were wanted so came back. I do want one so badly & am getting very stale.

Love,
Jacques

Emile was Sous-lieutenant Emile Foüan, one of Jacques's Tourcoing cousins who, like Jean, was killed in the Aisne and awarded the Croix de Guerre and the Légion d'Honneur. As for René, he could already have been suffering from the diabetes that carried him away four years later. In 1916 he had fought in the Somme. It is not known whether he was still with Jean in this last battle, though they had been together for most of the war. Eighty years later their cousin Marie described René as good looking but shy and *sauvage* (unsociable), speaking very little. He wrote long letters to her in very small writing, but unfortunately none remain.

Remembering the first Battle of the Marne in 1914, some Parisian newspapers expressed anxiety for the safety of Paris, which for some months had been experiencing bombing from *Gothas* (German bombers) at night, and shelling from the 'Big Bertha' gun 120 kilometres away by day.

It came as no surprise when on 15 July Ludendorff attempted a further advance to the west and east and even crossed the Marne river, establishing a bridgehead in the heart of the Champagne winegrowing district by the village of Dormans. Thirteen French and four US divisions, led by tanks, retaliated three days later and the enemy was obliged to recoil to safer positions north of the Marne, continuing to fall back in succeeding weeks and finally abandoning Soissons. Allied morale was greatly encouraged by this counter-attack, the second Battle of the Marne, and particularly by the successful battle fought by newly arrived US Marines at Belleau Wood near Chateau-Thierry, only 96 kilometres from Paris. Foch stated to the Allied Generals that it was now time to pass to the offensive on all fronts.

Numerous convoys were by now disembarking American military personnel and equipment in massive numbers in Atlantic ports. Characteristically, the Americans were planning on a gigantic scale; one ship called the *Leviathan*, formerly the *Vaterland* of the Hamburg-Amerika Line, carried 12 000 soldiers at each crossing. They came with equipment and creature comforts that were to amaze their Allies. They built small towns for their military camps with streets, post offices, shops; they provided 3000 showers for 30 000 recruits, and their thousands of individual tents behind the battle lines were the joy of aerial photographers.

Ludendorff was now left with three bulges or pockets in the Front, in Flanders, the Somme and the Aisne; three considerable advances, but none of these quite deep enough to attain his main objectives. His near-success bore already the scent of eventual defeat.

15

1918: 'We Knew That You Would Fight'

At the time of Ludendorff's great push in the Aisne in late June and July, there was a corresponding lull in enemy activity in the Somme area. This respite gave the Allies the opportunity to reorganise themselves into their new positions and plan new strategies.

The Australian sector at its junction with the French sector south of the river Somme was still seen as vulnerable. Monash had only four divisions under his command, as the First Australian Division remained with the British in Flanders. The loss of Le Hamel and nearby Vaire Wood in April at the height of the Ludendorff advance had given the enemy a strategic advantage in observing Australian movements. Monash now proposed to his immediate superior General Rawlinson, the commander of the British Fourth Army, a comparatively small Australian operation around the newly fortified Hamel village. Although the American General Pershing had given specific orders that US troops were not to participate in anything more than a raid until they were fully trained, and then only under American leadership, it was hoped that some newly arrived Americans training with the Australians would be given their first battle experience at Hamel. The chosen date of 4 July was therefore not entirely fortuitous, as it was partly a tribute to the American national day.[1] In fact, only those Americans already at the Start Line and about to go into battle were permitted to stay, and the rest recalled.

By chance the Australian Prime Minister, Mr W. M. Hughes and the Minister for the Navy, Sir Joseph Cook, who were on their way to a meeting of the Inter-allied War Council in Versailles, paid a visit to the Australian troops. They were informed of the coming battle and were able to observe the men in full battle array.

Zero hour was 3.10 a.m. and the attack was to be secret and highly synchronised. General Monash's concept of a successful battle plan was to compare it to an orchestral score, every player coming in at the exact second at a signal given by the conductor. Brand new British-manned Mark 5 tanks were to be used to cut the barbed wire and accompany the advancing infantry. Aircraft would also be used to bomb enemy positions and drop ammunition by parachute. Recent reconnaissance and good large-scale maps were used to plan where the artillery and infantry Start Lines should be placed on the ground and thick white tapes to indicate them were accurately pegged out by the engineers without the enemy observing them. This enabled the artillery to bombard their targets precisely in front of the infantry, who lay on the ground while the barrage went on for an exact length of time. When the barrage advanced 100 yards, the infantry rushed forward 100 yards to catch up, and so on till the objective was reached. Secrecy and synchronisation are exemplified in the following extracts from the Report of Operations of the 13th Field Artillery Brigade which was covering the attacking battalions of the 11th Australian Infantry Brigade:

> ... Prior to the operation carried out on 4th July resulting in the capture of Hamel and high ground N.E. of Villers Bretonneux ... the 13th and 14th Brigades were recalled from rest near Abbeville, and came into action as part of the Centre group Artillery of the 4th Australian Division Front.
> ... In order to conceal the fact that additional troops had been brought into the area Wagon Lines were allotted along the banks of the River Somme, and all movement was restricted to hours of darkness.
> ... At Zero Hour minus 8 minutes a special program of harassing fire was carried out, finishing with all Howitzer batteries dropping down to their START LINE at Zero Hour. This was made to drown the noise made by our Tanks which were then moving forward ... At 8 minutes before Zero Hour 10% of smoke shells were fired to conceal movement ... 3.27 a.m. Brigade Liaison Officer reported that synchronization was good and that the barrage was well placed ... 3.44 a.m. Brigade Liaison Officer reported that the Infantry got a good 'jump-off' and all going well ... 4.20 a.m. More tanks visible and moving about freely ... 4.32 a.m. Brigade Liaison Officer report 43rd and 44th Battalions leap-frogging satisfactorily, casualties slight, more prisoners, others following, and that the tanks were busy and doing good work ... 4.45 a.m. Hamel captured, casualties slight ... 5 a.m. Battalion Liaison Officer reports all objectives gained.

It is interesting to note that, in this translated article, L'Ilustration was now perceiving les Australiens as a separate entity, and no longer described them as Britanniques:

> On July 3 south of the Somme, the Australians aided by a few elements of American Infantry and by tanks and aircraft, engaged in a useful action, and it was immediately crowned with success. They quickly seized the village of Hamel, the wood of the same name and that of Vaire, progressing at the same time to the east of Ville-sur-Ancre, capturing 1300 prisoners, a field cannon and about 100 machine guns. The positions of the plateau of Villers-Bretonneux were thus shoring up the northern flank of the plateau by several support points.

Although a small success in the wider strategy, Monash's masterly planning of the Hamel operation, using modern technology, was to serve as a model for future campaigns. The whole operation took only 93 minutes, with comparatively few Australian casualties.

† † †

Eighty years on, on 4 July 1998, a memorial park was inaugurated near the rebuilt village of Le Hamel on the site of the trenches captured by the Australians. A small group of veterans, some of them centenarians, flew from Australia to attend the commemoration ceremony. The Last Post was played, and the men were decorated with the Legion of Honour.

The trenches have been left exposd, and a walking trail has been designed, with 18 information panels describing the battle. The trail leads to a granite monument designed in Australia to honour the Australian Corps. Etched into the granite is a portrait of Monash and a picture of an officer adressing his troops before battle.

† † †

A new but unsuccessful German attack against the French sector south of the Somme marked their final attempt in this area. Similarly in the Aisne, the Allied victory in Chateau Thierry had spelt the end of the German push in that region.

The Australians were now immensely confident in their own abilities, even cocky, while the German soldiers, who lacked their adaptability, were further demoralised by a new Australian pattern of 'offensive patrolling' or 'peaceful penetration'. This was a method using small groups, sometimes even by daylight and without artillery protection, who crept stealthily into enemy trenches, casually gathering bewildered prisoners, weapons and booty in addition to useful information. This well suited the individualistic Diggers, who saw these patrols as a sporting event, but they astonished and intimidated their more docile German counterparts, who hastened to surrender. The campaign was especially productive as the enemy was thereby prevented from setting up new defences after the Hamel defeat. This meant that, without a battle, the Allied Front had crept forward several hundred metres.

In Amiens there was a sense of relief amongst the few inhabitants remaining in the city. Hundreds of people had been evacuated to escape the bombing by flights of *Gothas* and shelling from huge guns sited many kilometres away. The French national day on 14 July was celebrated in the semi-ruined town hall, and the Mayor invited representatives of the British armies to attend.

Four days later the French Prime Minister, Monsieur Clemenceau, visited the devastated city after the end of the Versailles conference, spontaneously extending his visit to speak to the Australian soldiers.

Speaking in English, he thanked them for their fine effort with these words: 'We knew that you would fight a real fight, but we did not know that from the very beginning you would astonish the whole continent with your valour' It would be wrong, however, to see this campaign from a purely Australian perspective, as the Canadians view the saving of Amiens as a Canadian feat of arms. Furthermore, the leadership was essentially still from the British.

Jacques was now granted leave in Paris, where he visited his family. His young cousin Marie had by now become a good friend, and delighted in sharing his visits to the theatre. Jacques returned to his Field Artillery Brigade in time to help in preparation for the next offensive, which was to commence 11 days later. On arrival he wrote to Marie (translation):

28 Juillet (July) 1918

Chère Marie

A note to tell you I have arrived safe and sound at my destination. The journey has been rather tiring. I spent the night on a bench at Corbeil and it was only at 7.43 that I found a train for the Front. I travelled all day but fortunately on arriving at the terminus I was able to find a good bed to rest in. It was the last time for how long? Yesterday I slept on the ground in a tent. The Boches came to announce it was night, and I was in a tight corner. Today I made myself a hole and I am now sheltered.

Love to your mother and yourself,
Jacques.

Don't forget you owe me a letter. Your address in the country please.

By 'Corbeil' Jacques probably meant Corbie, the railway junction east of Amiens, a town much frequented by Diggers on leave. It was just north of a swimming hole on the Somme river where the soldiers liked to swim in summer.

At the Allied General Headquarters the three chiefs, Pétain, Haig and the American General Pershing met to plan their future strategy and to decide when and from which point to launch a significant counter-offensive. As many of the German reserves had been transferred to the Aisne-Champagne area, the Generals chose to launch an immense Franco-British attack in the Somme with the aim of emptying the pocket remaining from Ludendorff's April advance.

It was to be planned with the utmost precision and secrecy, beginning at a point in front of the British Fourth Army which was situated astride the Somme under the command of General Rawlinson. The attack would be spearheaded by the five Australian divisions of the Australian Corps, together with the Canadian Corps of four divisions on their right, facing nine Divisions from Prussia, Bavaria and Wurtemburg. Further south the German 8th Army was deployed against the First French Army under General Eugène Debeney, which was to join in the attack. Further south again were the Second and Third French armies. In all, some 100 000 Allied soldiers were to participate, protected by 500 tanks and 800 aircraft. Today, Australians could visualise this number of men as comparable to a capacity crowd at the Melbourne Cricket Ground.

General Rawlinson convened a conference of his Corps Commanders on 21 July, and later fixed the date of 8 August for the action to begin. As this campaign was possibly the Australians' most significant advance in the whole war, it is interesting to identify the Australian part in this immense operation in detail.

Lt. General Monash was jubilant that finally the First Australian Division had been released from duty in Flanders to come under his command in the Somme, so that for the first time all five Australian Divisions were to fight together as the Australian Corps. Several conferences were convened at the chateau of Bertangles where, with masterly efficiency, Monash took many hours to organise his subordinates, basing his tactics on his previous Hamel success. Much emphasis was placed on secrecy and surprise so that, for example, tank and troop movements were to be made at night to avoid reconnaissance from the air, while using 'noise camouflage' to conceal the sound from enemy observation.

The tactic of 'leapfrogging' of divisions was to be employed, one fresh division overtaking the other at a given time to speed up the advance. This required meticulous preparation and coordination, and precise support from the mobile artillery. Each infantry brigade was protected by a brigade of field artillery steadily moving forward its horse-drawn guns and wagons in the 'creeping barrage' used so successfully at Hamel. In the days preceding the attack guns were accurately calibrated using a new technology to eliminate errors in range or line. Monash, the practical civil engineer, aimed to protect the infantry as far as possible by employing existing technical resources such as tanks, aircraft and artillery to prevent the carnage he had observed in earlier battles at Pozières, Bullecourt 'and other bloody fields'.[1]

Jacques' 13th Field Artillery Brigade was to cover the 8th Australian Infantry Brigade. The attack on 8 August achieved its purpose and the brigade diary sums up the day's actions thus:

> The operation was successful, casualties being very slight ... This was the first opportunity the Brigade has yet had of participating in actual mobile warfare, and considering the exceptionally small amount of training it has received, it can only be said it did remarkably well ...

The necessity of a motor cycle with side car, or some more rapid means of carrying out reconnaissance was most evident during the day. The advance of the infantry was very rapid, they arrived at their final objective before the time anticipated, and it was found that the batteries' advance and coming into action could not maintain their rate of advance.

It was a most interesting day, large numbers of prisoners were captured.

On that day the Australians and Canadians in the centre of the attack had moved forward some 12 kilometres, capturing thousands of prisoners, many large and small guns, useful stores, horses and ammunition. On each side the French and British also advanced, though not quite so rapidly. At last the Allies could begin to scent victory. General Ludendorff was later to write 'August 8th was the black day for the German army in the history of the war ... The war must be ended.'

A gentle viewpoint was taken by the painter Arthur Streeton, now an official War Artist. In his painting *The Somme near Corbie August 8th 1918*, the peaceful river undulates across the canvas, its poplar-lined banks not unlike his Yarra, but without the eucalypts. Yet the puffs of smoke in the hills are not bushfires in the Dandenongs. Over the slopes to the south 'The Front' is moving, and the smoke is from cannon fire. This delicate summer landscape is a more forceful condemnation of war than many a spoken word.

The Allied advance continued in the next few days, but against stiffening German resistance. As for the 13th Field Artillery Brigade and Jacques, the operation had begun on 8 August with infantry fighting their way east, supported by a creeping barrage. It then continued for five more weary days, with casualties for both men and horses before they were given any relief. Orders were issued for a two-day spell. The brigade diary then relates:

Fine warm day, country very dry and dusty. Day spent in overhauling equipment and preparing indents for stores lost and destroyed etc. and as far as possible, resting. As many men as possible sent to River for bathing, which was generally appreciated. H.M. The King passed through this area today.

Now came the accolades. That day, at the Chateau of Bertangles, King George V knighted Sir John Monash. Several days later on 15 August, the feast of the Assumption of the Virgin, a Mass was celebrated in the soaring gothic cathedral of Amiens, the interior piled high with sandbags and the stained glass windows removed for safe-keeping, so that white doves flew in unimpeded during the ceremony.

The city of Amiens had every reason for offering thanksgiving. Not only had the Allied armies saved the city from Ludendorff's troops, but in their rapid advance the Australians had captured a huge 280 mm calibre railway gun, together with its locomotive and trucks of ammunition. One of the Krupp factory's biggest, it had been wheeled out on its rails each day to bombard the city. This great trophy was examined on 18 August by M. Clemenceau in the company of Lord Derby the British Ambassador, Maréchal Foch and Field Marshal Haig. The visit followed a ceremony in which M. Clemenceau conferred on Field Marshal Haig the Médaille Militaire, the highest distinction available to a foreign officer. The gigantic gun, mounted on its two bogie carriages and its camouflaged railway truck, was later exhibited to crowds in Paris on the Champ de Mars. The camouflaged barrel is now displayed outside the main entrance of the Australian War Museum in Canberra.

† † †

In Amiens Cathedral a white marble plaque on a cluster of columns to the right of the altar bears an inscription 'To the glory of God and to the memory of the soldiers of the Australian Imperial Force who valiantly participated in the defence of Amiens March–August 1918 and gave their lives for the cause of Justice, Liberty and Humanity'. Similar plaques recognise the contribution of the Canadians and New Zealanders. In the ambulatory from the walls of a side chapel dedicated to St. James hang the Australian, American, Newfoundland and New Zealand Flags. Most significant is the inscription on a plaque: 'In Sacred Memory of the 600,000 men of the armies of Great Britain and Ireland who fell in France and Belgium during the Great War 1914-1918'.

16

1918: 'The Kaiser Must Be Starting To Scratch His Head'

In August the Allies were steadily advancing all along the Front. To the north, in Belgian Flanders, there were successful British operations; in the Aisne, French troops under Général Mangin advanced with the help of several Scottish regiments, thus emptying the pocket resulting from the Ludendorff operation in May. As for the Australians, good progress towards the east was still being made despite rearguard action by the withdrawing enemy. Jacques was able to depict this exhilarating experience to Marie in his next letter, which is translated from the French:

22 Août (August) 1918

Chère Marie

Only today did your letter of the 12th reach me. I am happy to hear that you are making the best of a well earned rest. As far as I can judge, there seem to be plenty of people over there, and the company of American doctors must be all the more appreciated as young men are rare now. And your improvement in tennis? I won't dare play with you soon.

You ask me what I have been doing these last weeks. I've led a rather hard life, but good and exciting. Sleeping rarely more than 2 nights in the same hole, not finding anything to ameliorate my ordinary life. I've eaten 'singe' ['monkey', a type of tinned meat] like a brave poilu.

Only pestered by the bombardment by planes and cannons, I followed our batteries 4 to 5 kilometres to the rear with the baggage. The first day it was through territory conquered only a few hours earlier that we progressed. The dead still where they had fallen, stretcher-bearers still at work, with many prisoners giving them a hand. Damaged English tanks, abandoned Boche artillery, often dragged by several horses trying to bring them back to the rear, dozens of plane combats. The Boches were defending themselves well and sprayed the highway with bombs even in full daylight.

Sometimes from certain vantage points I could follow the combat with the naked eye, the Infantry accompanied by Tanks, then when they had advanced a little, the artillery arrived at full gallop to get into action in the field. The Boches, completely taken by surprise, only began to collect themselves on the second day. The sector did not quieten again, and we are continuing to wrest pieces of territory from them, and to take prisoners. Today the cannon has been roaring since the early hours, and I have seen hundreds and hundreds of prisoners passing by.

The whole of yesterday afternoon they were bombarding us here in the waggon lines, but today nothing more. Probably they have been forced to withdraw their guns again. My official role until now has been only to send to the mission an account of the state of the villages which have been reconquered. It was very simple. The Boches had already long since evacuated towards the rear anything of value, and the artillery completed their handiwork.

Indeed the communiqués are marvellous. The Kaiser must be starting to scratch his head. But it is perhaps too much to expect the liberation of the north this year.

Love to yourself and your mother from cousin

Jacques

By 'the north' Jacques was referring to his and Marie's fathers' birthplace in Tourcoing, which had now been under German occupation for nearly four years. Despite Jacques' prediction, it was to be liberated in less than three months, for the enemy was now retreating to safer positions in the old Hindenburg Line, though German artillery and machine guns were still firing relentlessly. Consecutive Allied attacks were being made all along the Front, in Flanders, the Aisne and the Argonne.

From the inception of the great attack of 8 August, Monash's Australians, together with British, French Canadians and New Zealand units, were in pursuit of the enemy north and south of the Somme, capturing prisoners and enthusiastically gathering material abandoned in the rout. Later in the month, however, resistance stiffened. The day after Jacques' last letter, the 13th Field Artillery brigade was involved in a significant operation resulting in the capture of the villages of Chuignolles and Chuignes, close to each other on low hills south of the river. This Artillery Brigade was to cover the 1st Australian Infantry Brigade, and the official report of this engagement provides an impressive example of the protection given to the infantry by the artillery:

Zero hour was fixed at 4.45 a.m. when the barrage opened, and after remaining on the artillery START LINE for 3 minutes it moved forward by lifts of 100 yards each 3 minutes until the artillery HALT LINE was reached, where it remained for 15 minutes.

It then moved forward at the same rate until the Protective Barrage line was reached where it remained for 10 minutes before ceasing, each Battery ceasing fire alternately as it reached this line. Thus the Batteries firing on the Left [North] end of the objective, stopped firing before the advance of our Infantry in the centre was completed. This appears to have allowed the enemy who were strongly posted on the high ground ... to directly enfilade Machine Gun fire into the valley.

This trouble was observed by Lieut. W. F. Osmond, M.C. 49th Battery who occupied an O.P. ... and he succeeded in bringing fire from the 113th How. Battery and this with shrapnel from the 49th and 50th Batteries succeeded in driving most of the Machine Gun nests, and the hostile infantry away over the crest to the North. He then followed them with one 18 pdr Battery and inflicted serious casualties'

As the battle continued, the artillery brigade went on to support the advance of the 3rd Infantry Brigade with a creeping barrage well into the afternoon. 'This advance was successful and all objectives were captured including the town of Chuignes' was reported in the brigade diary.

As well as the strategic gain to the Australians in their advance east along the Somme Valley, this battle furnished them with abundant booty, dumps of engineering material, two complete trains and, best of all, the largest gun yet captured from the enemy in the whole war. It was a masterpiece from Krupp, a 380 mm calibre naval gun, even larger than the railway gun they had seized on 8 August. From its shelter in Arcy Wood near Chuignes it had been systematically bombarding Amiens some 30 kilometres away. It had been conveyed there by a specially built railway line and mounted on a platform over concrete foundations. As the enemy troops retreated they exploded its breech to render it useless to the Allies.

A pleasant interlude is described in the brigade diaries of 24 August, which Jacques would have found refreshing:

Arrangements were made for bathing and disinfecting clothing of personnel of Brigade. This has become very necessary owing to the length of time Brigade has been continuously in line and the few opportunities recently obtained for bathing ... Clean underclothing provided for the Brigade, and Foden Disinfector placed on bank of river for disinfecting blankets, clothing etc.

A couple of days later the Brigade marched through Fay and Asservillers past old, disused trenches to take up positions in an area near Barleux, where Marcel Playoust had lost his life in 1916, just south of the almost right-angled bend in the Somme near Peronne. Here the Somme, at some distance from the sea, was a series of ponds and marshes which acted as a natural north-south barrier to the Australian Corps' advance east, particularly as the enemy had destroyed the bridges.

Monash conceived the daring idea to bypass this difficult crossing by transferring most of his forces over improvised bridges across a narrower part of the river to the northern bank and attacking from an unexpected direction. In a surprise move he would rapidly seize the strategic hill of

Mont St. Quentin, though it had been heavily fortified by the Germans and was thought to be impregnable. This rise was not high, but the enemy had good visibility of advancing Allied forces and its artillery defended Peronne just nearby on the watery Somme bend. Peronne itself could then be taken more easily from the north. General Rawlinson was astonished by the audacity of the plan, but commented 'I don't think I ought to stop you. Go ahead and try — I wish you luck!'

Peronne is a small but ancient ramparted city which had already been occupied by the Germans in 1870, and then again in 1914. It stands near the confluence of the Somme with its tributary the Cologne river, and a canal. There are a number of ponds within the city itself, some of which had served in earlier centuries as moats to the castle. The surroundings were marshy and access to Peronne was made even more difficult by tangles of barbed wire remaining from previous defences. It could not be a set-piece battle this time, as speed was essential to prevent the enemy from preparing new defences. This was to be an entirely Australian operation using three Divisions, the 2nd, 3rd and 5th.

The surprise attack on Mont St. Quentin opened at 5 a.m. on 1 September, with some 70 officers and 1250 other ranks 'yelling like bushrangers'[1] and protected by artillery fire. It was a bloody uphill assault with bayonet charges and much hand-to-hand fighting. By evening they had established a foothold on the mount, and this in turn was of assistance to the 14th Infantry Brigade which was attacking Peronne. The protection of this Infantry Brigade was to be the responsibility of the 13th Field Artillery Brigade, who carried out their portion of this operation successfully, although the enemy's heavily entrenched position made infantry advance very difficult.

By 2 September Peronne was 'mopped up' and Mont St. Quentin secured, in effect opening the gate for the British 3rd and 4th armies to pass, for the enemy's defences on the Somme were now useless. *L'Illustration* sums up the battle in this way:

> The hill and village of Mont St. Quentin were taken by the
> Australians in the course of an audacious operation executed with
> magnificent dash.

† † †

The gentle hill named Mont St. Quentin at the edge of Peronne now overlooks farming land stretching towards Amiens, only 51 kilometres away. The road skirting the hill is named 'L'avenue des Australiens', and is crowned by a tall bronze statue of an Australian soldier in full battle-dress.

† † †

Not only the Australians were moving ahead, for all along the Front the Germans were being driven back by the Allies striking successive blows in a coordinated manoeuvre. In Belgian Flanders to the north, British forces under General Plumer advanced beyond Mount Kemmel, while further south of them near Arras Canadians and British had breached some outer defences of the Hindenburg Line by 2 September, reaching the Canal du Nord two days later. The New Zealanders had captured Bapaume on 28 August. South of Peronne, in strategic liaison with the British, the First French army under Général Debeney was advancing near Noyon and approaching Général Mangin's armies in the Aisne. To the east on 12 September, American troops under General Pershing erased the German salient at St. Mihiel in Lorraine. Systematically the Germans were retreating to their sturdy field fortifications in the Hindenburg Line, which Field Marshal Haig was confident he could pierce, while Foch believed that he could pursue his campaign to victory by autumn.

In the first weeks of September Monash, after reluctantly leaving his fine chateau at Bertangles for makeshift headquarters, moved his divisions forward in pursuit of the enemy. The Germans, though fighting to protect their rearguard, were leaving behind prisoners, ammunition and stores.

Mr Hughes had been visiting the troops for some days. He saw the site of the battlefield at Mont St. Quentin on 14 September, and the giant Krupp gun captured at Chuignolles by the 3rd Australian Battalion. According to *L'Illustration*, at Bray sur Somme Mr Hughes assembled those soldiers who had the privilege of wearing a brass 'A' on their arm, indicating the 1st Gallipoli contingent. He announced that they were to be granted home leave, the first in four years. To the wonderment of the French journalist, the boisterous Australians threw their hats in the air, cheering and calling their Prime Minister 'Billy'.

The hitherto impregnable Hindenburg Line, on which the Germans had now been working for several years, was no single string of forts but a complex network combining fortresses with natural barriers, which when seen from the air had the appearance of a broad band of tight wire lacework.

In the case of the area facing the Australia Corps and the British 4th Army the natural barrier was the 7 kilometre long St. Quentin Canal, connecting the Somme river with the Scheldt river further north. Built in the early 19th century with Napoleonic efficiency, the canal had required deep cuttings through hills and a number of tunnels averaging 16 metres below the surface. (The war artist, Arthur Streeton, painted a peaceful looking landscape now in the War Museum in Canberra, showing the entrance to the tunnel, with a barge floating in the canal). Now protected by thick wire entanglements and strategically slanted gun emplacements guarding the labyrinths of deep tunnels and interlocking trench lines, command and observation posts, this area provided a formidable obstacle. Trains brought in men and materials, and barges in the tunnels acted as electrically lit accommodation, storage space, even a well-equipped hospital. Army Intelligence had fortunately provided the Allied generals with an old plan of the original Hindenburg defences which had been found on a captured German prisoner in the previous year and on another front.

General Rawlinson called a conference of the three Corps Commanders of his Fourth Army, Butler, Braithwaite and Monash on 10 September to plan the next vital operations, the capture of the Hindenburg outpost lines, to be carried out in concert with the Third British Army and a French force. Monash was to use the First and Fourth Divisions, both of them Gallipoli veterans, together with machine gunners from other divisions and extra artillery, which included Jacques' 13th Field Artillery Brigade.

Monash, his commanders and men were now a clever, experienced team, understanding what was virtually the familiar choreography of a set-piece battle, knowing well that the precise synchronisation of artillery and infantry movements meant greatly reduced casualties. Monash doubled the number of machine gunners. There were few tanks available, so a scheme was devised to fabricate dummy tanks which would be left in view of the enemy. Artillery and infantry movements were coordinated in the well-rehearsed method used since the battle of Hamel. To quote from the 13th Field Artillery Brigade Report:

> Zero Hour was fixed for 5.20 a.m. at which time a creeping barrage was fired which moved Eastwards in lifts of 100 yards, the first being made after 3 minutes, the second after two minutes more, the 3rd to 11th inclusive at 3 minutes interval.

The attack continued all day and into the night. It was successful, with thousands of prisoners taken, but at the cost of 1260 Australian casualties. The main Hindenburg Line defences of the St Quentin Canal were now visible and within the reach of artillery fire. The First and Fourth Artillery Divisions, veterans of Gallipoli and Egypt, had fought their last battle on the Western Front, and were now sent by train and bus to rest areas near the coast to await shipping arrangements for the home leave promised earlier by 'Billy' Hughes.

17

1918: 'Hostilities Will Cease ... '

Parallel movements had been taking place all along the Front, gnawing away at the defences of the Hindenburg Line, which had first been breached by Canadians and British near Arras some weeks earlier. A concerted effort to push through the main defences was planned for 26 September.

In the Argonne the French Fourth Army and the US First Army attacked in wooded terrain which was so difficult and well defended that the advance came to a stop after about 15 kilometres. In Picardy the British 1st and 3rd armies reached Cambrai, and in Flanders, Belgian, British and French armies took the whole of the sinister Passchendaele Ridge, thus opening the way to the Flanders plain and its populous industrial agglomerations.

The attack envisaged by Monash for his own sector was not on the St. Quentin Canal tunnel itself, but above it, over the top of the hill between Bellicourt and le Catelet, in order to envelop the tunnel entrances. Bereft of his First and Fourth Divisions, Monash discussed his need of reinforcements with General Rawlinson, who proposed a joint attack strengthened by the addition of two American divisions. Monash welcomed the idea, for although the Americans were inexperienced they were fresh, enthusiastic, and had shown much affinity with the Australians in the battle of Hamel.

Monash was to find the planning for this battle more arduous and difficult than any in his whole war experience. Given command of the whole operation, he received friendly cooperation from the US General G. W. Read. At this stage the Australian Corps was a lean, highly efficient and well rehearsed team, so a mutual need to work and think together was recognised by both Australians and Americans. The latter were valiant but raw fighters who still had much to learn about organising supply systems, anticipating enemy actions and reducing infantry losses by strict synchronisation of movement. To iron out differences in technical language and customs Monash appointed an Australian Mission to enable his staff to relate with the Americans at all levels, as well as to educate and advise.

Monash's meticulous and orderly battle plans had to be explained in minute detail to the Americans, in particular the requirements for 'mopping up', which meant extracting enemy soldiers from their hiding places in dug-outs and underground passages and blocking the tunnel exits before allowing the infantry to advance further. This was to prevent a surprise attack from enemy soldiers hidden in their rear.

While Monash's final conference with his Australian and American commanders was under way Field Marshal Sir Douglas Haig called in unexpectedly to give them a few words of encouragement. Foch was launching a simultaneous attack on all fronts from Belgium to the Vosges, with Belgian, French, British, Canadian and American troops thrusting forwards.

This time there could be no element of surprise for the enemy when Monash launched his attack on 29 September. A massive artillery barrage was commenced. Batteries alternated with each other for a period of 60 hours, beginning with 12 hours of mustard gas shells. This was followed by 48 hours of high-explosive shells to destroy the artillery, coupled with sensitive '106 fuses' which exploded on meeting an obstacle above the ground, thus destroying wire entanglements.

Two American divisions were to lead the attack, followed by the 2nd, 3rd and 5th Australian divisions and a large number of tanks. The 13th Field Artillery Brigade was to support the 15th Australian Infantry Brigade following the two American Divisions. In their enthusiasm the inexperienced Americans drove ahead without taking the time to 'mop up' before continuing their advance. Germans then appeared out of tunnels and hidden trenches so that the Americans found themselves surrounded. Monash's careful set-piece battle plan fell into disarray, his inability to use his coordinated artillery movements resulting in costly hand-to-hand fighting.

A tight-lipped report of the 13th Field Artillery Brigade describes their inability to use the 'creeping barrage', of objectives not met, of mists clearing and finding no infantry in front. However, during the night of 30 September they received:

> instructions by telephone at 3 a.m. Through Brigade Liaison Officer [Captain H. K. Prior who was with the 8th Inf. Brigade H.Qrs.] from 5th D.A.H.Q. That a creeping barrage was to be fired at 6 a.m. in support of an attempt by the 14th Australian Infantry Brigade to capture the Le Catelet Mauroy Line N.E. of Bellicourt ... This attack was partly successful but much opposition was met with.

The liaison officer in question, Captain (later Major) H. K. Prior, who was with the 8th Inf. Brigade H.Q. was in later years to become, quite by chance, Jacques' immediate neighbour when Jacques returned to live in Sydney. Their families were to become close friends.

Welcome assistance came to the right of the Australians from the British 9th Corps, who crossed the St. Quentin Canal in a smoky mist by an imaginative assortment of portable bridges, lifebelts from channel steamers and rafts, then advancing several kilometres. The Australian Corps had reached most of its objectives on 1 October, rescuing several parties of trapped Americans on the way, entering le Catelet but not yet reaching the defences of Beaurevoir Hill. In these three days of action the 5th Australian Division had lost 73 officers and 1431 other ranks, but the 13th Field Artillery Brigade was more fortunate, with only seven other ranks wounded, although the loss of 43 horses was reported.

The Third and Fifth Divisions were now relieved, after being in almost continuous action since the battle of Le Hamel on 4 July.

Monash's last command in the war was the taking of Beaurevoir Hill and the village of Montbrehain, despite still unrelenting German rearguard action. Here for the first time Australians encountered French civilians hiding in the cellars; they had suffered under German occupation for four years and now joyously received their deliverers. Monash and the 2nd Australian Division were relieved by General Read and his 30th American Division. Although they did not know it, this battle was the last to be fought by Australians in World War I.

The dislocation of the German Front caused by this definitive piercing of the Hindenburg Line, coupled with the defeat of Bulgaria in the east and the successful Allenby offensive against Turkey, brought an admission of defeat by the German High Command and firmer action in Germany by those who sought peace. The virtual military dictatorship of Hindenburg and Ludendorff became less and less acceptable to public opinion, particularly in view of the possibility of Germany itself being invaded. The liberal Prince Max of Baden was appointed Chancellor to negotiate a peace proposal, and on 4 October he wrote to President Wilson asking the President for his support.

Negotiations were unfortunately protracted, and the exhausted Allies, lacking supplies and transport, were slow to cross the devastated territories to free the cobblestoned villages and industrial cities of Flanders and eastern Belgium. The enemy was still fighting a determined rearguard action while keeping the common soldiers in ignorance of the hopelessness of their overall situation. The Germans methodically destroyed as they retreated, flooding rivers, digging up railway lines, wrecking industrial machinery, collecting booty, and exploding buildings and bridges.

Although there were no more large scale battles, the killing went on all through October and into November as the Allies fought their way forward. King Albert of the Belgians, whose troops had been holding a tiny remnant of swampy Belgian territory throughout the war, was now able to advance, repairing roads across plains flooded by the enemy. Four British armies continued the pursuit in Flanders and entered Mons, their first battlefield in 1914, a few hours before hostilities ended.

An irony of the time was the death in action of Wilfred Owen, one of the greatest British pacifist poets, barely a week before the signing of the armistice, and a month after being awarded the Military Cross.

One city after another was being delivered from the occupiers, and official visitors and journalists from Paris were shocked by the scenes of devastation. Fortunately for the industrial agglomeration of Lille, Roubaix and Tourcoing, advances by Belgian and British armies had left German positions uncovered so that they were obliged to hasten their retreat. On 16 October an order was issued from the German Kommandatur for all the inhabitants of Lille to assemble in the Grande Place to meet the incoming British troops, thus protecting their own precipitate departure. British Tommies of General Birdwood's 5th Army marched in acknowledging the cheers, accepting bunches of flowers with wide grins on their pink faces. The Germans retreated also from Roubaix and Tourcoing, leaving their industries ruined but most buildings still standing.

Nearby the carillons of the ancient city of Bruges were ringing from its tall gothic belfries as the Belgians welcomed back their King, wearing his military uniform and tin helmet, and accompanied by his Queen. In Ypres, the sumptuous gothic Cloth Hall, one of the most architecturally significant buildings of its kind, was to lie in ruins for many more years.

Newspapers were now giving prominence to *la grippe*, the 'Spanish Flu', a virulent strain of influenza which was ravaging both soldiers and civilians on both sides. It caused respiratory failure, and was sometimes called 'Heliotrope Pneumonia' as patients' faces took on this colour through lack of oxygen. It had a short incubation period and was highly contagious, and later was to become pandemic, one of the worst of its kind in history, ravaging countries as far away as India and Australia.

For the Playoust family life had taken a sudden change. Just as the storming of the Hindenburg line was developing, the youngest son Roger, now of military age, sailed from Australia to report for duty. His sister Eugénie ('Ninie'), who wished to join her parents in Paris, sailed with him. Events overtook them both — the war ended before their ship arrived, and their father Georges, who had looked so saddened and ailing in his last photographs and much older than his 63 years, had died, possibly from this flu, just 11 days before the armistice.

This event was widely reported in obituaries in Sydney newspapers. They all stressed his patriotism and generosity, as well as his activities in cementing goodwill between the French and Australian communities, but went further in showing a personal affection seldom seen in formal eulogies. Letters of condolence were received from the Premier, from friends in pastoral families and the wool trade, as Georges had been a popular and influential figure in the state. Mr W. A. Holman, the Premier, wrote to Joseph Playoust 'he has lived a life of very great usefulness to his country, has been of inestimable service to the Wool trade of this state, and has closed a life of beneficent activity with signal service in the interests of his suffering countrymen'.

The German military situation had become desperate. At home anarchy threatened; the Kaiser had accepted Ludendorff's resignation and sailors of the German Navy had mutinied at Kiel. A conference of the Allied powers was held at Versailles to decide on the terms of capitulation and on 6 November a delegation of German parliamentarians left Berlin for the Front. The next evening the cortege of large open Mercedes–Benz convertibles proceeded along pock-marked roads through the battle lines, headlights illuminating their way through the fog, large white flags on a pole declaring their surrender. A bugler on the running board heralded their safe passage through groups of silent, muddy soldiers leaning on their guns.

The five plenipotentiaries were met by the commanding officer with chilly courtesy, given a frugal meal and taken to the train which was to serve as their home and office for the next three days. Highly charged with symbolism, one of the carriages was a splendidly decorated drawing room, upholstered in Empire green satin and trimmed with red, a relic of the Emperor Napoleon III who had been beaten so decisively by the Prussians in 1870. The train bore them to a clearing in the almost leafless forest of Compiègne, where they were informed of Foch's conditions for the preliminaries for peace. The delegates sought a cessation of hostilities during the discussion, but Foch refused as he wished to hasten the end. A courier was sent by aeroplane to German General Headquarters in Spa, and all conditions were accepted. Kaiser Wilhelm II abdicated, and General Ludendorff fled to Sweden.

In the small hours of the morning the plenipotentiaries were transferred to another train, traversing the sodden soil over duckboards before entering a railway carriage which had been Field-Marshal Foch's office during the campaign, and here they signed the documents in the presence of Foch and the British Admiral Wemyss. An announcement was signalled to all Allied armies that 'Hostilities will cease at 11 hours today, November 11th'.

The 13th Field Artillery Brigade diaries noted the news they had been waiting for:

11th November ... While on the road unofficial intimation was received to the effect that an armistice with GERMANY has been

concluded. Whistles and bells were heard in the distance, and
cheering passed down the column. The weather was fine and warm.

Jacques had been given compassionate leave, which allowed him to spend
time with his bereaved mother and family in Paris. Father, who had left
home and work to be in closer touch with his fighting sons, was dead.
For Jacques the war was over, but at the cost of two brothers, one brother-
in-law, and a cherished cousin, as well as numerous friends and relatives.
His early idealism had given way to a matter-of-fact pragmatism, but he
had the advantage of a resilient, extroverted personality to help him
overcome the horrors of the last four years.

He now wrote to his young cousin Marie (translation).

16th November 1918

Dear Marie

Firstly allow me to thank you and your mother for the affection you
showed me during my last visit to Paris. In terrible moments such as those
I have passed, the affection of those one loves is the only consolation
remaining.

I didn't find my unit on my return. It was on the move again, but finally
I caught up with it. We are stopping to permit the Boches to meet the
conditions of the Armistice before following them.

We spend our time flying. I went up in a Handley Page, the large English
bomber. You'll be able to imagine its size when I tell you it is able to carry
22 passengers. It was terrific. I then wished to try the fighter plane, but I
soon repented. The pilot made me do spirals, dives, gliding on the wing
etc. I assure you I will not be repeating the experience in a hurry.

Now, a little favour. I will spend all my next leave in Paris. For this I
will need a certificate of lodging. Ask your mother to have one made for
me.

I'm sorry I did not reimburse you for the batteries which you sent me.
Don't forget to claim for them next time.

I do thank you for your long letter. I will write to you at greater length
next time. I still haven't the spirit to write any more now.

your devoted cousin,

Jacques

No hurry for the certificate of lodging. I do not expect to arrive before
January.

The brigade, still south of Peronne at Athies, was in a state of limbo for
several more months, as the men could not be discharged until shipping
could be arranged back to Australia, and the detailed care of both men

and horses attended to. Jacques remained several more months with them, and his interpreting skills would have been useful in communicating with the newly liberated civilians. The Brigade diaries at this stage were taking on the tone of a boy's boarding school, reporting football matches, a few cases of influenza, sporting results and educational courses, including classes in French and German conducted by Interpreter Playoust. These classes would have suited Jacques admirably, as he always showed a real interest in teaching.

According to the War Office List of 1 December of British Decorations awarded to Allied Foreign Powers, Interpreter Jacques Playoust received the Distinguished Conduct Medal.

Towards March the Brigade issued lists of soldiers to be repatriated to Australia, but Jacques' date of discharge is not known. He did not return to Australia for three more years but remained in northern France to busy himself with reviving the family business.

† † †

In the suburbs of Australian cities the battles in which Australians fought in France are widely commemorated. In Sydney alone there are eight streets named 'Amiens', five called 'Bullecourt', four called 'Peronne', four 'Hamel', four 'Pozières', four 'Bapaume', three 'Fromelles', three 'Flanders', two 'Messines', two called 'Somme', two 'Armentieres', and one called 'Villers-Brett'.

For its part, no European nation shows greater respect than does France for the sacrifices made on her behalf by Australians. In Flanders and the Somme, the Australian presence remains vivid in people's minds, and throughout northern France the present generation treat the war cemeteries and monuments with great respect. Schoolchildren are ritually taken to visit them. North and south of the gentle Somme river signs marked with the emblem of a red poppy now lead numbers of pilgrims of many nations along the 'Route du Souvenir', a road that winds through rebuilt villages still bearing the names of old battles, and along fields now yielding rich crops.

Road maps indicate each monument and cemetery, signalling their tragic message all along the phantom of the old Front, not only in the Somme but in Flanders, and east through the Chemin des Dames, the Argonne and Verdun, each seen as a place of pilgrimage.

At Peronne, part of the ancient moated castle has been transformed into the 'Historial de la Grande Guerre', a fine historic museum of the Great War. It flies the European, French, British and German flags, and makes a wordless plea for reconciliation and peace. Mementos, documents, films in three languages are displayed with no sounds of glory, only an immense sadness, possibly best embodied in a picture of a German soldier in his spiked helmet standing by a heap of corpses and asking 'Why?'

† † †

This very personal or skewed viewpoint of the Great War (as it was known before World War II), with its emphasis firmly fixed on the Western Front and the involvement in it of one family, is best balanced by the casualty lists of all fronts, land and sea. These vary considerably, depending on the source, but the list below is an estimate from the US War Department (*Encyclopaedia Britannica*).

KILLED AND DIED FROM ALL CAUSES

Allies		Central Powers	
Russia	1 700 000	Germany	1 773 700
France	1 357 800	Austro Hungarian	1 200 000
Brit. Empire	908 371	Empire	
(of these 59 342 from Australia)		Turkey	325 000
Italy	650 000	Bulgaria	87 500
Romania	335 706		
USA	126 000		
Serbia	45 000		
Belgium	13 716		
Portugal	7 222		
Greece	5 000		
Montenegro	3 000		
Japan	300		
TOTAL	5 152 115	**TOTAL**	3 386 200

COMBINED TOTALS 8 538 315

Many have estimated the losses as considerably higher.

PART III
'The Children of Our Flesh and Blood'

18

Peace and Reconstruction

The poppies were beginning to bloom in Flanders fields, spreading a dramatic red flame along the tops of the deserted trenches. For a long time they were the only vegetation to grow. The obscene coil of 'The Front', which had stretched across the map for four years, was slow to be eradicated. The farmers of Picardy prepared to return to their fields; the vignerons of Champagne reappeared to plant new vines, in order to stock the deep chalk wine cellars which the Germans had completely emptied. It was some time before the farmers of the war zones could exploit their blighted farms and, if they were still able-bodied and not financially ruined, prepare to sow their crops and build up their herds. For many years to come, every ploughing would turn up armaments, shells and gruesome remains of the bodies of unknown soldiers.

The work of the 'French-Australian League of Help', initiated in 1914, was now to come to fruition as the huge task of rebuilding the war-ravaged towns, villages and farms began. However, now that Marie-Thérèse Playoust had seen her husband buried in her family vault in the cemetery at Tourcoing, she badly wanted to return home to Sydney with her ailing son, René. Bereft of the companion with whom she had been so involved in the distribution of the funds raised by the League, she relinquished her responsibilities towards this charity to Mademoiselle Augustine Soubeiran who had recently arrived from Australia. Mlle Soubeiran had acted as an effective secretary of the League in Sydney throughout the war and was now to remain throughout 1919 to take over the secretariat in Paris, together with her colleague Miss Louise Gurney, one of the treasurers.

Together they viewed the numerous institutions and villages which the League's funds were helping. In addition to the 300 000 articles of clothing that had already been sent, some £218 711 had been collected by March 1918, with more to follow.[1] Such a sum had great purchasing power at the time, and these funds 'so generously given in Australia in memory of the Australian soldiers who had died in battle' were now used to support a number of different ventures. The 'Waratah' and 'Australie' orphanages had already been established to accommodate some of the estimated million war orphans; in addition, hostels were organised for evacuees and money given to refurnish homes in devastated villages, buy agricultural machinery, and equip their schools. These two dedicated educationalists saw to it that these small village schools in the Ardennes and the Somme were provided with text books, exercise books, slates, chalk, pens and pencils. Letters of thanks poured into the League's headquarters from such dignitaries as Maréchal Foch and the Archbishop of Rheims and also, more touchingly, from individuals such as a mother of ten children whose husband, suffering from tuberculosis was incapable of supporting them. The League had given them clothing and, better still, shoes.

Similarly there were many letters from mayors of villages along the old Front who had been given aid to rebuild, particularly in the département of the Ardennes. One such village was the small but ancient Poilcourt, set on a tributary of the Aisne in an agricultural plain and just a little to the east of the Chemin des Dames ridge. As in Flanders, grazing sheep had been an essential activity, and the spinning of their fleeces was a cottage industry. The industrial revolution of the 19th century brought a spinning mill to the village in association with woollen interests in Rheims, which employed some 80 people. During a four-year German occupation the mill had been sacked, then used as army barracks, and now stood in ruins. The gate of its chateau had been desecrated during the occupation with a large inscription *Gott Strafe England* (May God Punish England). Its remaining inhabitants, old people, women and children had been forcibly recruited for forced labour on starvation diets.

Carefully handwritten municipal records of the period[2] relate an interesting occurrence:

> In the year nineteen hundred and nineteen on the thirtieth of the month of November at five o'clock in the evening, the Municipal Council and its inhabitants (men, women and children) were duly convoked by Monsieur le Maire to the Town Hall to be informed of a telegram from the Chief Assistant to the Minister concerning the adoption of the Commune by the City of Sydney, Australia ...
> Immediately the acclamations for the Godmother City burst out. Our people who have suffered so much from the war are happy not to feel abandoned, and allow their hearts to speak, overflowing with gratitude towards all the people who have cared for them, and for their kind Godmother the City of Sydney.

A vote of thanks was also expressed by the grateful population to the French-Australian League, who had raised the sum of 5000 francs donated to the commune and had organised the distribution of a case of excellent new warm clothing. A decision was made to have postcards printed with 'photographs of the village ruins caused by the wild barbarians in order to send to the municipality of our benefactors'. The main square was to be renamed 'Place de Sydney'. To perpetuate this happy event a marble plaque would be placed in the school which would read 'Honour to the Australian Soldiers fallen in France for the defence of Justice'.

More significantly, it was unanimously decided to change the name of the village to Sydney. It must be said that the name Poilcourt did not appeal much to its inhabitants since it translated as 'short hair', giving rise to some hilarity. The proposed name change led to more than a year of negotiation with government authorities, as it would have ramifications when the village was re-integrated into the national telephone and railway networks.

Archivists deplored the loss of a traditional name and explained the etymology of 'Poilcourt' as a corruption of the medieval Pauli Curtis (village of Paul), dating from at least the 9th century when a survey listed the village as part of the lands of the Abbey of Saint Remy. A final compromise was found by hyphenating the names of Poilcourt and Sydney, and this became its official name.

In 1920 the Mayor of Poilcourt-Sydney announced at a municipal meeting that Mademoiselle Soubeiran, secretary-general of the French Australian League, had put at the disposition of the commune a further sum of 10 000 francs for the purchase of a communal threshing machine for the use of the farmers. In addition, a clock was donated for the facade of the Mairie (Town Hall), which also served as the village school. When France honoured the village by awarding it the Croix de Guerre, the medal was engraved on this clock.

††

Seventy-five years after adopting the name of Sydney the mayor of Poilcourt-Sydney in the Département of the Ardennes wrote to the Mayor of Sydney, Mr Frank Sartor, sending his greetings. He referred to the clock given so long ago by the people of Sydney and which still stood on the top of their Town Hall, recalling their gift of farm machinery, and he expressed the wish to re-establish links between the two municipalities, especially between their young people.

Some time later, this writer visited this village, which had once spent years trapped behind the German lines but is now easily reached by a good road some 20 kilometres north of Rheims. She carried a gift of a book of photography from the Mayor of Sydney addressed to Monsieur le Maire, M. Michel Baudet, and was presented in return with a basket of biscuits and wine of the Champagne region, also an illustrated history of Poilcourt-Sydney. An Australian flag flew from the Mairie for the occasion. In this warm welcoming ceremony she also gave a miniature didgeridoo and cassette tape to the children of the school, and the didgeridoo tape was played loudly from a car radio to a fascinated audience as the champagne was poured. Great interest was shown in the other much larger Sydney in the Antipodes, and the coming Sydney Olympic Games.

Like many modern French villages, regional supermarkets and the use of motor cars have made the baker and other small shops and cafés redundant, and as people work away from home the shutters are often closed. But the village school in the Mairie now educates children from surrounding villages, the marble plaque on the school room wall still bears its inscription honouring Australian soldiers, and the teacher makes the pupils very aware of the involvement of Australia in their history.

† † †

Sydney newspapers interviewed Marie-Thérèse Playoust at length when she returned by the *Ventura* in the latter half of 1919 to her household at 'Murrulla'. Dressed in deep mourning, she spoke to them of her visit to the battlefields near Rheims to pray at her sons' graves, and how these areas, now ablaze with poppies, were already being visited by trainloads of conducted tourist parties. There was nothing to see but a great desolate waste of up-heaved land, pocked with shell holes, with here and there a wall standing to show what was once a prosperous town or village. The curiosity of the visitors was such that they were even prepared to sleep in the open, for hotels no longer existed in the ruined towns. The historic city of Rheims had been severely damaged by shelling, and its 13th century gothic cathedral was now open to the sky.

Marie-Thérèse gave lavish praise to the Australian soldiers ... 'magnificent, so brave' ... who, with the Canadians, had been given 'the hard tasks to do, and had thrilled France with their valour and initiative ... Whenever there was a tight corner the Australian soldiers were sent up, and never once did they fail'. The Australian soldiers were also liked in French homes because they were 'kind and good, and not hard to please'.

She spoke of the French-Australian League of Help and of how she and her husband had assisted in the distributions to victims of the war, widows and orphans, blind soldiers and refugees. Assuring the people of New South Wales of the good done by their generous donations, she described Mademoiselle Soubeiran's innovative scheme to assist destitute war widows to become self-sufficient by securing small parcels of land for them to farm.

Marie-Thérèse now moved back into the house at Centennial Park, and gradually the family dispersed. Jacques and Maurice were in France, Maurice still not discharged from the army. Her daughter Marie-Thérèse Polin was now reunited with her husband, who had fought with the AIF in the Middle East, and the couple settled in Mosman with their children. Marguerite, her widowed daughter, took another house alongside with her own family. René, now weakened by the onset of diabetes, had joined the swelling ranks of unemployed returned soldiers. He lived on with his mother, his sister 'Ninie', and his younger brother Roger, who was now a medical student.

In 1920 all four moved to a house in Mosman. This area had always been a favourite place for wool buyers of all nationalities because of the excellent ferry service to Circular Quay, near their offices and the Wool Exchange. Many of these families have remained in Mosman, and house names like 'Saint Cloud' and 'Beau Séjour' are legacies of former francophone occupants.

The responsibility for reviving the family's woolbuying enterprise now fell to the resilient Jacques. After his discharge from the army, and later with help from his younger brother Maurice, he returned to Tourcoing for the first time in four years and started work immediately in the newly liberated North. Under the occupation this narrow band of terrain had been cut off from communication with the rest of the world, by the Belgian border on one side (which the Germans had closed) and the Front, which had stabilised at about 13 kilometres from Tourcoing after the first battle of Ypres. They were totally isolated, as roads and railways had been destroyed, canals drained and their locks exploded.[3] People had suffered many privations and even their food supply had come mostly from the USA, who had sent them their surplus flour and lard via neutral Holland.

Aggravated by malnutrition, tuberculosis was rife and some 70% of school children had tested positive. On the initiative of Dr Calmette, the co-discoverer of the tuberculosis vaccine 'BCG' (Bacillus Calmette-Guérin), who was inspector of hospitals in Lille, a scheme was devised to prevent the spread of the disease and was based on good food and fresh air for the children. Several of Joseph Flipo's family, mostly very young people who had lived in Tourcoing throughout the war, died of 'privations'. One may wonder what exactly this meant for these poor children.

Jo Hollebecq, a former wool buyer now living in Sydney, had spent his childhood nearby in Belgium under German occupation, living close to the Front at Menin. The family lived in the cellar of their house because of bombardments, and always had their baggage packed in case of evacuation. Two hundred Germans had occupied his father's brewery, where soldiers did their cooking in the corridors of the building, which had been stripped of any metal fittings. He remembers trainloads of wounded soldiers constantly passing through, together with groups of prisoners to whom they would try to slip some bread.

For Jacques it was now time to start living again. He bought his first car, a Buchet Torpedo, and found a former British Army sergeant called Mitchell to act as chauffeur-mechanic. He drove around the damaged Flemish roads to visit former clients in the textile mills of Roubaix and Tourcoing, including the Leplat blanket factory which had belonged to his mother's family for almost a century. Like all the others, they were struggling to start up after being closed for the last four years and almost ruined by German requisitions. Every piece of copper in the mill, for example, had been taken for German military needs, and in any case there was no wool to process. Even the churches were stripped of their bells and organ pipes. Heating fuel was in short supply, as the retreating Germans had destroyed the coal mines, blowing up the underground galleries.

Most of the mills were incapable of functioning after the German withdrawal, and the owners told Jacques that, during the occupation, hostages had been taken after refusing to manufacture goods for the enemy; a number of them had died from the appalling conditions of the prison camps. The discovery of clandestine radios and newspapers led to further reprisals. Each morning at dawn a particular mill would be targeted by a team from the Militar-Polizei; all exits were guarded, then about 30 experts armed with hand screws, planks, spades, mattocks, hammers, pliers and crowbars would methodically remove whatever machinery could be of use to German industry, smashing whatever remained. There was no money, and the factories — which in many cases had been used as army barracks — were standing idle.

Ruined they might be, but the survival instincts of the diligent northerners now took over. They were determined to cooperate to get the mills working again, and implemented an energetic collective project using government credits. Centralisation of purchases, combined with a real effort to cut red tape, helped to set the wheels turning, proceeding in the set stages required for the manufacture of wool. Shortly after Jacques' discharge, the first combing mills were re-opened. Spinning, then weaving and dyeing followed in turn, so that by September 1920 the chimneys were smoking once more in 55 of the 57 mills in Tourcoing and 46 of the 48 mills in Roubaix.

The textile industries of Rheims had also suffered. The city had not been occupied, but had been shelled and bombed to such an extent that 31 spinning mills, 23 weaving mills and 10 dyeing works had been destroyed. The German reparations did not come as promised, and it was understandable that in these regions, perhaps more than any other, indignation was expressed to the government in Paris for not taking a firmer line over Germany's failure to pay up. Few could then imagine how aggressively Germany would react in the following 20 years to its own economic ruin, induced by its warlike activities.

Jacques had been in touch with the family firm's former agent in Roubaix before travelling to London to the first wool sales. Wool sales in Australia had still not resumed, as Britain had agreed to buy the whole Australian wool clip at a favourable price for the duration of the war and one year after. This agency had been founded by Edmond Delvas, who as a young man in the 1870s had travelled to Australia by sailing ship to attend a season of wool sales. He had died during the occupation, and his son, recently an interpreter with the British army, was now continuing his work.

There was also a ravishing daughter, Evelyne, whose dark good looks evoked the centuries of Spanish occupation in Flanders. She was 26 and had worked as a Red Cross aide for these last four years, at first nursing British wounded soldiers in Roubaix till they were sent into captivity, and then caring for civilian refugees from the battle lines. In the last year of the war, with a Red Cross team, she had accompanied a convoy of frail civilian evacuees on a prolonged and overcrowded train journey through German and Swiss territory to Evian on the French shore of the lake of Geneva. Here, remote from the war, she had spent an idyllic period of liberty caring for the sick amongst the thousands of evacuees now arriving, walking in the mountains on her days off, eating good food in this abundant region, and generally regaining her health.

Jacques had seen her with indifference as a child, but was smitten the first time he met her again. Never one to waste time, he proposed marriage and, rejecting the normal bourgeois family negotiations over dowries, they were wedded within three months. Above all they were united in their desire to put this terrible war behind them and to rebuild their lives together in peace.

19

Marriage and Homecomings

After a year's silence, Jacques wrote again to his cousin Marie from London (translation):

14th December 1919

My dear Marie

Do you still remember the writing? I would like to thank you for your congratulations. You blame me for not having written to you much, but what have you done yourself? And since I left you I have been plunged into business, working on an average of 14 hours a day. A thunderbolt had to strike me before I could take the time to become engaged. And in the three months since my engagement I have spent only three weeks with my fiancée. Have you ever met her? Even though she was willing to take me on, she is not bad at all! Naturally I myself find her perfect, but I am speaking as other people would. I hope you will come to my wedding and I will introduce you to this marvel. The wool sales will continue in London till the end of the week, and I will not be back till Saturday night.

My best wishes to your mother and to yourself, till very soon I hope,

Jacques

From 'Murrulla' in Sydney, Marie-Thérèse wrote a letter thickly edged in black to Evelyne, welcoming her in very affectionate terms into the family, where she enjoyed a special status as the daughter of Edmond Delvas, her late husband's friend.

Jacques and Evelyne were married on 23 December 1919 at the Église Saint Joseph in Roubaix, Evelyne wearing a dress in the new short mode, well above her ankles. The family wedding feast at home was in the copious northern tradition, despite scarcity of food and limited coal supplies for winter lighting and power.

The menu was:

Fillets of Sole Dieppoise
Haunch of Venison à la Diane

Artichoke hearts Chantilly, Peas Paysanne
Fattened pullets stuffed with truffles
Croustades of Foie Gras
Ice creams, Desserts, Fruit

This was washed down with the best of the wines that had been astutely hidden from the Germans in the walled-up cellars, along with other family treasures. Jacques' brother Maurice was present, as were their cousin Marie and her mother Tante Mathilde Leplat. There was also a good contingent of Jacques' Australian relatives from Strathfield who had returned after the war to visit France, where their son Jean had lost his life.

On this wedding day thoughts of the war were resolutely put aside. The wedding toast was proposed by Evelyne's brother-in-law, Maurice Dubrulle, whose two brothers had been killed in the fighting, one at Douaumont, the other at the Chemin des Dames. He himself had spent the last four years in a prisoner-of-war camp in Germany, escaping twice but recaptured before reaching the frontier. He was now a textile manufacturer and his typical wedding speech was composed in wool trade parlance, ribbing Jacques on his diminishing fleece, hoping the couple would carbonise any burrs on their road to happiness, and that they would be shepherds of an imposing flock of lambs. A few years on this very energetic man was to play an important role in the wool markets of the world when he became the Founding President of the International Wool Textile Organisation (IWTO) which is still in existence.

The couple's honeymoon was spent in Beaulieu on the Riviera, but it was of necessity brief because they had to hurry to London for the opening of the wool sales on 12 January.

They lived happily in England for almost two years at the start of their marriage. Evelyne had spent a year in an English school as a girl and, having few problems with the language, enjoyed life there to the full. No doubt London was more exciting to her as a young married woman than the cities of Flanders, and almost as close to the Paris she longed to know better.

During the war the whole Australian wool clip had been bought in bulk by the British Government, and was still being sold by auction in London and Liverpool. The post-war needs for quantities of wool to furnish the returning soldiers with civilian suits had created flourishing sales for a short while. It was not until 1920 that sales resumed in Sydney, where they gradually surpassed the London market in volume. French direct purchases of Australian wool were renewed, growing rapidly in bulk and financial importance to the point where Evelyne and Jacques decided to make their home in Australia. Letters had also been arriving from Marie-Thérèse, who was anxious to revive her late husband's Sydney office, recommending to Jacques that he should arrive well before the re-opening of the next season of wool sales.

It was a wrench for Evelyne to leave her family, as she had rarely travelled out of France, but this promised to be a huge adventure. Australia had always seemed a legendary country to her, as she had read her father's diaries relating his journey to the Antipodes by sailing ship in the 1870s. Her brother and sister farewelled them at Le Havre as they boarded the Compagnie Transatlantique's fine three-funnelled liner, the *Paris*. Packed in their huge trunks were a few antique objects and paintings to remind them of their past, clothes, books, and nine heavy bound volumes of every wartime issue of the journal *L'Illustration*. They made the six-day crossing of the Atlantic to New York in October 1921 and here Evelyne experienced the first New World culture shocks, when they were refused wine with their meals because of the new prohibition laws, and the waiters addressed them as 'Folks'. They visited Boston, at that period a flourishing wool centre, and also the great tourist attraction of Niagara Falls.

A train bore them across the snow-covered Canadian plains and when it made a halt at a country station, they were touched by the sight of a young couple being farewelled by their family as they climbed on board with a pile of luggage. This was an emigrating Canadian doctor and his wife named Dickson, who by chance were to live as near neighbours in Mosman for the next 30 years.

They traversed the Rocky Mountains to Vancouver, before making a leisurely journey on the *Niagara* across the Pacific. France was very remote as they played deck sports in tropical clothes, with Evelyne marvelling at the sight of exotic ports like Honolulu and Suva. When they sailed through Sydney Harbour Heads, the quarantine doctor came on board to verify they were not bringing in smallpox or any other infectious disease before they were allowed to go ashore.

There was a warm welcome from Jacques' family but the joy of their return was clouded by Renés deteriorating health. The two brothers, Jacques and Maurice, now set up their office near Circular Quay, calling themselves 'Playout Fils' (sons), and their lives settled into a peacetime routine of wool sales in Sydney and Brisbane, with biennial journeys to France free of any drama. For them the war was over, if not forgotten.

Jacques' physical legacy of the war was a limping walk requiring the aid of a stick. In the wool stores he was obliged to use the goods lift rather than climb the stairs.

After his demobilisation their cousin Fernand Playout ('Ferdie') was still suffering from the effects of gas when he returned with his parents to Strathfield. For a while he worked as a jackaroo, as he had always been interested in the land, then for a short stint in Melbourne as a buyer in the same firm as his father, Henri Cauillez, before deciding to work as an independent buyer. He married an Australian from Strathfield, Rita Adams, and their only child John was named after 'Brave Little John' who had died in 1918 near the Chemin des Dames. Fernand's younger brother, Charles, made his career with the Roubaix/Tourcoing wool firm of Wattinne Bossut, for whom he worked in Adelaide, Melbourne and Sydney and in time became its Australian principal.

Paul Wenz returned to Forbes in 1919. When he was working with the Red Cross in London during the war he had written a novel entitled *Au Pays de leurs Pères* ('In the Land of their Fathers') concerning an Australian soldier in England, and dedicated 'to the men who came from Australia and New Zealand to fight for France'. He lived with a certain financial ease, as the Wenz company was a large enterprise, and his mother was born a Peugeot, of the car-manufacturing family.[1] He had a reputation for generosity and donated a parcel of land near his property on which a school was built, and he also endowed it with a library. His own collection of books was later bequeathed to the Forbes library.

During the wartime hiatus in sales, those buyers who had remained in Australia had been employed by the Australian Government Wool Appraisal Scheme to examine the clip which was sent in bulk to England. Most of the old pre-war buying houses such as Cauillez, Dewavrin, Dewez, Fuhrmann, Eugène Gosset, Kreglinger, Leon Leroux, Masurel, Simonius Vischer, Wattine-Bossut and Wenz resumed their activities as soon as possible, sometimes with new partnerships, and often employing their former buyers returning from the war. Most of the wool buyers who returned from hostilities founded families which were to remain in Australia. These families are listed in Appendix II.

The names of 20 Sydney and Brisbane wool buyers who fell in the war are listed on a bronze memorial plaque which hung for many years in the Sale Rooms of the Sydney Wool Exchange in Macquarie Place. It was transferred to less grand surroundings in Yennora when the Wool Exchange was demolished. The majority of the names are French or Belgian and include:

Georges MORELLE, who was wounded by shrapnel and died of tetanus in January 1915. Aristide DESROUSSEAUX, a buyer at Masurel, was also killed in 1915, the same year that Georges WAUQIEZ died of typhoid. Both these men had sailed in the first contingent in 1914 on the *Malwa*. The second contingent, sailing on the *Sydney* a week later, included Alfred DECOUVELAERE, Francois LEFEBVRE and Paul WATTEL who also did not return. The list also names Marcel and Stéphane PLAYOUST.

Gervais PARMENTIER was killed fighting in the Belgian army.

Paul LEBLANC Croix de Guerre, lost his life in the Somme in July 1916.

A young Australian buyer, Phillip WOODFORDE, who had studied French before the war to work effectively with Wenz and Co., had enlisted in the 1st battalion of the 1st Division. According to his battalion history, in May 1917, near Bullecourt, 'Major Woodforde was mortally wounded by a shell, a calamity that all found hard to bear'.

All Australian links were not severed by these deaths. Although Paul Wattel had been killed in battle in 1915, winning the Croix de Guerre, his wife and son Marcel were to live on in Australia. His brother Benjamin, who arrived later from northern France, worked for the Roubaix-based Comptoir Louis Kint, finally settling in Australia with his South African wife. Their son Raymond later was employed by the same firm.

Gervais Parmentier's brother, Georges, named his son after him, and young Gervais made his career in woolbuying in Sydney.

A number of new Belgian and French houses such as Brunninghausen, Dassonville, Louis Kint, Prouvost-Lefèbvre,[2] Leon Marescaux, Moch et Odelin[3] and Voreux Cau swelled their numbers, bringing with them a wave of new buyers from abroad. Wool auctions were now inaugurated in Perth, and a number of the larger firms such as Dewavrin and Masurel opened branches in the West.

This was a time of star personalities, such as Theo Desmarchelier of Alphonse Six (a firm which specialised in black wool to be used for priests' clothing), with his shock of white hair and his horrendous mutilation of the English language. Like many others, he had been mobilised from Australia to fight in the French army in 1914, but had returned safely from the war. He drove round Sydney in a Delage, and even though his fine new house had a view to the blue Pacific beyond Sydney Heads, he chose for it the incongruous name of 'Roubaix'.

Another was Georges Parmentier, something of a dandy, who wore monogrammed silk shirts to the wool stores, and is remembered by John Wilton for the way his bow ties always slipped askew during the agitation of the auctions. He drove a Ballot. He also had a reputation for being a very fine cook, bred pigeons for his table, and collected sculptures by Rodin.

Camille Gheysens, like Georges Parmentier and Jo Hollebecq, was a native of Mouscron, and arrived in 1926 to work as an independent buyer. He had a strong interest in the arts, collected paintings and befriended artists. His portrait was painted by Dobell, and now hangs in the Art Gallery of New South Wales. He was also a composer whose work was on one occasion performed by the Sydney Symphony Orchestra.

Jo Hollebecq recalls another Belgian, Joseph Balthasar, slightly related to Frederick Hentze, who had arrived in Sydney before the war to work for Etablissements Pierre Flipo one of the larger Tourcoing firms, later to become CIL (Compagnie d'Importation de Laine). He was known always by his surname, with its biblical overtones, and directed the Sydney branch for many years. He was an imposing figure, tall, with red hair sticking up in tufts, a red moustache, little round glasses and high collars. Because he was rather absent-minded and eccentric, he was the central character in many anecdotes and caricatures. Quite happily he once broke a window in Winchcombe Carson's wool store on a Sunday afternoon in Brisbane, in order to get a sneak preview of the following day's offerings. John Lamérand remembers him playing the clown at the sales, leaping up athletically, and shouting 'Nothing!'. He was reluctant to retire and remained in the wool trade well into old age. Like his confrere at the head of CIL in Melbourne, the majestic Augustin Nopenaire, Balthasar acted as honorary consul for Belgium for a period.

His own son did not follow his father's career and instead became an anaesthetist. An original thinker, Tony Balthasar applied his knowledge of electricity to designing and making an external defibrillator, possibly the first in Australia, to reverse cardiac irregularities. Modern modifications of this equipment are now used every time physicians, ambulance officers and cardiac nurses attempt cardiac resuscitation.

Marcel Paroissien was a tall man with a gentle, polite manner. Some recall his British Indian Army Officer style, also his sense of humour, mocking his colleagues in an exaggerated northern French *patois*. The buyers were in such close contact in their daily routine that they ragged each other like schoolboys exchanging amiable insults.

The traditional gastronomic train journeys to the Brisbane sales resumed, and these groups of buyers could well have proven tiresome for other passengers, as a train guard who was allotting seats once asked 'Are you gentlemen or are you wool buyers?'

Since the war the price of wool at auction had been extremely volatile, making business decisions difficult. Furthermore competition was increasing with the participation of the Japanese houses of Mitsubishi, Mitsui, Kanematsu, Itoh, Japan Cotton Trading, Marubeni and Okura, who operated strongly until 1940. There were also a number of very active German houses. From the record prices reached in the English post-war sales early in 1920, when quantities of woollen cloth were being consumed as soldiers changed into civilian suits, the price per pound weight fell sharply the following year, just when Australian sales were resuming. Prices peaked again in the 1924–25 season, dropping again to less than half this value in the calamitous season of 1929–30 which followed the Wall Street crash.

20

Domesticity

Evelyne was always called so by her very formal mother-in-law, but was now known to her friends as 'Zine', and as 'Madam' to the neighbourhood in Mosman. She had a gregarious nature and adapted well to her new home, though she regretted its distance from her family in Roubaix. Her mother made the long journey by ship to attend the birth of her first Australian grandchild, curious to retrace the footsteps of her deceased husband. He had attended wool sales here half a century earlier and had been dissuaded from making his life in this 'country of savages'.

A weekly correspondence was dutifully maintained between Roubaix and Sydney, long letters which were always carefully answered, but it took at least two months to receive any replies due to the slowness of surface mail. Only in the 1930s was an airmail postal service to begin. It was possible to telephone abroad, but only in a crisis, as prices of international calls were astronomical.

By now Jacques and Zine had settled into a life of peace and domesticity, and bought a house in Mosman built shortly before the war in what is now called Federation Style. By a curious co-incidence found themselves living next to Ken Prior, a former major in Jacques' brigade in 1918. Both men, as they grew older, found a common interest in gardening, and liked to share a drink before lunch. On these occasions the Australian Major and the French Private reminisced on the past and solved the problems of the future in a complete Entente Cordiale. Their children became firm friends.

Jacques quickly installed a wine cellar under the house which he was able to fill with the best vintages from Bordeaux and Burgundy, for the French franc had plummeted. Wine was rarely drunk by Australians of the period and the quality was vastly inferior to that produced half a century later. Food was plentiful, but limited in variety and unsophisticated in presentation.

In these peaceful years, Jacques became an active member and office-bearer of the French Chamber of Commerce, which his father had founded before the war. Zine and he also busied themselves with the Alliance Francaise, which had managed to struggle through the war years entirely by voluntary help. Mademoiselle Soubeiran continued her involvement with the Alliance, sharing the presidency for a year with a wool buyer, Monsieur Doucet.

The year 1923 saw a great renewal of its size and activity under the presidency of Professor E. G. Waterhouse, renowned academic and camellia expert. The 'Presidents d'Honneur' that year were the French consul and Mlle Soubeiran; Jacques Playoust was Vice-President. Monsieur Edouard Dulieu was elected co-secretary with Mrs Jowett. Edouard Dulieu was a Belgian who, after fighting in the Belgian army during the war, had come to Sydney to take up an academic career in French Literature. After a time he was enticed into the wool trade by his brother Robert and became a member of the French firm of Wattinne-Bossut. He gave literary lectures to the Modern Language association and continued to play an important part in French cultural affairs in years to come.

Two women were elected to the Alliance committee, Lady Mallan and Madame Georges Playoust, the other members being wool buyers, Droulers, Flipo, Lamérand, Dulieu, Doucet, Joseph Playoust and Thévenet. A later president and long-time supporter of the Alliance was Alfred Wunderlich, London born but educated in French-speaking Switzerland and married to a Swiss woman. He lived to the age of 101 and variously became president of the Chamber of Manufacturers, President of the Royal Philharmonic Society and an office bearer in the French Chamber of Commerce, yet found time to conduct the Alliance examinations personally. He was to be awarded the Gold Medal of the Alliance in 1933, and was decorated with the *Légion d'Honneur.*

Jacques' uncle, Joseph Playoust, was awarded the *Légion d'Honneur* in 1922, for his contribution to the work of the French-Australian League of Help, and for his part in establishing the 'Union Francaise', a social group. The Union held a *Soirée Dansante* to celebrate, which was attended by the ex-Premier Mr Holman, K.C. The *Courrier* reported that they all danced far into the night.

Although Marie-Thérèse Playoust was now playing a less active role, she retained enough of her old form to give an afternoon reception with dancing at the Wentworth Hotel for the French Naval Squadron commanded by Admiral Gilly, which was paying an official visit to Australian cities that summer. There were many gestures of friendship extended between France and Australia during this visit. Admiral Gilly entertained Mr W. M. Hughes on board his ship in Melbourne and decorated him with the *Légion d'Honneur.* Curiously, 20 years later a Free French destroyer called *Le Triomphant,* which was based in Sydney Harbour in World War II, was commanded by this admiral's son who subsequently married an Australian. His descendants live in Sydney.

Marie-Thérèse, who had once managed a household of 10 children, now had a shrinking entourage. René Playoust's died at home in the winter of 1923. His death from diabetes, just a few days before his 29th birthday, occurred only shortly before the introduction into Australia of the newly discovered insulin treatment which might have saved his life. Marie-Thérèse, who had now lost three sons, bore this additional bereavement with her habitual sang-froid. Strangers found her a chilly personality, but she was capable of great kindness and generosity, and her children were extraordinarily devoted to her.

In her matriarchal way, expected her family and their children to join her for lunch every Sunday in provincial French style. They responded loyally and there were often some 16 people at table. The children were seated at the far end, where they found that under the table was an interesting place to observe people's shoes; for example Grannie wore a style of high buttoned boots which had to be done up with a shoe hook. The children were permitted to go to play in the garden between courses if they felt restive. Their grandmother provided superlative food, which they all liked a little too much. Afterwards there was bridge or tennis.

Her widowed daughter, Marguerite Decouvelaere, returned to France soon after René's death at the request of her father-in-law, who undertook to give her children a French education. However, their Australian background was to remain strongly implanted in these children into their old age.

Georges, Marie-Thérèse's handsome eldest son, was divorced and unfortunately this fact was never accepted by his straight-laced mother. He lived in Sydney with his second wife and their daughter Marcelle, but his former wife had left the country to live in the United States with their son. Life could not have been easy for this eldest brother of five soldiers, and the only one not in the army, since few people in those days could have understood the psychological impact of rejection for military service on medical grounds. Georges was now working with Wilhelmsen's shipping line, and his pleasant manner and good relations with wool buyers were useful to the company.

His brother Maurice left home in 1928 when he married 'Nin' Lamérand, a marriage uniting the son and the daughter of two pioneering French wool buyers of the 1890s. Roger finished his medical studies and married an Australian, Olga Burrell; they later had two sons.

Every second year, in the years of even numbers, Jacques and Zine's household was subjected to a week of packing; wardrobe trunks for the cabins, in which hung tropical clothes and evening dress; hat boxes, fitted beauty cases, and large rectangular trunks with drawers. These were intended for the hold and labelled 'Not Wanted on Voyage'. Even two

deck chairs were included. After the birth of Annette in 1922, and
Jacqueline in 1925, it was necessary to add a large basket of toys and a
nursemaid when they sailed on the *Ormonde* in 1926. On these trips there
were always joyous reunions when Zine returned to Roubaix, and equally
sad farewells three months later. With each return journey came a supply
of books for adults and children. The French books had characteristically
flimsy paper covers, and pages which had to be cut open with a paper
knife. Zine brought back elegant clothes from Paris for herself and her
two daughters, but they would have preferred something resembling their
school friends' style. The Dekyvère brothers were similarly embarrassed
by being sent to visit friends in smart sailor suits. As for women's clothes,
hems were creeping up to a scandalous level, just below the knee, while
faces all but disappeared under deep cloche hats.

Zine had her own adjustments to make to life in Australia. She gained
a practical insight into the egalitarian notions of Australians from an Irish-
Australian country woman from Nimmitabel, Minnie Shiels, her house-
keeper, who had wanted to leave in the first week as she didn't 'like
foreigners'. She was persuaded to try a little longer, and 40 years later,
having become an essential and well-loved member of the household,
she stated that she still didn't like foreigners but that the French weren't
really foreign. Minnie indeed was thoroughly corrupted by exotic styles
of cooking, picking up even more skills when she was 'borrowed' by
friends during her employers' many absences abroad. These new
experiences combined with her own country training to produce kitchen
craft of great renown.

There was a popular and lively consul-general for Belgium, Henri
Segaert, who had arrived soon after the war and stayed in this diplomatic
post for about 18 years, long enough for his three children to marry in
Australia. Monsieur Segaert enlivened the existence of his wide circle of
friends, as he had a genuine talent for producing amateur theatricals in
the French language. Many wool buyers were involved in these
productions, which were staged to raise money for charity. On one notable
occasion in the 1930s Racine's *Athalie* was played at the amphitheatre
(now regrettably extinct) overlooking Balmoral Beach towards the entrance
to Sydney Harbour.

Not all adapted to this new country easily, particularly the women
who had failed to master the English language. Middle-class women at
the time did not normally work outside their homes, and it was too easy
for them to find themselves isolated in a small world of their own kind.
Some marriages succumbed, or women prevailed on their husbands to
return, while many stayed on and made friends in their neighbourhood.
The children had no problems, and changed languages quite easily from

their earliest ages, knowing exactly which people expected to be addressed in French, and which in English. Their formal education was to be entirely Australian, with a few periods of tutoring from French text books, which gave them a balanced view of history from two varying viewpoints, together with a mistrust of stereotypes and overstated nationalism.

Children who were educated in this country felt totally at home, although there remained a strong pull to Europe that marked them for the rest of their lives. Years later this could manifest itself in an atavistic taste for French faïence or Louis XV panelling, or a craving for a good cassoulet with a glass of Bordeaux.

21
'Peace in Our Time'

Despite their peaceful and easy way of life, the memories of the Great War remained dominant in Jacques' and Zine's thoughts, and were often referred to in their conversations. Jacques liked to recount funny incidents, spicing his sentences with army slang, and while the real horrors were avoided, the war was never really left behind. Even from the early twenties, the old shadow of German militarism had begun to darken Jacques' perceptions. Through his commercial relations with Germany, which he visited every second year, he was well aware of the growing influence of the Nazi party. He subscribed to a German language newspaper *Die Brücke*, which he read in its gothic print in order to keep in touch. His concerns are easily understood when influential Germans wrote expressing not regret, but anger at the 'stab in the back'.

The enemy commander at Verdun, the Kronprinz, who was occupying his days of exile on the Dutch island of Weringen by writing his memoirs, showed no repentance, and stated:

> If only we had had a leader like Clemenceau, he would have won the War for us by his perseverance, his decisiveness and his appeals to national unity.

The following year the Kronprinz was diagnosed by his doctors as demented.

Even General Ludendorff, in his memoirs published soon after the war, could still not accept the German defeat. He had fled to Sweden in the unrest at the time of the Armistice, then later returned to be elected to the Reichstag as a member of the National Socialist (Nazi) party. As early as 1923, an article in the *Courrier Australien*[1] referred to the 'Bavarian Mussolini' whose name was 'Mr Hittler' (sic), quoting a speech he had made in Munich:

> What I want is to expel the Jews and dubious foreigners who are always found behind political upheavals, and who swarm in our country.

In New South Wales, the ex-premier, Mr Holman had consistently supported French policy. In a speech to the National Club he endorsed the French occupation of the Ruhr and condemned the Germans for defaulting on the reparations agreed to at the signing of the armistice.

But to most Australians such problems seemed very remote as more cheerful activities occupied their thoughts. The summer of 1927 brought the excitement of the visit of the French tennis team to participate in the Australian Tennis championships in Melbourne and Sydney. These were the grand days of Australian tennis, when Jack Crawford and Harry Hopman were the heroes, elegant in their long flannel trousers. The game attracted a popular interest rivalling even that of cricket. 'The Three B's', Borotra, Boussus and Brugnon were tremendous crowd pleasers, particularly the expert volleyer Jean Borotra, the 'Bouncing Basque', who had stage presence demonstrated by his leap over the net, while the competition was played in an atmosphere of good will and sportsmanship. The players were feted everywhere with government and mayoral receptions, as well as a party given by Sydney's French community at the new Romano's restaurant in York Street.

About this time Sydney was to benefit from a legacy from J. E. Archibald, the founding editor of the *Bulletin* magazine, which was then owned by Jacques' neighbours, the Prior family. Archibald donated a vast and very beautiful fountain which was built in Hyde Park to the design of a Frenchman, Francois Sicard. Its Parisian scale delighted Zine, who showed it proudly to her children. Better still, from her point of view, it had been donated to commemorate the alliance between France and Australia in the 1914–18 war.

Jacques' cousins were now on the move. In 1929, Joseph Playoust decided to retire from work and to return to France, probably at the wish of his wife, with the result that the large household in Strathfield split up. Two daughters went with them but several of their other children, Fernand, Charles, Paul and Blanche chose to remain in Australia. Another daughter, Gabrielle, who had been one of the early women graduates in medicine from Sydney University, relinquished her medical career when she married a Belgian wool buyer. They bore a large family, and later returned to Belgium; 40 years later all the daughters still retained their Australian accents. 'Woodside' was sold, and in a few years the paddock, the cow and the horse made way for a new housing sub-division.

In 1928 the Messageries Maritimes shipping line, on which the wool buyers dispatched much of their wool, added to their fleet a rapid new ship with square funnels called the *Eridan*, plying between Sydney and Marseilles. It was a mixed freighter, taking cargo, as well as about 60 passengers in considerable comfort. This was a favourite with the wool buyers, as the cuisine was particularly good, and the number of passengers ideal. They preferred it to the *Commissaire Ramel* which, despite its comfortable cabins and spacious decks, was so unstable that when crossing the Great Australian Bight the children could play slippery dips on the parquet floors. There was plenty of company for the children, many of whom knew each other, so the journeys were great fun, except when Jacques insisted on a few hours of school work for other people's children as well as his own. The coaching was effective, as the children usually came home well ahead in their syllabus, though confused as to who was the enemy in their English history books.

In Marseilles their language passed unselfconsciously into French mode as they enjoyed their bouillabaisse, before taking the two long train journeys to the north. While Jacques spent his days in consultation with agents and mill-owners, his daughters were happy to settle into a few months of northern hemisphere life, where they were petted and spoilt by an extended family of grandmother, aunts, uncles and cousins. They became acquainted with provincial decorum in the formal houses, secluded behind austere brick facades and tall shuttered windows, and lunches that lasted till five in the afternoon, interrupted by frequent escapes between courses to play in the garden.

Expeditions were organised along the tow paths, watching the horses draw the barges along the canals, becoming familiar with the functioning of the locks which raised the water levels so the barges could proceed. As a reward for good behaviour they were offered the characteristic flat sugared waffles of Flanders.

This Flemish region bore the scars of World War I well into the 1930s. Visits were planned to the sandbagged Canadian trenches at Vimy Ridge. The little girls were shown the ruins of the gothic Cloth Hall just over the Belgian border at Ypres, and the War Cemetery containing some Australian names near Wimereux, the coastal town which had once accommodated the No. 2 Australian General Hospital. The cemetery was within cycling distance from an aunt's holiday house. Swimming at Wimereux was considered chilly compared to Sydney, the beaches in Brittany no less so, though the tidal differences were dramatic. In Normandy there were high white cliffs and the sea was reached by hopping across enormous pebbles.

Parents were envied as they sometimes disappeared to the mysterious enchantments of Paris while the children stayed with grandmother and were expected to spend each morning with a tutor at their French grammar lessons. They wrote on exercise books ruled in squares, and learnt to cross their sevens as they acquired strange methods of long division. Educational tours were arranged for the children to visit the enormous mills which scoured, combed, spun and wove the bales of wool shipped from Australia. In time there were tearful farewells before the long journey home, and another adjustment into the English language and Australian culture. Soon they switched to reading Ginger Meggs again instead of Tin Tin, as they licked their threepenny ice-cream cones on sunny beaches. Father, on the other hand was very indignant that some of the French books he had imported were confiscated by the customs inspector as 'offending morality and good order'. Censorship laws at the time were strict indeed.

About this time, Jacques and Zine and some friends booked a passage on a freighter for a voyage of exploration to the New Hebrides, now Vanuatu but then a very remote Anglo-French condominium in the South Pacific. They were intrigued by the double administration in Port Vila: two government houses at exactly the same altitude, two schools, two courts and police forces. They visited the Big Nambas on an outlying island, where they were given to understand that cannibalism was on the way out, but could not entirely disappear till some of the older chiefs died. That generation believed that by eating the flesh of their enemies, their evil spirits could no longer come back to haunt them.

But worries were starting to intrude into this carefree life. Prices of wool had been falling steadily, with a calamitous drop at the end of the decade. The stock market crash on Wall Street in 1929 was followed by a corresponding fall in demand for textiles round the world, and therefore a fall in demand for wool. This was catastrophic for the growers as well as the buyers. Marcel Dekyvère recalled his father saying at the time 'the most I would bid for these lots and crutchings was minus a halfpenny'. Over the years some companies merged or simply disappeared, and buyers changed from one employer to another. Business was also more competitive, and an element of speculation entered the market. Some large firms 'sold forward', making it possible for them to sell at a lower price, but this was a risky procedure. In contrast to the larger subsidiaries of French-owned companies, Playoust Fils was a small family firm based in Sydney, so Jacques and Maurice preferred to play safe, simply filling the few new orders as they came in.

The Great Depression then struck hard. The French mills had continued buying a little until the season of 1931–32, then orders almost stopped. This meant a certain belt-tightening for all, and a number of wool buyers such as Henri Renault and Jo Hollebecq, working for large European firms, were retrenched. The salaries of others were reduced. Unemployment numbers in Australia had never been so high, standing at some 24% of the general workforce. There were bankruptcies and suicides.

Playoust Fils survived, but only at the cost of reducing staff, which they did with great reluctance. A letter to Charles Churcher, still in his son's possession, illustrates the human cost of these economic conditions. It was written from France by Jacques in his beautifully regular hand and with his usual bizarre spelling. He wrote on his business letterhead in the formal mode of address of his generation:

Roubaix, 8th March 1932

Dear Churcher!

I received on the 6th inst. your cable asking me to reply to an advertisement that appeared in the Herald of the 5th inst. I immediately wrote to London and gave these people the highest recommendation both as regards your moral worth and technical knowledge. I told them that I was at their disposal for any information they might wish to have.

I avail myself of this opportunity to tell you how terribly cut up I am to have to let you go — One does not meet men of your stamp every day, & your eleven years of devoted service to the firm certainly deserved a better fate. You cant immagine what the situation is in Roubaix-Tourcoing. Our most important clients with the loss of the English market are practically closed down. What will eventuate? God only knows, but one thing is certain is that we are in for a period of very hard times.

I am only too pleased to do anything I can for you. Do not hesitate to ask me.

Sincerely yours,
Jacques Playoust

Charlie Churcher overcame these difficulties by combining with André Parmentier in a changed type of business, buying 'star lots' (small numbers of bales which in the early days had been marked by a star in the catalogues) and repacking wool for Japan. His son John followed his father into the wool trade.

Jacques and his family were home in Sydney by May 1932, too late for the opening of the new Harbour Bridge, but in time to hear the news of the dismissal of the Labor Premier, Jack Lang, by the governor of New South Wales, Sir Phillip Game.

The Test matches of 1932–33 distracted the attention of the whole country from the financial gloom as people of all ages remained glued to the 'wireless' as the 'bodyline' battles were fought on the cricket field and Stan McCabe and Don Bradman took on hero status for their courageous batting. By this time the European wool buyers had become Australian enough to share in the national enthusiasm for Test Cricket, particularly Jacques who had been a keen cricketer as a young man.

Affairs seemed to be sliding into chaos for many. Jo Hollebecq remembers a profound depression which touched everybody; those lucky enough to retain their jobs suffered from reduced salaries. A Belgian from Mouscron, just across the almost illusory French border with Tourcoing, Jo had come to Melbourne after the war as a very young man to work with his brother for Louis Kint and Co. This important firm of merchants was owned by a Belgian, but its headquarters were in Tourcoing. After three years in Melbourne Hollebecq was called up for Belgian military service, but by the time this training was completed, his old job no longer existed and several others had also been retrenched. At the height of the depression he tramped the cobblestones of Tourcoing for months to find employment. Finally his sister saw a newspaper advertisement seeking a buyer to work in Australia for the Roubaix firm of Voreux-Cau. Jo was chosen from a large number of applicants because of his previous experience, and returned to Australia in 1933, just as business was beginning to pick up.

For a time there was increased demand, prices firmed and the good life resumed. Hollebecq well remembers these days, and many of the characters of the sale rooms, particularly his chief Ben Wattel, a home-loving pipe smoker with a conservative style. He recalls Maurice Sellosse, who had spent the war years as a stretcher-bearer in the army, and was now working as a buyer in Sydney. Both these men founded families in Australia. Like the others, Jo Hollebecq travelled regularly back to Europe by ship, and recalls these journeys as 'the grand life' wearing a 'smoking' or dinner jacket every night. He remained with his firm for the rest of his working life, eventually taking over its direction. Although married to an Australian and with several Australian children, he is a Knight in the Order of Leopold and chose to retain his Belgian nationality.

In June 1933, Mademoiselle Augustine Soubeiran died in Sydney. Her obituaries were very respectful, and it was regrettable that the medal of 'Chevalier de la Légion d'Honneur' was only awarded to her posthumously.

In 1934, during one of Jacques' business journeys to Europe, he visited Berlin for a few days. Staying at the Adlon Hotel on 30 June, he was unaware that a deadly power struggle was taking place between two factions of the Nazi party. Throughout the country the black-shirted SS, having first murdered Hitler's former friend, Captain Ernst Röhm, leader of the SA, were quietly exterminating large numbers of his semi-military 'brown shirts'. This was the infamous 'Night of the Long Knives', but Jacques only heard the truth once he was out of the country.

Australian wool prices continued to be volatile. Demand had risen in 1933–34 but there was another fall the following year, which saw the cessation of sales for several months due to lack of orders. This was followed by two seasons of good prices, then six years of severe drought between 1935 and 1941.

There were about 70 French wool firms in Sydney at the time, but not all resumed after World War II.[2] Most of the big French and Belgian firms had interstate branches. Jacques Playoust attended all the Queensland sales, still travelling by the increasingly shabby old Brisbane Mail. To shorten the journey a little he was driven to Hornsby to board the train. Special compartments were reserved for groups of buyers, who still vied with each other to bring the best bottle and the best delicacy for their suppers to help pass the long night. Minnie's most famous dish, which he took with him on these journeys, was a terrine made of hare, which had been specially caught for her by Sydney butchers.

In Brisbane the buyers stayed mostly at the Bellevue, a hotel adorned not only by its lace verandahs but by the three beautiful Maguires, daughters of the proprietor; one of them, Mary, became a cinema star. Towards the end of the 30s the new Lennon's Hotel was favoured, and the more adventurous buyers were choosing to fly up in the small aircraft operated by Australian National Airways.

In 1936 and 1938, Jacques and Zine were again in Europe, leaving their daughters in boarding school in Sydney — Jacques was emphatic that women should be educated to their full potential, not a common idea at the time. On one occasion they travelled on the magnificent new flagship of the Compagnie Transatlantique, the *Normandie*, which had won the Blue Riband for the fastest crossing from Le Havre to New York. (This fine ship was later trapped by the war at a dock in New York, and met its end in a mysterious fire).

Political conversation in France was now extremely pessimistic. In Germany Jacques visited his business agent, Herr Welter, who was a committed Nazi. Nevertheless Jacques, with his usual candour, talked politics during a family lunch. He was discreetly taken aside in the garden by Frau Welter, who suggested that politics was not an appropriate subject of conversation when the children and the servants might overhear. From that time Jacques, dismayed by everything he had observed, kept a close eye on German political developments.

For most Australians, few of whom had ever left the country apart from war service, the Nazi problem understandably seemed to be very remote. For Jacques this was a source of frustration, as no one around him showed any alarm or any interest in discussing it. His old Major, gardening friend and neighbour, Ken Prior of the *Bulletin*, was an exception. A silent man, he was prepared to listen patiently as they shared a morning glass and reviewed world affairs. These two old warriors observed with growing apprehension the *Anschluss* (annexation) of Austria and the fall of Czechoslovakia to the Nazis with little opposition from the rest of Europe.

The first refugees from Hitler began to arrive in Australia from Europe, tangible proof of the tyranny of the Fascist regimes. They swelled the musical audiences of Australian cities to such an extent that, to Jacques' joy, orchestral concerts required repeat performances, and Sydney discovered chamber music.

About this time Hitler froze foreign funds in Germany. Irate and highly inconvenienced, Jacques took the unusual step of telephoning his German agent, who was visiting England. If Herr Hitler had frozen Jacques' funds in Germany, Jacques was quite prepared to reciprocate by freezing Herr Welter's funds in London. Angry words were spoken, but the situation was amicably resolved by a large shipment of Rhine and Moselle wines which were stored away in Jacques' cellar some months later.

The Munich pact between Chamberlain and Hitler, 'Peace in our Time', deceived the optimists for a while, but war in Europe now seemed inevitable to Jacques and to Zine. They had been firmly warned of this by Maurice Dubrulle, their French brother-in-law. When visiting Berlin on textile affairs in the late 30s he was told privately by the French Ambassador, Monsieur André Francois-Poncet: 'War is coming. Make your preparations'. The preparations were indeed carried out quickly by the Dubrulles, who remembered all too well the occupation of 20 years back. They bought a commodious house in the fertile countryside of Normandy which adequately provided their family and their friends with accommodation and food in the black years to follow.

Another who shared the Playoust's view was the Sydney wool buyer Maurice Paroissien, who had sailed to France with the first contingent on the *Malwa* in August 1914, and had been so badly wounded the following year. He now returned to France with some of his family. His son Bernard, like him a wool buyer, was mobilised to serve in a French tank corps.

22

War Again

Following the invasion of Poland by Nazi troops, war was declared on Germany by Britain and France. The whole Polish countryside was quickly overrun with the assistance of the USSR as Stalin, who had not long before signed a Non-aggression Pact with Hitler, came quickly in from the east to claim his portion. Mr Menzies announced on the radio that Australia was also at war and Australia prepared itself to send another expeditionary force to Europe. Loyal young men in Australia again rallied to the flag, while a few Stalinists demonstrated in the city streets calling for peace.

Many of the younger French and Belgian wool buyers had lived in Australia all their lives and were more inclined to join the Australian forces than the generation who fought in World War One. These included Bob Sellosse and Jacques' cousin, Charles Playoust who joined the Australian army. Pierre Cau, Paul Gilet, Charles Martel's son Maurice and Marcel Dekyvère joined the RAAF and Gerald van Rompaey joined the RAN.

For Marie-Thérèse Playoust, World War II was a renewal of the old nightmare. The matriarch, now almost 80, had to watch while her last child, Roger, who had missed fighting in France in 1918 by only a few weeks, was on this occasion one of the first to enlist in the AIF. He had no military training, but as a medical practitioner he was commissioned with the rank of Captain, and before long he farewelled his wife and two small boys before embarking in a convoy to North Africa.

He was to serve in the Middle East for some time before taking part in the 1941 Greek campaign and the withdrawal to Crete. When the Allies were forced to withdraw from that island, Australians and New Zealanders fought a rearguard action to protect the retreat across Crete's mountainous ridge, zig-zagging along precipitous tracks towards the south coast. Lots were cast to determine which doctors would stay behind to care for a party of severely wounded Australians, who were lying in a cave and too weak to make the journey. Roger remained with the wounded, to become a prisoner of war in Germany for several years. Possibly because he spoke French as well as English, and had made friends with French prisoners of war in the same 'Oflag', the Germans looked on him with suspicion, and transferred him to the infamous Colditz fortress. There he remained till the fighting ceased in Europe in 1945.

As in the previous war, wool exporting from Australia had come to a sudden end with the declaration of war, and those wool buyers who were too old to fight found themselves without a job. Any German buyers who still remained were interned. However the British government again announced that in order to prevent leakage of commodities through neutral countries to enemy powers, it would purchase the entire Australian and New Zealand clip for the duration of the war and one year after, for the equivalent of 10.75 pence sterling per pound, a price based on the low prices of the two previous seasons.[1] From 1941 much of the top quality wool was sold on by the British to the USA for the production of military uniforms.

It was necessary for skilled appraisers to assess the different grades of wool, and most wool buyers, including Jacques, were glad to be signed up for this scheme (*Le Skime*), which was administered by a Central Wool Committee headed by the buyer Sir James McGregor. This organisation kept most of the buyers in quiet but steady employment. It was dull work, but it provided them with a measure of financial security, and sometimes their schoolboy sense of fun masked the unhappiness of their situation. The Sydney appraisers were also responsible for assessing the wool offerings in Brisbane. The old pleasures of the fine hampers en route had vanished as the shabby trains crawled north on their wearisome journey, stopping a while for the passengers to catch a quick swim near the station at Coffs Harbour.

Jacques and Zine this time were seeing the war from a distance, for Australia was once more almost entirely spared hostilities on its own soil. Anxious hours were spent around the bulky walnut cabinet 'wireless', where overseas news could just be heard through the static. The old French-Australian League of Help was re-established, with the veterans Marie-Thérèse Playoust and Dr Crivelli from Melbourne as patrons, and with Zine and the legendary Mrs T. H. Kelly as Co-presidents. Mrs Kelly, who was an office-bearer in the Alliance Francaise as well a many other organisations, used her formidable social skills to manage the fund-raising and public relations. Zine's responsibility was the workshop, which was quickly set up in the top floor sample room of Dewavrin to make comforts for the troops. A group of diligent women worked self-effacingly at this task till the end of the war, including the impressionist artist Ethel Phillips Fox, who had spent much of her youth in France. Few had the wit to buy her paintings, which are now fetching phenomenal prices.

The first European autumn and winter of 1939 were months of *drôle de guerre* (phoney war), with little military activity, but in the following Spring

Norway was overrun. Luxembourg, Belgium and Holland were invaded on 10 May by a massive German panzer tank attack, again on the Schlieffen pattern, moving rapidly again through the neutral countries to by-pass the strongly fortified Maginot Line and enter France from the rear. Remembering the four-year occupation of World War I, the population of Flanders began a mass civilian exodus, encouraged by the enemy in a deliberate attempt to block the roads and obstruct French troop movements. The roads were clogged with distraught refugees. They travelled on foot, or by car, truck, bicycle, by anything that rolled, while the Luftwaffe created panic by spraying them with machine gun fire.

Zine's family, who were now living in the Normandy countryside, sheltered dozens of people on their flight towards the south. Joseph Playoust, now widowed and very old, who had been living in an apartment near Lille since his retirement, set off towards the south on foot with his two daughters. The country was so quickly occupied by the Germans that they decided to turn for home, but the old man suffered a stroke and had to be pushed home by his daughters in a wheelbarrow. Their apartment, fortunately, had remained intact.

Unlike 1914, the French and British troops were this time speedily defeated by a highly mobile, better organised and more warlike enemy. Bernard Paroissien, a former Australian wool buyer, was wounded in this attack, and subsequently died in a hospital in Carcassonne. His brother, meanwhile, was serving in a regiment in Indochina. Soon after the defeated British Expeditionary Force was successfully evacuated from Dunkirk, France capitulated and made a separate peace with Germany. This effectively severed diplomatic relations with the other Allies.

René Deschamps had a rather different war experience. After his first child was born in August 1939 in Roubaix, where he and his Australian wife were taking leave, he was called up for military duty, became an interpreter with an English regiment in northern France and remained with them until they were evacuated from Dunkirk. Some 1000 French troops, including René, reached England, though most of them returned to France further south to continue the fight. The French defeat and armistice were not long in coming, and René was demobilised in the southern town of Perpignan, near the Spanish border. Despite the chaotic conditions he was able to get messages through to his wife, and she and the baby managed to join him. The Spanish border was now closed, and as there was no way to escape back to Australia they spent the four years of German occupation in Chateauroux in the 'free zone' of France, where the Masurel company was continuing some commercial activity. Another son was born there. It was not for a year or so after the liberation of France that the family was able to return to Australia.

Postal communications between French and Australian civilians completely ceased for the next four years, save for a rare terse message through the Red Cross. Germany occupied Paris, Flanders and the Atlantic coast, leaving the south-eastern part of France as a nominally 'free zone' to govern itself. A puppet Government led by the aged Maréchal Pétain, the former victor of Verdun, was installed at Vichy in the hope of unifying a crushed people who could not grasp the reality of their defeat.

In Sydney one of the pioneer wool buyers, Victor Dekyvère Sr, 'Old Vic', died suddenly in the sample room at Masurel's shortly after hearing news of the fall of France. The irony of their hero Pétain submitting to German rule was not lost on Jacques and Evelyne and for them, as for all their compatriots, this was a time not only of shock but also of grief and disillusion. They applied for naturalisation papers and were subsequently granted Australian citizenship. This was to be the turning point in the lives of many, who now wished to identify their loyalty to the country where they had made their home by becoming Australians.

They were heartened on the 18 June by a dramatic message delivered by an unknown voice, beamed from the BBC in London. This was General Charles de Gaulle making his first broadcast, declaring that 'France has lost a battle, but France has not lost the war!', and urging French men and women everywhere to continue the fight. He had Churchill's immediate support. Nine days later it was announced from Free French Headquarters in London that, with the agreement of the British Government, a French Volunteer Legion would be formed in Britain to continue the fight against the Nazis and liberate France. Expatriate French citizens rallied to his banner and were joined by other fugitives who had contrived to leave France for Britain in fishing boats and other craft. A small naval force was also to be assembled, using sailors from the French Navy and Merchant Navy who had defected, and ships that had been commandeered from British ports.

In Sydney there was immediate collective action, not least in *Courrier Australien*, which bore the banner 'The Organ of French Interests in Australia'. The bland second-hand articles from France which had been the basis of its literary content were now to be replaced by more pithy journalism.

André Brenac played a key part in momentous events in Sydney's French community in the next few days. Brenac had come to Sydney in 1927 to set up an enterprise with his brother Georges to buy sheepskins for the family enterprise in Mazamet. Two years later he married 'Yette' Segaert, the dynamic daughter of the Belgian consul-general; they were close friends of Jacques and Zine Playoust. When trade in skins virtually ceased during the depression, the Brenac business closed and André and his brother-in-law Paul Segaert, also a former wool buyer, became importers of glass, carpets and blankets from Europe.

The *Courrier* later described André Brenac as a man of 'ardent sincerity' who was the 'animator' of a momentous meeting of French citizens who had been summoned to the consulate in Sydney to hear an address by the consul-general, Monsieur Jean Trémoulet. The events of this meeting were dramatically recounted by Brenac himself in his private memoirs. He thought the consul's speech was pessimistic, implying that in these hard times it was a matter of each man for himself, as worse could be expected. Outraged, André Brenac asked for permission to speak. He agreed that the situation was lamentable, but asserted that retreating was no solution, that they should go forwards, fighting on and presenting a strong, united front in the face of adversity. He concluded by saying 'We must all demonstrate our feelings towards General de Gaulle!' He was given a standing ovation. At the end of the meeting a statement was prepared attesting that the French people of Australia were rallying behind the action of de Gaulle. This rebellious text was actually written on the typewriters of the consulate, and was cabled to de Gaulle.

Since they were now *persona non grata* at the consulate, André Brenac, Joseph Flipo, Jacques Playoust, Pierre Rémond, the importer Maurice Pelletier and a group of like-minded people then repaired to the Alliance Francaise rooms, where André Brenac was then secretary and Jacques vice-president. An executive committee was formed which later set up the management structure of the Free French Movement in Australia.

On his way home André Brenac encountered by chance Monsieur Magrin, owner of the *Courrier Australien,* and asked him if he would lend his support to the cause. Monsieur Magrin did not hesitate. In the issue of 28 June the *Courrier* announced in an editorial that it had lost the help and support of the French consul. Monsieur Magrin, who described himself as the proprietor, administrator and editor of this 47-year-old paper, was forbidden access to the consulate and had been requested not to communicate with any of its employees by telephone.

A week later a rejuvenated journal, prepared by André Brenac and his friends, featured a photograph of the little known de Gaulle on the front page and claimed that it was 'determined to pursue the fight for the liberation of France' and asked for the support of all French nationals and Australian francophiles. At the end of the month the *Courrier* announced that it had sent a cable to General de Gaulle stating that 'the paper placed itself at his disposal to transmit his messages to the French in Australia'. Contact between Sydney and London were particularly difficult at this time, as Germany had launched heavy bombing raids (the blitz) on London, causing havoc in communications systems.

Now in an invidious position, the consul-general, Monsieur Trémoulet, was not seen until a few weeks later, when he was photographed by a newspaper as he boarded a homeward bound ship. The vice-consul, Monsieur F. Puaux took a more independent line and left Sydney to join the newly formed Free French administration in New Caledonia.

The Sydney branch of the Alliance Francaise rallied to the Free French Movement in an extremely diplomatic way, in view of the fact that the institution was by nature apolitical. Sir Hugh Poynter, the President, wrote an article in the *Courrier*[2] defining the role of the Alliance Francais now that it was separated from its headquarters in Paris. He stated that the committee had decided unanimously to continue its work of propagating French language and culture, and to be 'a rallying place for the French and their English and Australian friends who are convinced that the eclipse of la belle France that we all love is only temporary'.

Sir Hugh Poynter was an Anglo-Australian who had inherited a baronetcy from his father, the artist and director of the National Gallery in London, Sir Edward Poynter. As a widower he had married Jacques' very amiable secretary, which created a certain bond between the two men. Jacques succeeded him as President of the Alliance in 1943, and wrote an article on its foundation for the *Courrier Australien*.[3] This is today one of the few sources of information on the history of the Sydney branch of the Alliance, as their archives appear to have been lost in one of their moves.

The French in Perth, encouraged by Dr Louis Gellé, were quick to respond to General de Gaulle's call. The French-Australian League of Help in Perth gave its support, followed by the Sydney branch, which decided to raise money and make clothing for both the Free French and the British Civilian War Fund. The League of 'Anciens Combattants', led in Sydney by Joseph Flipo, were on the whole pro de Gaulle, but Joseph Flipo respected the opinion of those who remained loyal to their old leader Maréchal Pétain, who still wore a halo as the Saviour of Verdun. According to Paulette Flipo, there was a strong feeling in the League that France and French people everywhere would go on fighting.

Monsieur Albert Sourdin, who had been Magrin's assistant, took over the direction of the *Courrier Australien* in July/August 1940, together with an editorial board consisting of André Brenac and a number of his sympathisers. The *Courrier* was in top form, proclaiming the paper's mission to 'promote in people's hearts and minds the will to win'. Public relations were also addressed: on General de Gaulle's behalf the *Courrier* sent a message of condolence to the Australian Prime Minister, Mr Menzies, after the tragic air crash which killed three of his ministers, James Fairbairn, Sir Henry Gullett and Geoffrey Street.

By September the paper was labelling itself as 'The Weekly Journal of the Free French Movement in the Pacific', with the symbolic Cross of Lorraine alongside, and patriotic blue, white and red stripes on its front page. It commended the re-election of Franklin D. Roosevelt as President of the United States, as the candidate most sympathetic to the Allied cause.

At the end of the year General de Gaulle invited André Brenac to become his representative in Sydney, thereby launching him into a new career in diplomacy. He was later to promote the Free French Movement throughout Australia with diplomatic status. Dr Louis Gellé represented the Free French in Perth, and Pierre Mann in Melbourne.

More importantly, French islands in the South Pacific were rallying to the Free French, despite efforts from the metropolitan Vichy government to keep its colonies out of the war. The Resident Commissioner of the New Hebrides, Henri Sautot, was quick to voice his support of de Gaulle, offering to send volunteers to join him. Initially the Governor of New Caledonia would not commit himself, however with encouragement from the majority of settlers and the masterly diplomacy of Captain H. A. Showers, RAN, commanding officer of HMAS *Adelaide* standing by off Noumea Harbour, the people of Noumea were soon able to acclaim Monsieur Sautot as their new Governor.[4] The Vichy sloop *Dumont D'Urville* was provisioned and invited to leave New Caledonian waters, the Vichy supporters in the former administration were quietly evacuated to Saigon, and the government of the island could now declare its loyalty to the Free French Movement.[5] When Japan came into the war at the end of the following year it was denied this important source of nickel, and these islands were to serve as crucial bases for the Army and Navy of the USA in the coming battles of the Coral Sea and Guadalcanal.

With the Japanese entry into the war announced by the surprise bombing of Pearl Harbour in December 1941, the threat of hostilities came very close to Australian territory and gave a whole new dimension to Australia's war effort. Jacques' neighbour and friend, Ken Prior, had three sons. When they turned 18, each of them joined the army and spent the rest of the war in New Guinea.

As the Japanese advanced from the Philippines, Malaya, Singapore, Borneo, Timor and northern New Guinea, Australians prepared for an invasion as best they could, with pitifully few defences. A number of schools were evacuated to the country. Waterfront houses in Sydney were sold for a song. Civilians kept in their garages a store of petrol to permit a quick escape, for petrol was now severely rationed. Households practised serious air raid drills, and learnt to black-out their windows, expecting that Australian cities would be subjected to something like the London blitz, but only Darwin and Broome really suffered.

Sydney had one adventurous night when a few Japanese midget submarines followed the Manly ferry through the wire boom that stretched across the entrance to Sydney's main harbour. They released a number of torpedoes, seeking to damage several American warships which were in port. As depth charges were dropped there was considerable noise and light over the Harbour, particularly around the Mosman peninsula where one of the submarines was sunk. The warships remained intact, but a number of civilian workers at the naval dockyard who were sleeping on a ferry boat, the *Kuttabul*, at Garden Island lost their lives when it sank after the wall alongside was hit by a Japanese torpedo.

Jacques' depleted wine cellar now had a reinforced ceiling so that it could serve as a shelter in an air raid. The shelter was used once only, for ten minutes, in response to the air raid siren which sounded after another submarine sent a few shells across Bondi and slightly damaged a block of flats. Sydney's people felt heroic, but Jacques and Zine reacted more calmly to the raid, as they had seen worse in earlier days. They suffered much more anguish as the government of Occupied France conceded more and more to the Nazis, fearing for their relatives, now living mostly in Normandy. They gave all their efforts to supporting the Free French movement, which continued to broadcast its messages of encouragement from London through the BBC.

The bitter divisions with certain of their compatriots who retained loyalty to Pétain's government saddened them greatly. These people regrettably remained blind to Laval's compromises with the Nazis. In some cases friendships were severed, and even brothers were separated by incompatible opinions, not unlike the divisions caused by the Dreyfus case half a century earlier.

The Free French now had a small presence in the Pacific, with the rallying of New Caledonia, New Hebrides and Tahiti to the Free French Movement, and Australians became more conscious of their island neighbours. Volunteers were recruited from the Pacific region for the Free French Army, and Tahitians were to see combat against the Germans in Africa in 1943. A Free French destroyer, *Le Triomphant,* used Sydney Harbour as its repair base and its officers were frequent visitors at Jacques and Zine's house. A Seaman's Hostel was established by the Free French Movement for the sailors and the French Australian League contributed clothing and comforts. The navy and white sailor berets with red pompoms were a frequent sight in Sydney streets, a variation from the white American gob caps. They made friends all over the city. A number were to return to live here after the war, and 32 of the crew married Australian women.[6]

Along with several others living in Australia, Jean Pierre Sourdin, the son of the director of the *Courrier Australien,* joined the Free French Navy as a matelot and served on another Free French ship, the *Cap des Palmes,* which visited Sydney Harbour several times between 1941 and 1944. Like all recruits to Free French forces, he was put on a condemned list by the Vichy government. Another Free French vessel, the submarine *Surcouf* also visited Sydney.

After Pearl Harbour the wool appraisers' tedious train journeys to Brisbane became even less attractive. Hundreds of thousands of American troops were now crowded into the city, and General Macarthur and his staff had appropriated Lennon's Hotel for their own headquarters. Its dining rooms were crowded with their female escorts, sporting enormous orchid corsages. As accommodation was extremely tight, some of the wool appraisers were allotted rooms in a small shabby hotel across the river in South Brisbane, an area designated by the US authorities as a recreation place for Negro servicemen. Jacques, who was never fazed by finding himself in a different milieu, liked to go down to the bar for a chat but he may well have fazed the Americans by his stories which began with 'In the LAST war ... '

23

Indo Chine

A sad and little known campaign had taken place during the early years of World War II which caused a great deal of mental and physical suffering to those involved.[1] At the outbreak of war young French-Australians of military age had once again found themselves called up for army duty, this time receiving orders through the French consulate to travel to Saigon, the capital of Indochina, for military training before being sent to France. Saigon is now Ho Chi Minh City and Indochina at present exists as the three separate states of Vietnam, Laos and Cambodia. However, Indochina was then a protectorate which had been acquired by the French around 1862, and in 1939 was under threat from the Japanese who had invaded and conquered southern China. Two years before its attack on Pearl Harbour the Japanese empire was still consolidating its conquest, and troops were massing along the Indochinese border.

The first contingent of about 30 left for Saigon in early December 1939 on the *Pierre Loti*, a Messageries Maritimes freighter which plied the South Pacific. The journey took about a month, picking up nickel in Noumea and copra in Port Vila. The reservists included a number of wool buyers, among them René Dumortier, André Gaillard and Robert Mortelier. Two of them, Jean Paroissien and Pierre Scamps, were sons of men who had left Sydney to join the French army in World War I. André Flipo was the nephew of Joseph Flipo, who had sailed on the *Malwa* with Jacques Playoust in August 1914, and who had become a firm friend. Twenty-five years after their own departure, these two veterans watched the departure of the *Pierre Loti* with great sadness.

Three months later the same ship carried another larger French-Australian contingent bound for Saigon, again including a good number of wool buyers: Henri Bel, Fernand Bourgeois, André Cau, René Dutriez, Jacques Fourlinnie, Adrien Fiévet, Emile Gaillet, René Moniez, Pierre and Paul Robin, Marcel Richard, and several of their wives and children. Jacques' cousin, Paul Playoust, the younger brother of 'Little John', sailed with this group in the *Pierre Loti*. Another reservist was a Western Australian farmer and wool grower, Henry Jacques Stanley de Pierres who, like his French-Australian father the Vicomte G.C.B de Pierres, had responded to France's call in 1914. In 1971, Stanley's son Paul de Pierres was to serve in southern Indochina, but this time with the Australian forces in the Vietnam war.

The special problems of men of dual nationality are illustrated by the two Australian-born Dekyvère brothers, Victor and Marcel. Both reported as ordered to the French consulate for medical examinations, but Marcel was less than enthusiastic about participating in this exercise and ignored his mobilisation orders. He felt himself to be an Australian, and he longed to use his flying skills, therefore he chose to enlist in the RAAF. He trained in the Empire Air Training scheme, and was sent to Britain as a pilot. There he was assigned to air-sea rescues flying a Walrus, a small flying boat, and his log-book describes the daily sorties to pick up bodies, dead or alive, from the Channel. His D.F.C. was awarded for a brave and effective rescue when he was flying his Walrus close to the Normandy coast near Cherbourg. Although under attack from big guns on shore and aircraft from above, he brought down his small aircraft into very rough seas to save 13 of the crew of a ditched Flying Fortress. A measure of his laconic 'Australianness' could be made from his cheerful warning to the rescued airmen that they were probably safer in the sea than taking off with him.

The French bureaucracy, however, could not handle this problem. Marcel was now categorised as *insoumis* (insubordinate) and was threatened with sequestration of property and being shot on sight. A little concerned, he tried when in London in 1942 to regularise his situation with the authorities at the Free French headquarters in Bedford Square. He placed his problem before General de Gaulle, who agreed that the administration was incompetent and assured the young airman that he would fix it. The General pointed to a shelf containing a heap of passports, saying 'I am sponsoring these people to be flown in to France to fight with the Resistance and they will do it for me'. He thought it would take six months; 30 years later Marcel was still being chased by military officialdom.

Raymond Wattel, like Marcel, ignored his mobilisation orders and joined the AIF. When called up for duty in Indochina he was delighted to be able to appear at the ship in his Australian officer's uniform to explain why he could not embark with the other reservists. He was in the 9th Division and later fought in the Middle East and New Guinea. Victor Dekyvère, unlike his brother, had obeyed the order to report to Saigon for military training.

Roger Pelletier, who represented the importers Ballande & Co. in Australia, had sailed in the first contingent and in his memoir described the campaign in Indochina as 'neither gorgeous nor glamorous'. It was to be a futile and demoralising exercise. They were mostly raw recruits, and were submitted to basic training under seasoned Corsican sergeants of the regular colonial army. They were badly equipped, and conditions were primitive. A number found themselves in hospital in Phnom Penh with a variety of tropical diseases caused by infections, poor diet and humid conditions.

On completion of their training they were sent to defend the northern border against the Japanese who, though still not at war with the Allies, were claiming the use of the crucial seaport facilities at Haiphong. There were some skirmishes around the border town of Lang Son after the French refused this request. Paul Robin, now a Lieutenant, was sent on patrol into the mountains and lost his life, either killed by the Japanese or, as Jeanne Renault thought, shot in the back by an Annamite sniper, for already Ho Chi Minh was forming the nucleus of the Vietcong.

European events were now overtaking military plans in the colony. Nazi tanks had rapidly smashed their way through France, leading to her defeat in June 1940 — this was devastating for the morale of the French recruits. Other powers recognised a military opportunity. Thailand, then called Siam, took advantage of the situation by attempting to annex Cambodia. During 1941 the Axis Powers coerced the government of a crushed France to allow the Japanese to occupy the whole of Indochina and to appropriate its resources without any resistance whatsoever. Indochina became part of the Japanese 'Co-Prosperity Sphere', with Vichy French Government officials in nominal command. This later facilitated the Japanese push south to Malaya and Singapore.

Conditions deteriorated for the contingent from Australia, which was left for months to its own devices. The French-born men were at first forbidden to return to Australia to their families and were offered instead a passage to France, which was now dominated by Germany. None of them chose this undesirable option. Those actually born in Australia and therefore of dual nationality, such as Victor Dekyvère, André Gaillard, Jean Paroissien, Roger Pelletier and Paul Playoust, were more fortunate and were the first allowed to leave. They secured passages at their own expense on the *Suwa Maru*, travelling back via the Philippines in May 1941 on the last Japanese freighter to come to Sydney before the attack on Pearl Harbour.

Finally they all managed to get home to Australia as best they could. The *Neptuna*, later to be sunk in a Japanese raid on Darwin, brought back other wool buyers: Henri Bel and his wife, Charles Bourgeois, René Dutriez, Auguste Dalle, René Dumortier, Albert Fievez, Jacques Fourlinnie, Marcel Richard, Julien Sémat and his wife. They were thin and in varying degrees of ill-health, as well as severely depressed by the national defeat. Jean Paroissien was suffering from hepatitis. Marcel Richard spent months in Prince Alfred Hospital feeling the effects of tropical ulcers and amoebic dysentery. Both he and Victor Dekyvère later tried to join the Australian army but were rejected on medical grounds. Jacques Fourlinnie joined the RAAF. The tall West Australian woolgrower Stanley de Pierres volunteered for the AIF on his return but was 'manpowered', as his farming work was considered an essential industry. After a few weeks of recuperation André Flipo tried to enlist in the Free French forces, but failed the medical test. He then assisted André Brenac with the supply side of the Free French Movement, mostly in provisioning New Caledonia.

Another wool buyer in the group mobilised for service in Indochina was Henri Renault, but this sorry exercise proved indirectly to be of great benefit to Sydney gastronomy. His story is a saga splendidly described by his widow Jeanne Renault, who is now a lively woman of 90. Henri Renault came from the great silk centre of Lyon but as his father had a woollen mill in Normandy he was drawn to a career in wool rather than silk. Having gained experience at a Bradford mill, he performed his compulsory military service, graduating as an artillery officer.

In the late 20s he was sent to Melbourne as a buyer for the Tourcoing firm of Mote Meillassoux, but the Depression in the early 30s resulted in his being retrenched. He returned to France to look for employment and was back in Australia in 1933 as a freelance buyer. In 1934 he worked for himself as a client of the brokers W. M. Haughton, buying wool directly from growers.

Henri had a strong interest in food and wine — almost inevitable in those raised in Normandy and Lyon — and Jeanne, whose family was from Roubaix, shared these tastes. The couple took pleasure in entertaining like-minded friends, and they often met in the 1930s at the Rhine Castle cellars under the Royal Exchange in Pitt Street, Sydney. This establishment was owned by J. K. Walker, a man who was keen to promote good quality wine in a city where beer and spirits predominated.

Renault persuaded Walker that if the cellar could provide a light lunch, he would encourage a number of his wool buyer friends to meet there. An old second-hand stove was bought at Lawson's auctions, on which Henri and his friends took turns to present a satisfying dish for each other every Tuesday. Jo Hollebecq specialised in crépes, also a Flemish dish made with rabbit, prunes and red wine which he liked to call 'Wild Duck'.

Rhine Castle Wines quickly became a favourite rendezvous for a group of French, Belgian and Australian gourmets and it was here that the Wine and Food Society of Australia had its origins. By the outbreak of war it had 180 members. In 1940, before Renault sailed to Indochina, the Society presented him with a fine silver tray which was signed with names of wool buyers like Max Brunninghausen, Edouard Dulieu, Jo Hollebecq, and wine authorities, Douglas Lamb and the neurosurgeon Dr Gilbert Phillips. The inscription thanked Renault for his 'invaluable and unselfish service to the Society since its inception'.

After Renault arrived in Saigon in 1940 he was detailed to a battery at the Cape Saint Jacques (now Vung Tau) at the mouth of the Mekong River as an artillery officer. The battery consisted of a beautifully polished and ancient cannon which was not to fire a single shot. Jeanne who, with their baby, had joined him in Saigon, described the scene when thousands of Japanese troops arrived by ship into Saigon harbour, lining the decks of their ships in full uniform with very long swords trailing on the ground, and standing in strict formation like small tin soldiers. As the puppet government in Vichy had instructed, not a shot was fired and the Japanese were allowed to enter unimpeded to take over the entire administration of the city. The Japanese were under orders to behave correctly, and the French soldiers had no contact with them. Four or five months went by in an atmosphere of gloom as the whole contingent refused the offer to be repatriated to France. Soon goods became very scarce and a curfew was imposed.

While they waited, Henri Renault built up some useful experience in running the canteen and providing food for the officers' mess. He was in his element, and learnt quite a lot about Vietnamese cooking. He even set up a piggery to provide the canteen with good pork. When the repatriation orders were finally changed and the men were allowed to go home by whatever means they could find, the Renaults had a difficult and roundabout passage to Australia, finally boarding the *Neptuna* — probably the last available ship — at Manila. The Philippines were invaded by the Japanese only a few months later.

Henri, Jeanne and their baby arrived back in Sydney in September 1941 to find that there was no work in the non-existent wool trade, which had been replaced by the government wool appraisal scheme, and all the jobs in this scheme had already been assigned. Henri was not only penniless but he was also seriously ill with cerebral malaria complicated by diabetes.

After a fantastic welcome home party given at Prince's restaurant by the Wine and Food Society, a group of old friends headed by the President, Gilbert Phillips, suggested that the couple should open a restaurant. The Society would provide the capital to initiate it so as to have a permanent home in which to hold its meetings. A company was bought, and space in Ash Street was leased from Paling's music firm. An advertisement was placed in the *Courrier Australien* in 1942 announcing the opening of a Restaurant Francais by Monsieur and Madame Renault. It was to be called 'The Hermitage', and specialised in *cuisine bourgeoise* (middle-class home cooking), with a private room for meetings. This became one of the first seriously French restaurants in Sydney to be opened since the demise of the turn-of-the-century Paris House, and survived for 16 years. Henri and Jeanne Renault were dedicated epicures and naturally talented restaurateurs, despite the lack of formal training.

Henri and his many friends had always liked to *faire la popote*, to cook and dine at each other's places, at a time when there were few opportunities to find any sophisticated cooking in a Sydney restaurant. He was the mainstay in the kitchen of the Hermitage till he succumbed to his illness. The restaurant would certainly have failed had Jeanne Renault not shown the capacity to work extremely hard, looking after the marketing, the staff, the linen, the garbage, as well as the kitchen. Since it was wartime, there were inevitably shortages of staff so René Dutriez, an unemployed wool buyer after his return from the Indochina campaign, filled in for a while as a grill cook. The reputation of the restaurant was quickly established as a centre of gastronomy, particularly with the wool buyers, despite the difficulties of complying with wartime shortages and restrictions which, among other things, capped the prices of meals at five shillings. The Wine and Food Society now met in its private room for lunch every Tuesday.

The restaurant also promoted the name of Maurice O'Shea of Mount Pleasant in the Hunter Valley, who was making high quality wines. For some time this vigneron's reputation had been well known to wool buyers and, after attending the wool sales in Newcastle, they would seek him out in his vineyard at Pokolbin to purchase his wine.

Maurice O'Shea was born of an Irish father and a French mother. A small man with thick glasses, he was spoken of with great respect by his colleagues as an idealist, dedicated to achieving the highest standards in his craft, and by Jeanne Renault as a *pur sang* (thoroughbred). He had studied oenology at Montpellier, loved Bordeaux wines and tried arduously to raise the quality of wine making in Australia, and to interest a population of beer drinkers in the pleasures of drinking fine wine. His friends liked to try his ability to name different wines in blind tests, bringing in ring-ins from other states, but he never failed. O'Shea had a real affinity with Henri Renault, and a close friendship developed between the two epicures. The link still existed between the Hermitage and Johnny Walker's Wine Cellar, to the point that Walker Wines now advertised themselves as suppliers to the Free French Forces.

24

The War Ends

D–Day came at last. When the landings were made on the bleak beaches of southern Normandy everyone crowded round the radio, French men and women listening for every detail, seeking clues to the location of the battles in a countryside many of them knew. There was joy at the hope of liberation, and also anxiety — in Zine's case, her family's house a little south of Lisieux appeared to be very close to some of the fighting. Time seemed to pass very slowly for her till the area was finally cleared of Germans, when Red Cross messages began to arrive concerning her mother, her brothers and sisters stating that they were all safe and well and the house was intact. The newsreels brought emotional images — the Allies entering Paris in fine August weather, with General Leclerc's Free French tank division very visible, and the figure of General de Gaulle, towering above the rest, as they marched down the Champs Elysées to a Mass of Thanksgiving at Nôtre Dame Cathedral, ignoring the German snipers still hiding on the rooftops.

In mid August American and Free French, with the help of an American-British airborne division, landed in the bay of St. Tropez as part of 'Operation Anvil'. The little Free French destroyer *Le Triomphant*, which had been a popular visitor to Sydney, assisted in the landing but was badly damaged and a number of its crew were killed or injured, to the sorrow of their Australian friends.

Gradually prisoners of war were released to the Red Cross from their camps in Germany. Roger Playoust, who had spent some years in the chilly stone castle of Colditz, was in poor health. He had been afflicted with actinomycosis, a lung infection which was not easily treatable in the days before the availability of modern antibiotics. His mother, Marie-Thérèse, was not to see him again; she had died suddenly on 23 October, 1944 at home, as she was finishing her meal. At least she had known that Roger was liberated and was on his way home. He returned to his wife and children and his medical practice, but he never fully recovered his health.

After the liberation of France by the Allies, the first letters to Zine began to arrive from France, now by an improved airmail service. It was a joyous time, full of optimistic plans for reunions with her 87-year-old mother and siblings, for the end was at last in sight.

Despite the crucial American naval victory in the Coral Sea, the Pacific war was still dragging on as Americans and Australians fought to push back the Japanese, one island at a time. Marcel Dekyvère was now back after four years of service in Britain, and was acting as personal assistant to the Chief of Air Staff with the responsibility of Air Sea Rescue operations in the islands. Gerald van Rompaey was also serving there in Air-Sea Rescue, but on a naval reconnaissance vessel. At the end of the war he was using his language skills as a Royal Australian Navy liaison officer with the Netherlands Navy in what is now Indonesia. Maurice Martel lost his life in the RAAF.

Then came the bombing of Hiroshima and Nagasaki, and it was over. Little by little, Australian soldiers and prisoners of war happily returned home, to discover that peacetime life would present them with many difficulties to face.

After years of government control, the private wool sales resumed throughout Australia. The first post-war wool season in 1945–46 opened with great excitement, with 140 buyers at the auction. The buyers held their catalogues tensely, unused now to the process of bidding after years of routine appraisal for the government. They were buying for most manufacturing countries, although German and Japanese houses were still banned. The Sydney Wool Exchange, situated opposite the statue of Thomas Sutcliffe Mort in Macquarie Place, now needed three sale rooms for simultaneous selling; the big lots were sold in the number 1 room, the 'star' lots of less than five bales in the number 2 room, with number 3 room designated for the sale of cross-bred wool. The return to civilian activities had resulted in strong demand, and prices rose quickly.

These were the first competitive sales to take place after the wartime regime but there remained an accumulated surplus of 10 million bales of appraised wool acquired by the British Government, and a plan was devised to release the bales progressively over a long period to ease the stockpiles in such a way as to avoid a slump. An agreement to this effect was made in 1946 between the governments of Britain, South Africa, Australia and New Zealand, but it was to take nine years before profits were finally distributed.

Many of the old French and Belgian firms such as Brunninghausen, Cauillez, CIL, Comptoirs Louis Kint, Dassonville, Dekyvere, Dewavrin Fils & Cie., Dewez, Dreyfus, Leroux Brame Fils, Fuhrmann, Gheysens, Kreglinger & Fernau, Lahousse, Masurel Fils, Moch & Odelin, Prevost & Co., Prouvost Lefebvre, Segard, Simonius Vischer, Vanlaine, Wattinne Bossut, Henri Wattinne, Wenz and Co. resumed business.

The system was still dynastic and they recruited sons and sometimes grandsons of their former buyers:

- Victor and Marcel Dekyvère revived their late father's firm.
- Rene Deschamps, after his return from Occupied France, resumed his career as a wool buyer for Masurel, and later became a director of its Australian subsidiary.
- Jim Dewez succeeded his father 'Gus', the third generation to work in the firm.
- Xavier Droulers joined his father, Jean, at Masurel and was to work there for 42 years, finally managing the New Zealand branch.
- Jo Flipo joined his father at Dewavrin, where his uncle Jean Lamérand was already well established, and Andre Flipo took over the direction of Dewavrin in Melbourne.
- Armand George followed his father into Moch et Odelin.
- Phillip Hentze, son of Frederick, became manager of L.H. Bell Pty Ltd.
- Marcel Leman Jr and his brother, Raymond, also followed in their father's footsteps.
- Georges Nopenaire continued his career with CIL in Melbourne; like his father Augustin, he also acted as honorary Belgian consul.
- Gervais ('Boy') Parmentier and his brother, Paul, joined their father at Henri Wattine, and Gervais succeeded his father as director when he retired. Their cousin Andre Parmentier was employed by Camille Gheysens.
- Jean Paroissien, also a third generation wool buyer, resumed work for Moch et Odelin after a long convalescence following the Indochina campaign.
- Two of the late Joseph Playoust's sons continued in wool. Charles, after his Australian Army service, became the principal of Wattine-Bossut, and Fernand worked independently.
- Bob Sellosse returned from army service to work as a buyer, like his late father Maurice. He was employed by Voreux-Cau.
- Maurice Van Den Driessche Sr and his son Maurice Jr both worked for the French firm of Vanlaine.
- Alfred Van Rompaey's son Leslie, and his grandson Gerald resumed their careers in wool, now buying for Harry Ervin.
- Raymond Wattel, after his discharge from the Australian Army, was employed by Louis Kint, with whom his father Benjamin had worked in the 1930s.

As for the Australians, Charles Churcher now had his own company, with K. G. Churcher as a junior buyer. His son, John Churcher, joined Prévost and Co., an Australian firm founded by an expatriate Frenchman. Charles

Mort, a great-grandson of Thomas Sutcliffe Mort, was a buyer for Felt and Textiles of Australia.

With his usual resilience, Jacques planned to revive the family woolbuying firm with his brother Maurice, as he had done successfully after World War I. A photograph in a Sydney newspaper of Jacques Playoust in shirtsleeves examining a bale of wool in the stores bore the caption 'Continental Eyes on Our Wool'.

In early 1947 Jacques booked a passage, with Zine and their two daughters, in order to visit the mills in northern France. This time, however, his health was no longer strong, and his passport photos showed a thinner, tired face.

A few weeks before the departure date he became ill, and was diagnosed as having an inoperable cancer of the lung. He returned from hospital to spend his last weeks with his family in the home he had loved so much, for a time able to find the interest to re-read his old volumes of Plato. His brother Roger, now a civilian and back in general medical practice, looked after him with great devotion. It was not a long nor an extremely painful illness and he faced it with uncomplaining courage, in the way he had borne the physical and mental sufferings of two wars, calmly accepting the inevitable. He died on 2 February, 1947 aged 63, the exact age at which his own father had died as the first war was ending and, appropriately, in the country he had adopted and which had taken him and his family as its own.

Epilogue

Several months after Jacques Playoust's death, Zine and her daughters booked passages to Antwerp on the *Abbekerk*, a Dutch freighter, despite the difficulty of finding a berth at the time. They were able to spend almost a year in France with their family, where each had their various wartime adventures to tell, giving a more subtle slant to the stories of the Resistance when it appeared, sadly, that many old scores had been settled. The mills in Roubaix and Tourcoing were beginning to turn, and once again were using beautiful Australian wool. An uncle presented his nieces with lengths of his fine fabric woven from wool bought by Jacques before his illness.

Although business was reviving it was a period of great political instability in France, with Stalin's supporters playing a devious game. It was the beginning of the 'Cold War', and Zine was envied for living in Australia, as many seemed convinced another invasion would come from the East and that France would go the way of Hungary and Czechoslovakia.

A new wave of young wool buyers were now sent to Australia by northern French and Belgian firms to buy Australian wool in order to re-establish their textile industries, which had once again suffered under German occupation. After a youth spent under a tyrannical Nazi regime, these men saw Australia as a land of sunshine and abundance.

For example, Gérard Demeulemeester was sent from Tourcoing in 1947 with his wife and children to take over the direction of CIL after José Balthasar, who had founded the Sydney office of this company in the early 1900s, was persuaded that 90 was a suitable age to retire. Demeulemeester had spent the years of the occupation working for this company, using false identity papers and ration cards to avoid forced labour in Germany, and leapt at the opportunity to make a new life in the Antipodes. After some years of adjustment to a new language and new customs, this family is now permanently settled in Sydney.

The new generation of buyers participated exuberantly in the phenomenal wool boom in the 1950–51 season, thinking the good days would never end. The high prices were partly due to the demand for uniforms during the Korean War, and partly to the emergence of Japan as a buyer, still dealing unofficially through other firms as the Japanese were as yet not allowed to trade independently in Australia.

The inevitable slump was not far behind, to such an extent that the auctions ceased for months.[1] The improvement in synthetic fibres, which involved only three procedures to produce a fibre, became a real threat to wool which required nineteen. Furthermore cheaper labour costs in the developing Third World countries presented insurmountable competition for the European woollen textile industry.

In the 1960s and 1970s the great woollen mills in Bradford, Roubaix-Tourcoing, Rheims and Verviers simply closed and stood empty after more than a century of prosperity, and their looms were sold off to Asia. A number of Japanese mills followed suit when their labour costs increased as their country became wealthy. Most of the great French merchant houses such as Cauillez and Masurel ceased business in Australia. Prévost and Co. closed in 1961, Henri Wattine in 1967, Wattine Bossut in 1970, Wenz and Voreux-Cau in 1979.

Some French companies survived the slump. CIL was first established in Sydney about 1907 under the name of Etablissements Flipo-Segard. It is still under the same family ownership in Tourcoing, and buying Australian wool, but has also diversified into other activities. Prouvost-Lefèbvre is now owned by a conglomerate, Chargeurs, one of whose ventures is an important topmaking mill in Wagga Wagga. Anselme Dewavrin, which in 1992 celebrated its centenary in Australia, is still concerned with wool as well as a number of other interests.

Some buyers returned home to France and Belgium, but many simply moved to other employment, remaining in the country to which they had become so attached. Post-war arrivals from France and Belgium had included Albert Bribosia, Albert Byrom, Claude Cagé, André Catteau, Claude Davrain, Robert Debuf, Henri Deldicque, Gustave Deltoer, Gérard Demeulemeester, Raphael Desplechin, Francois Devos, César Esterman, Jacques Goebbels, Jean Hourez, Paul Lamblin, Bernard Lehembre, Jean Lieutenant, Felix Manchoulas, Pierre Marecaux, Georges Mathon, Jean Mourez, Guy Pascal, Michel Poulain, Emile Quennoy, Jacques Roussel, J. Van den Heyden, Jacques Vanderhaegen, and René Vandervaere. All these men and their families finally settled permanently in Australia. Groups of these nostalgic old 'woollies' still meet regularly for lunch recalling the camaraderie of the Sales, even the smell of lanolin in the wool stores. Their own children, however, work in other fields.

The venerable wool exchanges at 11 Macquarie Place in Sydney, and in King Street, Melbourne, which had witnessed the generation of so much of Australia's wealth are today defunct. The sales now take place in bleak warehouses in the outer suburbs. The Sydney sales have been held for some years in Yennora, a vast covered space of over 1° hectares, all on one floor, which is said to be the largest slab of concrete in Australia, but the future of this site is also under question. The remaining buyers complain of chaotic marketing conditions.

The outlook of the individual wool buyer is indeed tenuous, as there is little use for his ancient craft skills, and the whole system is to be streamlined in a way which is still unclear. Already the wool can be measured objectively by instruments capable of determining width, colour and yield, and could well be sold by description, sight unseen, by a form of mail order catalogue. Not all would agree that this is desirable.

The early Belgian pioneers in wool have left several generations of Australian progeny. The great-grandchildren of Jules Renard, Alfred van Rompaey and Frederick Hentze live in Australia but work very successfully in fields other than wool. A number are prominent in the legal profession.

The old established Dewez firm, like many others, went into liquidation in the 1974 crash, but Jim Dewez, the grandson of Toussaint, continued to buy wool on his own, largely for Italy, till he retired at the end of 1996 when, for the first time in 116 years, no Dewez attended the sale room floor. His children chose other careers, as did the many Australian descendants of Toussaint Dewez in Victoria and New South Wales. Toussaint's granddaughter Margaret used her European experience and proficiency in languages to work with the Good Neighbour Council and the Migrant Resource Centre.

The firm of S. H. Ervin, who had employed several Belgians, closed in 1963 and 14 years later Harry Ervin died.

Families like the Lamérands, the Droulers and the Flipos had numerous Australian progeny, with the Droulers possibly holding the record. Jean Droulers' marriage to a French woman from his own region had produced eight children in Australia, and there are now 90 Australian descendants from this union. Their sons and daughters and grandchildren work in many disciplines. Xavier Droulers followed his father working for Masurel, and remained with this firm for 42 years until what he called the 'bleak and hard years' during the slump in French woollen textiles, when the firm finally closed down.

Some of the Paroissien family remained in Australia. Possibly the best known is Victor Paroissien's grandson Leon, who was Director of the Sydney Museum of Contemporary Art from its inception in 1989 until 1997. He was then appointed Chairman of the Public Art Advisory Committee of the Olympic Coordination Authority, preparing for the Sydney Olympic Games in 2000. He also holds a number of international editorial and committee responsibilities in the field of modern art.

The Hermitage restaurant in Ash Street lasted for 16 years, and Henri Renault died shortly before it closed. Jeanne remained in Sydney, and her daughter married an Australian. René Dutriez, who had worked in this restaurant after the Indochina campaign, resumed his career in wool.

He was to lose his life in an air crash in India while on a business journey to Europe.

Jean-Pierre Sourdin, once the young Free French matelot, took over from his father the direction of the *Courrier Australien* and is still at the helm.

André Brenac had a successful career in the French consular service. Port-Said was an adventurous posting, as he was in office at the period of the nationalisation of the Suez Canal by the Egyptian government, followed by military intervention by Britain and France. He was responsible for the successful evacuation of French nationals in the area. He remains in France in retirement, but one of his sons still lives in Sydney.

As for Marie Leplat, Jacques' cousin and correspondent throughout World War I, she later married René Delos, and after living in Montana (USA), Indochina and Geneva they returned to Paris. She retained her great friendship for Jacques, which she extended to his wife and later on to their daughters. She celebrated her 101st birthday in 1998, remaining very youthful mentally and greatly intrigued by her Australian connection.

There are now no descendants of Georges and Marie-Thérèse Playoust in the male line, despite their six sons — in part a legacy of World War I. Their eldest son Georges had one son, the Rev. Alfred Playoust who lives in California, and a daughter Marcelle Cowdrill, who has several grandchildren, all in Australia. Jacques had two daughters. Maurice had no children. Roger had two sons, Mark and Anthony, before leaving for World War II and prisoner-of-war camp. Mark followed a scholarly career of the very first rank in medicine, then decided to train as a Jesuit priest. Shortly before his ordination he was killed in a tragic car accident. Anthony, also deceased, had an only child, Catherine, who has combined her mathematical genius with a career in music.

The grand double wedding of 1908 resulted in many descendants, but Marguerite's progeny live in France. Her son 'young' Alfred Decouvelaere visited Sydney with his wife after an interval of 60 years in France. He was still a British subject as well as a French national. He asked in a strong Australian accent to see the 'new bridge' across the Harbour and to eat a meat pie. An invitation was arranged for him to visit the much embellished 'Murrulla' by the then owner, the impresario Harry M. Miller and, as children do, he remembered best the kitchen and pantry. His brother Georges Decouvelaere returned to Australia with his wife to convalesce after his imprisonment by the Japanese in Indochina in World War II. The ties with Australia remain very strong and a number of their own children have visited the country in search of their roots.

The other bride, Marie-Thérèse Polin, had many great grandchildren from her daughter's marriage to John Lamérand, who all live in Australia.

The sons of Georges' brother Joseph were more prolific. Paul, who had participated in the Indochina campaign, was the father of an Australian boy of the same name, whose own daughter chose a career in medicine. Charles' sons live in France. Fernand Playoust worked all his life as a wool buyer, but his only son John became an architect in Sydney, a profession taken up in turn by his own sons. A century after his grandfather's arrival in Australia, however, traditional interests came to the fore. John is now engaged in growing wool in New South Wales, and more recently superfine wool which is admirably suited to the weaving of fine textiles. He is also concerned in topmaking,[2] thereby adding much needed value to Australia's venerable export.

Evelyne Playoust, 'Zine', lived on in the house where she had raised her children, helped by the beloved Minnie. The strong, forthright Minnie, who had instilled so many 'Aussie' values into the family, was deeply mourned when she died of cancer in the late 60s. Zine moved into smaller surroundings, but still in her village of Mosman. She was a diligent and loving grandmother, and also cherished her weekly conversation groups at the Alliance Francaise till she died at the age of 80.

Her six Australian grandchildren pursued careers in teaching, architecture, medicine, health administration, commerce and law. All have retained a special and affectionate link with France as do their own offspring.

In retrospect, it can be said that Georges Playoust demonstrated great prescience when, in 1907,[3] he foretold:

'No doubt some of us will end our days in Australia, and when the time comes will lie down in deep eternal rest, but better than our bones we will give Australia the children of our flesh and blood.'

Appendix I

Under the classification of Wool Merchants or Wool Brokers, Sands Directories for Sydney before 1914 list the following French and Belgian firms. In some cases the firms were not listed under their own names but under those of their buyers. Hyphenated names are often the two surnames in a marriage, as was the custom in northern France.

Roubaix and Tourcoing firms:
Henri Cauillez et Cie 1895
Flipo-Segard 1907
Segard and Co. 1908
Etablissements Pierre Flipo 1909 (which became CIL in 1935)
  represented by J. Balthasar
P. Lamérand, representing Anselme Dewavrin & Fils 1907
Lorthiois Frères 1907
Masurel Fils 1907
Mathon-Bertrand & Fils 1907
Motte-Meillassoux was unlisted, but G. Wauqiez's obituary stated that
  he was a buyer in this firm
Pierre Nutte representing Henri Wattinne & Co. 1907
Paul Wattel representing Emile Lahousse 1913
Wattinne-Bossut & Fils 1898 represented by Edouard Gaillet
A. Roussel and Co.

Other firms had their headquarters in Rheims, another woollen textile centre, including:
Etablissements Wenz 1890
Picard-Goulet Fils 1907
Eugène Gosset 1898–1907

Other French firms:
Auguste Assemaine & Co. 1907
Brial Frères 1909 (member French Chamber of Commerce)
Paul Brial 1913
Dreyfus & Moch 1913
Armand Guilhou (skins), represented by P. Puech & N. Puech 1907

APPENDIX I

Leon Leroux 1909
Alphonse Six was represented by Alfred Decouvelaere in Sydney and
  Theo Desmarchelier in Melbourne before 1914 (member of French
  Chamber of Commerce)

Belgian firms:
Fuhrmann and Co. 1890
Fuhrmann Troost & Co. 1907
Kreglinger 1913
R. Lhoest and Co. 1895–1907
Kurth Weyhmann and Co.
Ostermeyer Dewez 1890
Ostermeyer Dewez & Van Rompaey 1898
Jules Renard and Co. 1890

Possibly French or Belgian firms:
Francart G. B. and Co. 1895
Wallon & Lamy 1913
E. Jouy 1898
P. Bertrand Co. 1907

Appendix II

Most of the buyers mentioned below founded families whose descendants have remained in Australia:

After his demobilisation Jacques' friend Joseph FLIPO returned to Sydney in 1919 to his former job with Dewavrin and Co., now one of the largest buying firms. After being severely wounded in the battle of the Mort Homme, he had been sent to the United States as part of a French Military Mission which was assisting the American Army with the organisation and training necessary for the Western Front. One of his first activities on returning to Sydney was to found an association of French returned soldiers, La Ligue des Anciens Combattants, and he remained President of this group for half a century. He married Paul Lamérand's daughter, and was to succeed his father-in-law in 1934 as General Manager.

Phillipe SCAMPS returned from the War to be greeted on Turramurra Station by a brass band, and also to be handed an illuminated address. He returned to work for Cauillez and Co.

Eugène CAU had been a prisoner of war in Germany, but had managed to escape to neutral territory in Switzerland, where he was greeted by his wife. Cauillez and Co. assigned him to attend the London wool sales for several years after the war and he and his family did not return to Australia till the early thirties. He remained with the same firm for many more years, and all his children are still in Australia.

Marcel PAROISSIEN, who had been so severely wounded, returned to work for Wattine Bossut, and his son Jean, after his schooling at Cranbrook and a year's practical experience in Roubaix, followed his father into the wool trade.

Armand GEORGE had fought on the Belgian Front as an infantry soldier, but because of his Australian experience was able to become an interpreter with the British Army. He returned firstly to New Zealand, working again with Dewez, then Wattine Bossut and Moch et Odelin.

Jean DROULERS returned from the war with his French bride to work with Masurel Fils, which he later managed. Their youngest child, Xavier, was to head the New Zealand branch of Masurel 40 years later.

Marcel LEMAN, who had fought in the Belgian artillery, joined Henry Wattine & Co., and a generation later his son Marcel Jr also became a buyer.

Victor DEKYVÈRE had been invalided back in 1916 and worked in the government wool appraisal scheme till private buying resumed in the Australian auction rooms some time after the war.

During the war Alfred van ROMPAEY, now in his sixties, had lived on the outskirts of Paris, as his country of Belgium was now overrun by German forces. He had understandably developed a loathing for Germany, and could see his German shipping agency as a potential liability. No wool trading with Australia had been possible during the war, but it was now time to consider the future. He therefore summoned G. and C. Kreglinger, the principals of an Antwerp firm which was already functioning in Australia as wool buyers. In 1917 Van Rompaey made them the extraordinary offer to take over his woollen interests in Australia at no cost, provided they gave a written guarantee that the numerous staff, including his son Leslie, now in Australia, would be 'well-looked after'. This offer was accepted. Leslie remained with Kreglinger and Fernau until 1938, when he commenced his own firm L. van Rompaey, Wool.

Toussaint DEWEZ'S Belgian–Australian company resumed business after the war and was now administered by his two sons, Toussaint Jr (known as 'Tue') in Melbourne, and his brother 'Gus' in Sydney.

The second generation of HENTZES in the wool trade was represented by Phillip, who returned to Sydney from his experience in European woollen mills to work with his father for Simonius Vischer in Sydney in the 1920s.

Appendix III

A probably incomplete list of French and Belgian wool buyers who came to work in Australia under contract and who settled here, or whose families stayed on. This list was compiled in large part by René Vandervaere, former Chairman of the Australian Council of Wool Exporters. Sons who worked in the wool trade are also included:

Jos. Balthasar

Daniel Blom

Charles Boggio

Fernand Bourgeois

Jean Bourgeois

André Brenac

Georges Brenac

Emile Brial

Albert Bribosia

Maurice Brisbout

Max Brunninghausen

Albert Byrom

Claude Cagé

Desiré Carney, son Pierre

André Catteau

Eugène Cau

André Cau

Georges Corne

Auguste Dalle

Claude Davrain

Robert Debuf

Robert Degraeve

Victor Dekyvère, sons Victor, Marcel

Paul Dekyvère, his brother

Jean Delbarre

Henri Deldicque

Gustave Deltoer

Gerard Demeulemeester

Pierre Deschamps

René Deschamps

Theo Desmarchelier

Raphael Desplechin

Francois Devos

Toussaint Dewez, sons Tue, Gus, grandsons Jim, Arthur, Peter

Numa Dezarnaulds (via New Caledonia)

Edouard Douez

Jean Droulers, son Xavier

A. Duboc

Marcel Dugard, son Jean-Baptiste

Edouard Dulieu

Robert Dulieu, his brother

René Dupuche

René Dutriez

Cesar Esterman

Adrien Fievet

André Flipo

Joseph Flipo, son Joseph

Jacques Fourlinnie

Camille Gheysens

Maurice Gilet

Gérard Gilet, his brother

Armand George, son Armand

Jacques Goebbels

Frederick Hentze, son Phillip

Jo Hollebecq

Jean Hourez

Charles Jaeger

Paul Lamblin

Paul Lamérand, son Jean

Bruno Leclercq

Jean Legrand

Bernard Lehembre

Jean Leman

Marcel Leman, sons Marcel, Raymond

Jean Leveaux

Jean Lieutenant

Felix Manchoulas

Pierre Marecaux

Charles Martel, son Maurice

Georges Mathon

Max Mazzetti

René Mouniez

Jean Mourez

Augustin Nopenaire, son Georges

Georges Parmentier, son Gervais, grandson Paul

Joseph Parmentier, his brother, son André

Guy Pascal

Anatole Paroissien,

Victor Paroissien, his brother, son Marcel, grandson Jean

? Pinel, skins

Georges Playoust, sons Jacques, Maurice, Georges Jun.

Joseph Playoust, his brother, sons Charles, Paul, Fernand

Ben Prevost (Perth), son Michael

Michel Poulain

Maurice Pycke

Emile Quesnoy

Jean Quint

Jules Renard

Henri Renault

Marcel Richard

Roger Richard, his brother

Pierre Robin, son Michael

Paul Robin

Auguste Rousseau

Jacques Roussel

Phillipe Scamps, son Albert

Paul Segaert, (son of Belgian Consul-Gen., briefly a buyer)

Maurice Selosse, son Robert

Fernand Sémat

Maurice Vandendriessche, son Maurice

J. Van den Heyden

Jacques Vanderhaegen

René Vandervaere

Alfred van Rompaey, son Leslie, grandson Gerald

Paul Wattel, son in Australia

Ben Wattel, his brother, son Raymond

Paul Wenz, linked to wool buying firm

J. Wischer

Appendix IV

Wool buyers in photograph of Sydney Sales Room, early 1920s. (Photograph courtesy of the Australian Council of Wool Exporters.)

From left to right:

1st row: J. Droulers (Kreglinger or Masurel), R. Randall (Hinchcliffe Holt), Bersch, W. Coss (Kanematsu), J. Martin (W.P.Martin), Utsumi (Mitsui), T. Ayrton (Biggin & Ayrton), T. Packer (Wenz).

2nd Row: ? (M&O), R. Carver (Dawson's), Ockajeba (Iida), C. Waite (Lemprière), P. Slessinger, Pohl (Pohl & Krech), S. Sawada (Okura), J. Inglis (Haughton's), K. Heckmanns (P. Schreiterer).

3rd Row: H. Paton (Beaumonts), R. Longworth (A.W.M.), E. Moore (Sidney Moore), M. Paroissien (Wattine Bossut), J. Playoust (Playoust Fils), H. Andrews (Laycock), J. Blackwell (Jowett), A. Lord (K&K), F. Booth, Schall, ?.

4th Row: Lund, Carney (Dassonville), J. A. Burton, E. Lough (Herrons), Vouet (Dehaye), Brunninghausen, T. Swinbourne, Bert Hilliger (Biensen), F. Rush (Kirchner), A. J. H. Marshall (Sandersons), ?.

Not all those seated in subsequent rows can be named, but they include:

5th Row: P. Spring (F. Willey), F. Wade (A.W.P.), Reid (Kanmatsu), A. Bruce (Wright & Bruce), Hiegen (North German Woollen), Wyslog, J. Parmentier (Wattine), R.B. Archer, S. Wright (Vicars).

6th Row: Glass, Wedemeyer, Carrados (Sims Cooper), Bennett (Bennett & Gillman) Melb., P. Dekyvère, Russian Buyer, M. Lieno (Mitsubishi), G. Love, J. Callachor.

7th Row: E. Cook, S. Gilfillan (Martins), B. Devereaux (Martins), A. Grundy (Globe), J. Mather (Brown & Dureau), Hat, Shackleton (Pickles & Ray), J. McLeod (A.C.Ltd or P.S.& B), J. Ellis.

8th Row: J. Brassil, Kelly (F&G), J. Allmark, J. Beanland (Tankards), Baxter (Estates Bris), T. Leitch.

Centre Gangway: J. Schneider (Reda) front, N. Fox (Gedge) with catalogue.

Endnotes

CHAPTER 1

1 H. Austin, *Australia v. London as the World Wool Depot*, S.T. Leigh & Co., 1894.

2 ibid.

3 R. Aldrich, 'Commercial Relations between France and Australia', in A. M. Nisbet & M. Blackman (eds), *The French Australian Cultural Connection*, University of NSW, 1983.

4 Margaret Dewez.

5 A. Stuer, *The French in Australia*, ANU, 1982, also P.D. (Paul Dekyvère) 'La laine et les Francais d'Australie', *Courrier Australien*, 13.9.1943.

6 A. Barnard, *The Australian Wool Market 1840–1890*, Melbourne University Press and Australian National University, 1958.

7 W. H. Chard, *Australian Wool Markets—Historical Sketch*, W. H. Chard & Co., 1926.

8 *South West Pacific*, No. 15, 1946.

9 Anon., 'Les Activités Francaises en Australie Occidentale', *Courrier Australien*, 8.7.1943.

10 Carbonising wool is the process of removing burrs or vegetable matter content to their natural state of carbon by treatment with sulphuric acid.

11 Fell mongers are skin dealers. In Mazamet the fleece was stripped from the hides, the leather was tanned and the wool sent on to be processed into felt, etc.

12 J. Eddowes, *The Language of Cricket*, Carcanet Press, 1997.

13 *Le Monde Illustré*, 5 March 1923, p.21.

14 Roving: Sliver of wool drawn out and slightly twisted. *(Oxford English Dictionary)*.

CHAPTER 2

1 Sands and McDougall Melbourne Directory 1895.

2 R. J. & R. A. Sullivan, 'Pastoral Strikes 1891 and 1894', in D. J. Murphy (ed.) *The Big Strikes*, University of Queensland Press, 1993.

3 NSW Year Book, 1894.

4 M. Herman, *Architecture of Victorian Sydney*, Angus & Robertson, 1956.

5 Jocelyn Middleton, 'Augustine Soubeiran' M.A. Thesis, University of NSW.

6 *Sydney Morning Herald* 31.7.1899 and *The Daily Telegraph* 1.8.1899.

7 *Courrier Australien*, 13.1.1900

8 Bulletin of the French Chamber of Commerce of Sydney, 1901–1905.

9 ibid.

CHAPTER 3

1 After prospecting for gold in Victoria, the Frenchmen Auguste Nicolas and Joseph Reymond had settled in Forbes and engaged in agriculture, flour milling, saw milling and wine growing. Reymond was mayor of Forbes in 1883–4, also

representing the area in the Legislative Council in 1895–1905. He owned a property called 'Champsaur' on the Lachlan and could well have attracted Wenz there.

2 M. Blackman, Introduction to Paul Wenz' *Diary of a New Chum*, Angus & Robertson, 1990.

CHAPTER 4

1 The former convent in Paris is now the Rodin Museum, near Les Invalides.

2 *Australian Leather Journal*, 15.10.1907

3 Australian Imperial Forces Notes on the French Army, 1911.

CHAPTER 5

1 *Encyclopaedia Britannica.*

2 J. Robertson, *Anzac and Empire*, Hamlyn Australia, 1990.

3 J. Beaumont, *Australia's War*, Allen & Unwin, 1995.

4 E. Vedel, 'La Guerre à Tahiti', written almost three years after the incident. *L'Illustration*, 25.5.1918.

5 P. Moss, *Modern World History*, Hart-Davis, 1978.

6 *Courrier Australien*, 23.10.1914.

7 J. Middleton, *Augustine Soubeiran*, M.A. Thesis, University of NSW

8 P. Wenz, Letter to André Gide, with *Diary of a New Chum.*

9 J. Playoust, 'The Alliance Francaise', *Courrier Australien*, 8.2.1943.

10 Anon., 'Les Activités Francaises en Australie Orientale', *Courrier Australien*, 8.2.1943.

CHAPTER 7

1 French-Australian League Papers, Mitchell Library, MSS717.

2 The 'Mr. Moore' referred to was possibly an old family friend associated with the wool firm Harrison Jones and Devlin.

3 Marcel gave the day as Thursday without a date, but the card is postmarked 1 July, which fell on a Thursday in 1915. It was addressed to Mme Playoust, Hotel Métropole, 37 Rue Francois 1er, Champs Elysées, Paris, which was her address in 1915.

4 French-Australian League Papers.

CHAPTER 8

1 A. Horne, *The Price of Glory*, Macmillan 1962. This admirable account of the Verdun battle gave much of the background to Pétain's assumption of leadership of the campaign.

CHAPTER 9

1-6 All translated from April–May 1916 issues of *L'Illustration.*

5 'The enemy's main effort bore towards our positions on the left bank of the Meuse from the Mort Homme to Hill 304. The bombardment has attained an unheard of violence.'

6 'The Germans did not give up their assaults on Hill 304—all the night of the 8th to the 9th they rained bombs on it and at 3.00 a.m. tried another fruitless attack.'

7 A. Horne, *The Price of Glory.*

CHAPTER 10

1 J. Terraine, *The First World War 1914–18*, Macmillan & Co., 1965.

2 *L'Illustration*, 29.7.1916.

CHAPTER 11

1 *L'Illustration.*

2 J. Terraine, *The First World War 1914–18*.

3 A. Horne, *The Price of Glory.*

CHAPTER 13
1 J. Terraine, *The First World War 1914-18.*

2 London *Daily Telegraph,* 2 June, 1997.

CHAPTER 14
1 This and other quotations from War Diary, 13th Field Artillery Brigade, 5th Division. Microfilm, Australian War Memorial

2 W.H. Downing, *Digger Dialects*, Lothian Book Co., 1919.

CHAPTER 15
1 J. Monash, Lieut-Gen. *Australian Victories in France in 1918*, Lothian Press, 1920.

CHAPTER 16
1 Taken from inscription on the plaque of the Australian Memorial at Mt. St. Quentin.

CHAPTER 18
1 French–Australian League Papers.

2 Municipal records of Poilcourt-Sydney (Ardennes). Photocopy of relevant details in possession of the author.

3 Details of reconstruction drawn largely from an article in *Le Monde Illustré*, 5.3.1923, 'La reconstruction des Regions Devastées Roubaix-Tourcoing 1918–23'.

CHAPTER 19
1 According to Julie Sinclair (Dewez), who knew the family.

2 Sands Directory, 1922.

3 Possibly the former Dreyfus Moch of 1913.

CHAPTER 21
1 *Courrier Australien,* 9.2.1923.

2 According to Paulette Flipo.

CHAPTER 22
1 B. Hitches & T. O'Keefe, *Wool in Australia 1788–1988,* Australian Wool Corporation, 1988.

2 *Courrier Australien*, 9.4.1940.

3 *Courrier Australien*, 9.8.1940.

4 J. Lawrey, 'The Cross of Lorraine in the South Pacific', *The Journal of Pacific History,* Canberra, 1982.

5 *Bulletin Scientifique de la Société D'Etudes Historiques de Nouméa* No.106, also the personal recollections of Roger Pelletier.

6 A. Stuer, *The French in Australia.*

CHAPTER 23
1 This account of the Indochina campaign is drawn largely from reminiscences of Roger Pelletier, Jeanne Renault and Paul de Pierres' article 'Australians in Vietnam' in *Sabretache*, Vol XXX, April–June 1989, the journal of the Australian Military Historical Society.

EPILOGUE
1 Recollections of John Lamérand.

2 Topmaking is the process of combing the wool into 'tops', or bundles, in preparation for spinning.

3 From a speech on the French national day, 14th July, reported in the *Courrier Australien.*

Bibliography

Aldrich, R. 'Commercial Relations between France and Australia'. in A. M. Nisbet & M. Blackman (eds), *The French Australian Cultural Connection*. University of NSW, 1983.

Anon. 'The Australian Wool Trade'. *New Nation* Magazine, 1.6.1933.

Anon. Anzac Memorial. Published by NSW. Branch Returned Sailors and Soldiers Imperial League of Australia, 1919.

Anon. Municipal Records of the Commune of Poilcourt-Sydney, 1921.

Anon. Notes on the French Army. Australian Imperial Forces, 1911.

Anon. War Diary 13th Field Artillery Brig. 5th Div. Microfilm, Australian War Memorial.

Austin, H. *Australia v. London as the World's Wool Depot*. S.T. Leigh & Co., 1894.

Australian Dictionary of Biography

Barnard, A. *The Australian Wool Market 1840–1900*. Melbourne University Press & Australian National University, 1958.

Barnes, J. 'Evermore'. *Cross Channel*. Jonathan Cape, 1996.

Bean, C. E. W. *Gallipoli Correspondent*. Allen & Unwin, 1983.

Bean, C. E. W. *Anzac to Amiens*. Australian War Memorial & Penguin Books, 1946.

Bean, C. E. W. *The Story of Anzac*. Australian War Memorial, 1921.

Beaumont, J. *Australia's War*. Allen & Unwin, 1995.

Bulletin of the French Chamber of Commerce in Sydney, 1901–1905.

Carter H. B. (ed.) *The Sheep and Wool Correspondence of Sir Joseph Banks*. Library Council of NSW, 1979.

Chard, W. H. *Australian Wool Markets–Historical Sketch*. W. H. Chard & Co., 1926.

Chedgey ?. *First Battalion A.I.F. 1914–19*. First Battalion History Committee, 1931.

Churchill, W. *The Second World War*. Cassell & Co., 1949.

Clark, A. *The Fall of Crete*. Anthony Blond Ltd., 1962.

Clark, M. *History of Australia: Part III*. Melbourne University Press, 1973.

Clarke, F. G. *A Concise Political and Social History of Australia*. Oxford University Press, 1989.

Coombs, R. *Before Endeavours Fade*. Battle of Britain Prints, 1983.

de Gaulle, C. *Memoires de Guerre, Vol 1, l'Appel*. Plon, 1981.

Dekyvère, Paul (P.D.) 'La laine et les Francais d'Australie'. *Courrier Australien*, 3.9.1943.

Downing, W. H. *Digger Dialects.* Lothian Book Co., 1919.

Dunstan, A.S. 'Selling Wool'. *The Bulletin.* May 1956.

Dysart, D. 'The Ervin Legacy'. *National Trust Quarterly,* October 1992.

Eddowes, J. *The Language of Cricket.* Carcanet Press, 1997.

French-Australian League papers, Mitchell Library, MSS717.

Gibson, R. *Best of Enemies.* Sinclair Stevenson, 1995.

Gilbert, M. *The First World War.* Weidenfeld & Nicolson, 1988.

Guide Michelin, Michelin et Cie, 1997.

Henderson, G. *Menzies' Child.* Allen & Unwin, 1994.

Herman, M. *Architecture of Victorian Sydney.* Angus & Robertson, 1956.

Hitches, B., O'Keefe, T. *Wool in Australia 1788–1988.* Australian Wool Corporation, 1988.

Horne, A . *The Price of Glory.* Macmillan & Co., 1962.

Ingpen, R. *Pioneers of Wool.* Rigby, 1972.

Inscriptions on Australian War Memorials at Villers-Bretonneux, Pozières and Mont St. Quentin. French War Memorials at the Chemin des Dames, Douaumont, summit of the Mort-Homme, Newfound-land Memorial Park at

Beaumont-Hamel, British War Memorial at Thiepval.

Kurtovitch, I. 'Du Conseil d'Administration de la Nouvelle Calédonie pendant la Seconde Guerre Mondiale'. *Bulletin Scientifique de la Société d'Etudes Historiques Nouméa* No.106, 1996.

L'Illustration weekly copies from August 1914–November 1918 in possession of the author.

Laffin, J. *Guide to Australian Battlefields on the Western Front 1916–18.* Kangaroo Press & Australian War Memorial, 1992.

Laffin, J. *The Cost of Victory.* Time-Life, 1988.

Lawrey, J. 'The Cross of Lorraine in the South Pacific'. *Journal of Pacific History*, Canberra,1982.

Le Courrier Australien. Microfilm archives, State Library of NSW

Le Monde Illustré 'La reconstruction des Regions Devastées Roubaix-Tourcoing', 5.3.1923.

London *Daily Telegraph.* Letters to the Editor, 2.6.1997.

Loughlin, J. 'The Rites of Wool'. *South West Pacific* No.15, 1946.

Melbourne Directory, Sands & McDougall, 1895

Middleton, J. *Augustine Soubeiran.* M.A. thesis, University of NSW

Molony, J. *Penguin Bicentennial History of Australia.* Viking, 1987.

Monash, J. Lieut-Gen. *Australian Victories in France in 1918.* Lothian Press, 1920.

Moss, P. *Modern World History.* Hart-Davis, 1978.

Murphy. D.J. Ed. *The Big Strikes—Queensland 1889–1965*. Univ. of Queensland Press, 1993.

Origo, I. *The Merchant of Prato*. Jonathan Cape, 1957.

Pamphlets. Historial of the Great War (Museum at Peronne, France.)

Passant, E.J. *A Short History of Germany 1815–1945*. Cambridge University Press, 1969.

Personal memoirs of André Brenac, Paul de Pierres, René Deschamps, John Lamérand, Robert Pelletier, Ian Renard, Jeanne Renault, Gerald van Rompaey.

Pointing, K. *The Wool Trade Past and Present*. Columbine Press, Manchester, 1961.

Proceedings, Australian Council of Wool Exporters Melbourne 1890–1893.

Remarque, E. M. *All Quiet on the Western Front*. Putnam, 1929; Pan, 1993.

Robertson, J. *Anzac and Empire*. Hamlyn Australia, 1990.

Rountree, P. 'Pasteur in Australia'. School of Microbiology University NSW Historical Review *Journal of Pathology*.

Sassoon, S. *Memoirs of a Fox Hunting Man*. Faber & Faber, 1930

Sassoon, S. *Memoirs of an Infantry Officer*. Faber & Faber, 1930.

Slutzkin, L. & Pearce, B. *Bohemians in the Bush*. Art Gallery of New South Wales, 1991.

Stuer, A. *The French in Australia*. Australian National University, 1982.

Sydney Directories between 1890 and 1914, Sands.

Sydney Morning Herald microfilm archives, State Library of NSW

Terraine, J. *The First World War 1914–18*. Macmillan & Co., 1965.

Wardell, J.E. 'The Wool Customers of Australia'. *New Nation* Magazine, 15.7.1935.

Wenz, P. *L'Écharde*. Republished by La Petite Maison,1986.

Wenz, P. *Contes Australiens*. Plon, 1911.

Wenz, P. *Diary of a New Chum*. Collins, Angus & Robertson, 1990.

Wharton, J.C. 'The Wool Industry'. Royal Agricultural Society Annual, 1910.

Index